SCANDINAVIAN INSTITUTE OF
ASIAN STUDIES MONOGRAPH SERIES

Foreign Investment and Development
Swedish Companies in India

Klas Markensten

Studentlitteratur

© Klas Markensten 1972
Printed in Sweden
Studentlitteratur
Lund 1972
ISBN 91-44-06891-3

CONTENTS

Chapter 1. Theoretical Outline   7
    Theoretical Benefits   8
     Direct benefits   9
     External economies   13
    Costs of Foreign Investment   17
     Indirect costs   18
     Benefits and costs   21

Chapter 2. India and Foreign Industry   28
    Industrial Development   28
     Industry before independence   28
     Foreign capital and colonialism   33
     New objectives of industrial development   38
     Policy implementation   43
    Foreign Investment   46
     Foreign capital after 1947   46
     Foreign exchange and foreign control   50
     Policies towards foreign capital   53
     Foreign investment and priorities   58

Chapter 3. Swedish Companies   63
    The Swedish Companies and Their Environment   63
     Swedish Match and Wimco   63
     The new Swedish companies   67
     Location   70
     Swedish companies in Poona   76
     Infrastructure and physical environment   78
    Production and Priorities   81
     Swedish companies and priorities   81
     Industrial linkages   84

Chapter 4. Employment   88
    Employment and Productivity   88
     Employment and turnover   88
     Productivity   93
     Choice of technology   97
    Recruitment   102
     Work-force characteristics   102
     Recruitment policies   105
     Women and casual labour   110
     Mobility and promotion   115

Chapter 5. Labour Conditions   119
        Wages   119
           Wage levels in the Swedish companies   121
           Wages and standard of living   127
           Wages and productivity   129
        Welfare   133
           Social benefits   133
           Present benefits in the Swedish companies   136
           Welfare   140
        Labour and Management   143
           Trade unions and negotiations   145
           Industrial disputes   148
           Labour and management   151

Chapter 6. Education, Culture and Politics   154
        Education   155
           Workers' training   156
           Staff-training   159
           Technology and know-how   162
           Organization and personnel   166
        Culture   169
           Caste and religion   170
           Commitment and absenteeism   174
           The industrial order   177
           Fundamental cultural values   179
        Politics   182
           Big business   185
           The Government and the companies   190

Chapter 7. Capital Inflows and Foreign Trade   196
        Foreign Capital Inflows   196
           Savings   198
           Foreign ownership   201
           Foreign-exchange inflow   204
        Exports and Imports   208
           Exports   208
           Export restrictions   211
           Imports   214

Chapter 8. Profits and Outflows   222
        Profits and Benefits   222
           Profits   222
           Profit distribution   225
           Taxes   229
           Tax concessions and wage benefits   232

Outflows and Costs   235
    Dividend outflows   235
    Royalties and fees   238
    Foreign-exchange costs   242
    Benefits and costs   245

Chapter 9. Competition and Opportunity Costs   250
    Competition   250
        Benefits to consumers   250
        Competition and monopoly   254
        The new Swedish companies   256
    Opportunity costs   260
        Foreign and domestic companies   260
        Opportunity costs of Swedish companies   264
        Transformed benefits and costs   267

Chapter 10. Conclusion   272
    Benefits and costs again   272
    Location and employment   274
    External economies   276
    Training, culture and politics   278
    Final considerations   281

Bibliography   287

Chapter 1

THEORETICAL OUTLINE

This study is an empirical contribution to the discussion on the impact of private foreign investment in underdeveloped countries. Data will be presented on the activities of a few Swedish companies in India, and their possible effects on Indian development will be discussed. The obvious framework of such a study is the Indian national political, social and economic objectives. The effects and variables in this study will be related to the policies of the Indian Government, which thus will in a sense be the "value premises" of my study. [1]

Like most other countries, India wants higher living standards, a high level of employment and more equality. In the words of the first five-year plan: "Maximum production, full employment, the attainment of economic equality and social justice...constitute the accepted objectives of planning ..." [2] But these major objectives of the Indian Government are not always consistently pursued, and the detailed policy measures enacted to fulfil the major goals are therefore open to discussion and criticism. [3]

The material for the present study was mainly collected in India in 1969. A few studies of foreign investment in India in general have been of value, but the facts about the Swedish companies are derived from primary sources through interviews and documentary research. Cross-checks between different sources and personnel groups have been made as far as possible. Where the data are particularly weak, this is indicated. The busy reader

---

1) Myrdal, G., Asian Drama, New York 1968, pp. 49 ff. Cf. India. Industrial Licensing Policy Inquiry Committee, Report, Delhi 1969, p. 196; Prest, A.R. and Turvey, R., Cost-Benefit Analysis: A Survey, in Surveys of Economic Theory III, Macmillan, New York 1967, p. 157.
2) India. Planning Commission, The First Five-year Plan. A Summary, Delhi 1952, p. 8.
3) I share to large extent the basic economic and political ideas of the Indian Government, but in the absence of consistent practical policies, the concept of Indian Government policies as "value premises" becomes rather vague.

will get a superficial but fairly comprehensive view of the material by reading Chapter 10. [1)]

Theoretical Benefits

Foreign private investment has long been discussed within the framework
of the theory of international capital movements. This might have been
adequate when portfolio capital constituted a large proportion of international investments, but at present the direct manufacturing investments dominate the picture, and they cannot be conveniently analysed with only the
traditional tools. The simple reason is that direct investments are not
primarily transfers of a homogeneous production factor, capital.

> ... most current foreign investment in manufacturing and services
> does not lead to major international movements of financial assets.
> The crucial resources transferred (i.e. the resources which "move"
> across national frontiers) are typically of the organizational and
> technological kind described in the previous chapter. The major
> addition to the host country's stock of capital does not come about
> through capital transfer from without, but through promotion of ca-
> pital formation from within, through both reinvestment of profits
> and local borrowing, i.e. stimulation of local savings. It is, to re-
> peat, not capital but intangibles which are the core element of the
> resource transfer taking place in the course of direct investment. [2)]

The analysis of direct investment (from the point of view of the investor)
therefore belongs more to the theory of industrial organization than to the
theory of international capital movements. [3)] The major elaboration of this
view has been made by Stephen Hymer, who concludes: "The theory implies that the relevant units of study are particular industries and particular
firms and not the aggregates of international operations." [4)] The investment

---

1) For readers with a special interest in the histories of the individual
   Swedish companies in India, a mimeographed set of case histories has
   been prepared and may be obtained from The Scandinativan Institute of
   Asian Studies (Kejsergade 2, 1155, Copenhagen K., Denmark).
2) Gabriel, P.P., The International Transfer of Corporate Skills. Management Contracts in Less Developed Countries, Boston 1967, p. 85.
3) Kindleberger, C.P., American Business Abroad, New Haven 1969, p.
   11.
4) Hymer, S.H., International Operations of National Firms. A Study of
   Direct Foreign Investment, Diss., Massachusetts Institute of Technology 1960, p. 91.

8

of capital that takes place in the course of direct investment is primarily motivated by the investor's desire to get control over the new venture.[1] Control has a value in itself, and the distinguishing feature of foreign direct investment is that control is in foreign hands.[2]

My main interest here is the possible effects of direct investments in the receiving countries. Here, too, the theory of capital movements is insufficient, and I shall mainly use conventional investment theory with a sprinkling of sociological and anthropological findings. In fact, a specific body of theory relating to private foreign investment in the poor countries has been evolved. However frail this body of theory may be, I shall follow the theoretical tradition, so that my empirical findings may be related to familiar concepts. The underdeveloped countries are in focus here, but much of the analysis that follows has been suggested by authors writing on developed countries, notably Australia and Canada.

Direct benefits

In the remaining part of this chapter I shall briefly enumerate some possible benefits and costs of foreign investments. My attention will be focussed on the manufacturing industries and the special problems of the extractive industries and plantations will therefore be given less attention. The classification of effects as "benefits" and "costs" can only be made within a specific framework.[3] In this connection I shall take a very instructive discussion of benefits and costs by Gerald Meier as my point of departure.[4] His classification of benefits and costs was made from the viewpoint of a "national development program", which is a useful classification also for my purposes. Underlying the development programs of different underdeveloped countries are various concepts of growth theory, which cannot be fully discussed here.

---

1) Ibid., pp. 163, 184. Cf. Desai, A.V., Potentialities of collaboration and their utilisation, in Hazari, R.K.(ed.), Foreign Collaboration, University of Bombay, Bombay 1967, p. 124.
2) Cooper, R.N., The Economics of Interdependence, New York 1968, p. 81.
3) See p. 7.
4) Meier, G.M., The International Economics of Development, Tokyo 1968, pp. 131 ff. An earlier version of his argumentation was published in Meier, G.M., International Trade and Development, Tokyo 1964, Ch. 5.

All possible costs and benefits cannot be included in an analysis, but I hope that nothing essential will be left out and that the effects enumerated here will, on the whole, be on the same "level of importance". As usual, the benefits pose many more problems than the costs. [1] Both the enumeration and the evaluation of benefits are very difficult, and double counting is an ever-present danger All types of cost-benefit analysis suffer from the limitations inherent in partial analysis. I shall not go into all the theoretical difficulties here - to some extent these problems will be discussed later in connection with their empirical application.

Capital inflow. New foreign investment brings capital, skills and techniques Of these, capital is probably the least important contribution. [2] Fresh capital provided by the foreign investor adds to the domestic supply of savings and makes new investment possible.

The capital inflow is not only an addition to savings, but also to the supply of foreign exchange at the disposal of the host country (without any double counting). In many countries, notably India, the shortage of foreign exchange is a more serious bottleneck for development than savings, and in such cases the foreign-exchange contribution of new investment is more important than the addition to savings. [3] In so far as the foreign investment is financed locally or in kind, the potential foreign-exchange contribution may be reduced. [4]

The fact that the capital inflow is in foreign exchange can be taken into account in the form of a foreign exchange premium. The main positive effects from the initial increase in savings are realized through the higher output resulting from the foreign investment. The increase in output is in fact the main economic benefit of foreign investment. "The case for direct investment is simply that more is produced..." [5] The fresh capital and other production factors produce jointly a higher output, and this output less costs constitutes the main economic benefit of foreign investment.

---

1) Prest, A.R. and Turvey, R., op. cit., p. 201.
2) See p. 8; pp. 196-98; Cairncross, A.K., Factors in Economic Development, London 1962, pp. 63, 88, 114, 118; Gårdlund, T., Främmande investeringar i u-land, Stockholm 1968, p. 20.
3) Chenery, H.B., Foreign assistance and economic development, in Adler, J.H. (ed.), Capital Movements, New York 1967, p. 275.
4) See p. 204.
5) Humphrey, D., Direct foreign investment and economic growth, in Economic Weekly, Special Number, June 1960, p. 928.

Output less costs is an expression of profits, so we could in principle say that the main economic benefit from foreign investment is the profit it produces. But we have then to distinguish between private and social profits (social benefits). To arrive at the social benefits, private profits must be corrected for differences in social and private valuations of output and costs. The main difference is that dividend remittances to the foreign owners are included in private profits but should be excluded from an estimate of the social benefits. Other adjustments should also be made, but, properly adjusted, private profits can serve as an indicator of the economic benefits accruing to society.

But society is not indifferent to the different uses of the adjusted social income generated by foreign investment. Both the objective of economic growth and that of equality may be affected. Used in one way rather than another, the income from the foreign investment can in different degrees promote economic growth or influence the distribution of income. In principle, the use of every single rupee of the adjusted private profits should be traced and given weights to make the various uses comparable. [1] If the social income from the foreign investment is saved, this might be better for economic growth than if it was consumed, and a comparison could be made by discounting future consumption ensuing from the investment of the savings. If the project is located in a poor part of the country, it is likely to promote economic equality more than if it was located in a wealthy area.

The gross profits of a foreign company are either re-invested, distributed as local or foreign dividends or paid as taxes. Re-investments increase the company's capacity to produce future profits and reduce the scope for immediate payments of costly dividends to foreign shareholders. From society's point of view, this is probably a positive effect, but at the same time re-investments are likely to increase the future burden of foreign dividend payments - a long-term obligation is created. Continuous re-investment also means increased foreign control over industry.

Dividends actually remitted to the foreign owners are not included in the adjusted social income from the foreign investment, but local dividends are. Income distributed to local shareholders is either put to more or less productive use or consumed. The higher the total average income of local shareholders, the less value should be placed on the additional social income, in the form of dividends, consumed by them. [2] Taxes paid to the

1) Little, I. M.D. and Mirrlees, J.A., Manual of Industrial Project Analysis, OECD, Paris 1968, p. 43. Cf. Prest, A.R. and Turvey, R., op. cit., pp. 159, 173.
2) Little, I. M.D. and Mirrlees, J.A., op. cit., p. 130.

12199

Government presumably replace re-investments or dividends, which is a positive effect, in so far as the Government makes a sensible use of the money. [1]

Employment. If the foreign investment is not a substitute for domestic investment, the employment opportunities created constitute a positive effect. More employment is an explicit policy objective in most underdeveloped countries. The employment objective is often a synthesis of a genuine employment objective and a distribution motive. [2] Higher employment is, strictly speaking, an independent objective only in so far as it is considered better for a person to be working than not working, regardless of his wages and consumption. But higher employment is often desired in the first instance because one worries about the low consumption of the unemployed, and higher employment is then regarded primarily a means of increasing the number of wage-earners and thereby promoting the objective of a more equitable distribution of income.

If labour recruited by a foreign enterprise is drawn from other occupations, there is no direct employment effect. Instead, there are indirect effects throughout the industrial structure, and the ultimate employment effect is probably that fresh labour is drawn from agriculture. [3] A labour-intensive technology in the foreign enterprise promotes the employment objective more than a capital-intensive technology, but the latter may have other advantages. [4]

In the calculation of the social income accruing from a foreign investment, the costs and benefits used should be social-opportunity costs and benefits. In underdeveloped countries, there is often a difference between the private and social costs of industrial labour. The social cost of employing labour in a foreign investment is the value of its alternative production in former occupations. Under conditions of underemployment, the social cost of the best alternative use of labour is often lower than the private cost for the foreign company, and the difference should then be considered as a social gain. Social-welfare outlays can be regarded for analytical purposes as part of wages.

Consumers may benefit from foreign investment. If the foreign investment reduces production costs, and the cost reduction is reflected in lower

---

1) See p. 229.
2) Little, I.M.D. and Mirrlees, J.A., op. cit., p. 45.
3) Ibid., p. 158.
4) See pp. 97 ff.

prices, this constitutes a real gain to the consumers. Foreign investments can also benefit the consumers by offering new products, better products and better product service.

External economies

I am aware of the recent trend in welfare economics of not using or redefining the term "external economies", because of its ambiguity. But my main aim here is to present some empirical material concerning the developmental effects of a few Swedish companies in India, and I therefore prefer to stick to the established body of theory on foreign private investment. This includes an emphasis on "external economies", as exemplified by Gerald Meier:

> From the standpoint of contributing to the development process, the major benefits from foreign investment are likely to arise in the form of external economies. Besides bringing to the recipient country physical and financial capital, direct foreign investment also includes non-monetary transfers of other resources - technological knowledge, market information, managerial and supervisory personnel, organizational experience, and innovations in products and production techniques - all of which are in short supply. By being a carrier of technological and organizational change, the foreign investment may be highly significant in providing "private technical assistance" and "demonstration effects" that are of benefit elsewhere in the economy.[1]

"External economies" usually means goods and services provided by a firm without remuneration, an unpriced output. External economies are external to the individual firm but not to society in general. As is evident from the quotation above, many external economies are difficult to quantify, but this does not mean that they are less important than the quantifiable effects. At the same time, one should be careful not to overrate the role played by external economies. Scitovsky, for example, complains about "the impression one gains from the literature on underdeveloped countries that the entrepreneur creates external economies and diseconomies with his every move".[2]

1) Meier, G.M., The International Economics ..., p. 141.
2) Scitovsky, T., Two concepts of external economies, in Arrow, K.J. and Scitovsky, T. (eds.), Readings in Welfare Economics, London 1969, p. 246.

Of the many possible ways of classifying external economies, I have chosen to distinguish here between "external economies in a narrow sense" and "external economies in a wider sense". The former category would comprise physical external economies and diseconomies, for example, air pollution from a factory chimney, and industrial linkage effects. [1] The latter category would include more intangible effects in relation to technical knowledge, skills and attitudes.

The industrial linkages are of two kinds. A "forward linkage" is the market relation between two companies seen from the seller's point of view, and a "backward linkage" is the same relationship seen from the point of view of the buyer. [2] A foreign investment can break bottlenecks in production and stimulate new investment by offering a steady supply of a new or a cheaper product - a forward linkage. [3] A backward linkage comes into effect when, for example, the demand from a new foreign investment make possible the realization of economies of scale for suppliers. The linkage concept has been extensively discussed. [4]

The "external economies in a wider sense" are much more difficult to define than the former category. As we have seen, they have to do with education, transfer of know-how and cultural transformations. One reason for making this book as voluminous as it is was the desire to specify these effects more than is usual. They are very often only mentioned in passing and not analyzed, but at the same time they are designated the "main benefits" or the "major contribution" of foreign investment. [5] They are exemplified by Singer:

> In the economic life of a country and in its economic history, a most
> important element is the mechanism by which "one thing leads to
> another", and the most important contribution of an industry is not

---

1) By tradition, the term "external economies" generally includes also diseconomies.
2) The term "linkages" was coined by Hirschman. Cf. Hirschman, A.O., The Strategy of Economic Development, Yale 1958.
3) Meier, G.M., The International Economics ..., p. 142.
4) See pp. 84 ff.
5) See pp. 13,15.

its immediate product (as is perforce assumed by economists and statisticians) and not even its effects on other industries and immediate social benefits (thus far economists have been led by Marshall and Pigou to go) but perhaps even further its effect on the general level of education, skill, way of life, inventiveness, habits, store of technology, creation of new demand, etc. And this is perhaps precisely the reason why manufacturing industries are so universally desired by underdeveloped countries; namely, that they provide the growing points for increased technical knowledge, urban education, the dynamism and resilience that goes with urban civilization, as well as the direct Marshallian external economies.[1]

In connection with employment, external economies of this type can be produced by the foreign enterprise by training and educating the employeés. The external economy in question is realized when the trained employee leaves the firm to take up employment elsewhere, or when the foreign enterprise has to raise the wages of the employee to retain him.[2] When the employee is paid a low trainee or apprentice wage during the training period, the company is to some extent compensated for having to pay higher wages in the future. A more long-run external economy is created by the demand of the new enterprise for additional and more efficient government training institutions.[3]

As I have already pointed out, foreign direct investments are not primarily movements of capital but of other resources like technique and organizational knowledge.[4] Technical and organizational know-how is commonly regarded as the essence of foreign investment. Apart from this, it is also widely held that technique and organization spread from the foreign firm to

1) Singer, H.W., The distribution of gains between investing and borrowing countries, in The American Economic Review, May 1950, Papers and Proceedings, p. 476.
2) Little, I.M.D., and Mirrlees, J.A., op.cit., pp. 27, 211; Meier, G.M., The International Economics ..., p. 142.
3) Behrman, J.N., Economic effects of private direct investment, in Mikesell, R.F. (ed.), U.S. Private and Government Investment Abroad, Eugene 1962, p. 149.
4) Cf. p. 8.

the surrounding society, and that these spread effects constitute the main
benefit reaped by host countries from foreign enterprise. [1]

Technical know-how and new technology can be spread to other companies -
and thus become an external economy - by imitation and through the selling
and purchasing activities of the new enterprise. It can also go along with
employees who leave the foreign firm to take up employment elsewhere
or to start businesses themselves. Organisational know-how is spread in
the same way.

Over and above the organizational effects there are what I shall here call
cultural effects - "more general external economies, such as the inculcation
of non-traditional attitudes (consciousness of the benefits of change and
new methods, a disciplined attitude to work, punctuality, etc)". [2] Attitudes,
institutions and habits are often important obstacles to development, and
the belief is widespread that industries, particularly foreign ones, can
change attitudes in a way conducive to economic growth. [3]

.

1) "There are two types of benefits realised from foreign investment:
   additional supplies of capital, on the one hand, and, on the other,
   new techniques of production and management, entrepreneurial skill,
   new products, new ideas... But it is primarily in the second category
   that the special advantages of direct investment lie. The benefits
   of direct foreign investment, when it takes the form of the establishment of new foreign firms, the introduction of new technology and
   the provision of experienced managerial and technical services can
   hardly be exaggerated" Penrose, E., Foreign investment and the
   growth of the firm, in Economic Journal, June 1956, pp. 232-33. Cf.
   Gabriel, P.P., op. cit., pp. 84, 90; Cairncross, A. K., op. cit.,
   pp. 63, 88; Meier, G.M., The International Economics..., pp. 141,
   158-159; Lewis, A.W., The Theory of Economic Growth, London 1965
   (1955), p. 258; Gårdlund, T., op. cit. p. 142; Subrahmanian, K.K.,
   A Study of Foreign Private Investment in India since 1950. Diss., University of Bombay 1967 (unpublished), pp. 17, 111; Mason, R.H., An
   Analysis of Benefits from U.S. Direct Foreign Investments in Less-
   developed Areas, Diss., Stanford Univ., no date, pp. 32-37; Mikesell,
   R.F. (ed.), op. cit., p. 579.
2) Little, I.M.D. and Mirrlees, J.A., op. cit., p. 74.
3) See pp. 154-55, 169 ff. Cf. Behrman, J.N., op. cit., p. 139; Lewis,
   A.W., op. cit., passim; McLaughlin, R.U., Foreign Investment
   and Development in Liberia, New York 1966, p. 192.

A word of warning is warranted. The scope for external economies is often exaggerated. [1] It is not always true that foreign industry changes attitudes, knowledge and techniques. [2] The realization of external economies from training and the transfer of know-how is dependent on sometimes uncertain spread effects. [3] And the benefits in the form of external economies are usually largest in the early years of the life of an investment, while costs often have a tendency to rise over time. [4]

Costs of Foreign Investment

The most obvious costs of foreign investment are the remittances of dividends, royalties and other foreign payments. There is a difference here between private and social costs. For the investing concern, dividends and royalties paid by the subsidiary to the parent company are only intra-company transfers. But the host country sustains a real loss. [5]

In addition, the host government may have to incur costs for "locational concessions". To attract foreign investment to the country and to a certain region, the government may have to spend money on special facilities, additional public utilities and subsidized inputs to foreign enterprise. [6] Tax concessions given to foreign investment constitute a cost in the sense that the government has to forgo taxes that would otherwise have been paid. If a foreign company, regardless of concessions, is located in rich, metropolitan areas, the costs of public amenities per money unit invested will be relatively large, there will be a non-quantifiable cost of congestion, and the distribution of wealth within the country will be adversely affected, with ensuing economic and political costs. [7]

Much attention has been given in the literature to the effects of foreign investment on the terms of trade of the host country. If there is a deterioration of the terms of trade as a consequence of foreign investment, the

1) Little, I.M.D. and Mirrlees, J.A., op. cit., pp. 37, 59, 219.
2) See p. 155.
3) Kurian, K.M., The Impact of Foreign Capital on Indian Economy, New Delhi 1966, pp. 280 ff.
4) Wells, D.A., op. cit., p. 498; Meier, G.M., The International Economics ..., p. 156.
5) Cf. p. 235.
6) Meier, G.M., The International Economics ..., p. 143.
7) Cf. Wells, D.A., op. cit., p. 486; Little, I.M.D. and Mirrlees, J.A. op. cit., p. 43.

benefits from foreign investments are reduced and vice versa. Without making a number of assumptions on the strength and direction of the pertinent structural changes, supply and demand conditions, elasticities and government policies, it is not possible to predict the movement of the terms of trade. I shall not take up the discussion of the terms of trade here, because there seems to be a consensus of opinion that the effects of foreign investment on the terms of trade are insignificant anyway, and that the ultimate direction of possible changes caused by foreign capital is therefore of little practical interest. [1]

Indirect costs

One type of indirect costs of foreign investment is associated with the balance of payments. The inflow of foreign savings is a direct benefit to the host country, and the subsequent outflow of profits is a direct loss. But the fact that inflows and outflows are effected in foreign exchange is a complication. It sometimes happens that outflows from foreign investment bear additional indirect costs of balance-of-payments adjustments.

Dividends are sometimes the first charge on profits earned by foreign investment, and in such cases they do not therefore vary with business cycles. The remittances of dividends from foreign investments then become an invariable foreign-exchange obligation, which in situations of balance-of-payments pressure may be a considerable embarrassment. The recurrent balance-of-payments crises in countries like India have to be remedied by

[1] Meier, G. M., The International Economics..., p. 144; MacDougall, G.D.A., The benefits and costs of private investment from abroad: A theoretical approach, in Oxford University Institute of Statistics Bulletin, 22:1960, p. 204, 210; Streeten, P.P., Economic Integration, Leyden 1961, p. 89; Arndt, H.W., Overseas Borrowing - The New Model, in The Economic Record, Vol. 23, August 1957, p. 258.
[2] See p. 226.

costly measures, often of a disinflationary nature, which might then to some extent be regarded as costs of foreign investment. [1]

The issue is complicated by the fact that also other foreign-exchange effects than the simple inflows and outflows have to be taken into account. Re-investment of profits in foreign enterprises may reduce the immediate foreign-exchange burden of dividend remittances, but at the same time the re-invested capital adds to the long-term foreign-exchange liabilities of the host country. The inflow of foreign capital would normally be disinflationary, but the increased domestic investment and consumption caused by foreign investment might, on the other hand, be inflationary, with negative effects on the balance of payments. The impact of foreign enterprise in connection with import savings and export gains is of great interest from the foreign-exchange point of view, as is really the total impact of foreign investment on production, technology and comparative advantages. It is evident that the total balance-of-payments effect of foreign investment must be very difficult to estimate and quantify.

Some of the external economies treated earlier have their counterparts in the form of external diseconomies. But in conformity with the traditional view that external diseconomies are included in external economies, I shall not enumerate all these possible costs here. One example will suffice. Foreign firms may bring about external economies in the form of new technology. But at the same time foreign-owned subsidiaries in a country sometimes carry on less research activity than indigenous firms. There are economies of scale in research, and foreign companies may concentrate their research activities in the respective parent companies. The potential dynamic benefits from research activities would thereby be lost to the host country. [2]

---

1) "External measures, such as import quotas, tariffs, and exchange restrictions, may suppress the demand for imports, but they do so at the expense of productivity and efficiency. To eliminate the excess demand, internal disinflationary measures - higher taxation and credit tightness - are necessary, and these involve the costs of reduced consumption and investment. Alternatively, the country may have to devalue its currency and incur the costs of a possible deterioriation in its terms of trade, changes in income distribution, and necessary shifts of resources. When foreign investment leads to balance-of-payments difficulties, we must include these indirect costs of a depletion of international reserves, direct controls, disinflation, or devaluation in any assessment of the benefits and costs of foreign investments" (Meier, G.M., International Trade and Development, Tokyo 1964, pp. 105-6).

2) Södersten, B., International Economics, New York 1970, p. 465.

19

As a very special kind of effects, one may single out the political effects of foreign investment. It might be argued that such effects should not be included in this type of study, as they are often merely manifestations of xenophobic attitudes, but they are no doubt a reality in a number of countries. As Cairncross says, "No country likes to depend upon foreign capital, when it can mobilize domestic capital for the same purpose". [1] The possible political effects will be discussed in more detail in Chapter 6.

Opportunity costs. Foreign investment may have indirect negative effects in relation to existing domestic industry. If opportunities of domestic production or investment are forgone because of a foreign investment, this could be called an opportunity cost. The appearance of a foreign firm on a sometimes limited market in an underdeveloped country may result in lower sales and profits for domestic firms already in the field. To meet increased competitive pressure from a foreign company, domestic firms may have to secure costly technical collaboration agreements with other foreign firms. [2]

Cases are known in which domestic firms have been forced to shut down completely, with a resulting capital loss. Even more serious may be the possibility that the presence of a strong foreign company may deter domestic entrepreneurs from entering the market to begin with. In many

---

[1] Cairncross, A.K., op. cit., p. 58.

[2] In comparison with foreign investment, domestic enterprise with foreign technical collaboration may be an attractive alternative: "Finally, the true alternative to the joint venture is not complete foreign ownership but rather no foreign equity participation at all. To the host country, the advantages of a joint venture is the acquisition of the intangible benefits and the nonmonetary transfer of resources associated with foreign investment without incurring the costs of 100 per cent foreign equity... If, however, the foreign know-how, managerial talent, and training facilities could be acquired without the foreign equity from the start, the developing country would then completely escape the costs of foreign financial involvement. To this end, contractual devices involving engineering and construction agreements, technical services agreements, management contracts, or license or franchise arrangements may be superior to the equity joint venture. These contractual devices provide an extremely flexible means of directly transferring specialized technical and managerial knowledge of a proprietary nature from a foreign enterprise, which is the outstanding - and the early - benefit of foreign investment, without the higher costs - which mount over time - of a foreign equity interest" (Meier, G.M. The International Economics ..., pp. 158-160).

underdeveloped countries, non-industrial investments offer a remunerative
alternative to industrial investment, and the prospect of having to compete
with an experienced foreign company may not be very attractive. Especially the early foreign investment in underdeveloped countries is therefore
often found in monopolistic positions. [1]

Even though domestic companies may be affected negatively or prospective
entrepreneurs are deterred from investing, as a consequence of investment by a foreign company, the loss is not always great. The existing companies can perhaps re-orient their activities so as to become more efficient
or to avoid competition with the foreign firm, and the resources of capital
and know-how possessed by prospective entrepreneurs may also be profi-
tably used in other industrial fields.

Benefits and costs

Once the costs and benefits of foreign investment are known, they can be
compared. In an ordinary cost-benefit analysis this is done by discounting
benefits and costs accruing at different points in time, usually in the
future, to a base year, using an uniform discount rate. The discounted
value of costs is then subtracted from the discounted value of benefits, and
the figure obtained is the result of the cost-benefit calculation, which can
then be compared with results from similar calculations for other projects.

Cost-benefit analysis is commonly used to compare future chains of events.
When applied to the history of existing foreign investment, the comparison
with alternative events is most conveniently included in the analysis in the
form of opportunity costs. The assumptions concerning the alternatives to
the foreign investment that actually occurred are often very important for
the final outcome. [2]

In calculating the benefits from foreign investment, the private calculation
of profits may be taken as a point of departure. [3] Private costs and benefits should be corrected for differences in private and social valuations,

---

1) Giesecke, H., Betrachtungen zum Entwicklungsbeitrag überseeischer
   Privatinvestitionen, in Wirtschaftsdienst, 43, 1963:1 pp. 15, 18.
2) Cf. Pazos, F., The role of international movements of private capital
   in promoting development, in Adler, J.H., op. cit., p. 200; May, S.
   and Plaza, G., The United Fruit Company in Latin America, New
   York 1958, p. 219; Baran, P.A., The Political Economy of Growth,
   New York 1967, pp. 150,230.
3) See p. 11.

and external effects should be taken into account. All costs and benefits of foreign investment should in principle be first identified, then quantified and finally transformed into money units, using proper weights. The costs and benefits in money units should then be discounted to a point in time and compared.

All effects on all objectives should be taken into account and made comparable, by transforming them, for example, into money units of present consumption for a specific group. [1] Benefits in the form of savings result in future consumption, which may then be compared with present consumption via the discount rate. Benefits to different groups or geographical areas should be given different weights, a special accounting price may be used for employment, and similarly the effects in terms of economic independence, power and prestige should be identified, quantified, and valued in money units. All external effects should in the same way be quantified and made comparable.

All this is, of course, impossible. For one thing, many effects cannot be quantified in money units. More effects can be identified than quantified, and more can be quantified than transformed into money units. [2] The effects expressible in money units often give a very limited picture of the impact of a project, and to fulfil the aim of guiding decisions, many effects not expressible in money or even not quantifiable at all have to be taken into account. It is possible that the final weighing must sometimes be what Myrdal calls an "intuitive political judgment". [3] Many practitioners and politicians seem to feel this way. [4]

1) Cf. Little, I.M.D., and Mirrlees, J.A., op. cit., pp. 39 ff.
2) Thorburn, T., Nyttokostnadskalkyler, in Lundberg, E. and Backelin, T. (eds.), Ekonomisk politik i förvandling, Stockholm 1970, p. 146.
3) Myrdal, G., Asian Drama, p. 1812.
4) "The practitioners were very sceptical and inclined to doubt whether the most important social effects of government investments could ever be appraised quantitatively by cost-benefit analysis or any other formalized method. One of them likened the problem to appraising the quality of a horse-and-rabbit stew, the rabbit being cast as the consequences that can be measured and evaluated numerically, and the horse as the amalgam of external effects, social, emotional, and psychological impacts, and historical and aesthetic considerations that can be adjudged only roughly and subjectively. Since the horse was bound to dominate the flavor of the stew, meticulous evaluation of the rabbit would hardly seem worthwhile" (Dorfman, R., (ed.), Measuring the Benefits of Government Investments, Washington 1967, p. 2).

Quantification should, of course, always be aimed at. "The goal must always be to quantify facts and relationships between facts, and until we can measure them, our knowledge has not proceeded far from the initial a priori". [1] Non-quantified analysis often leads to exaggerations one way or the other. [2] But the price of the overall view necessary for responsible decision-making is often a relatively high degree of uncertainty and qualitative reasoning. [3]

As for the evaluation of the impact of private foreign investment, the main benefit is, as we have seen, usually considered to be the technical and organizational know-how transferred, which is seldom amenble to precise quantification. Many effects of foreign investment, for example, the cultural and political effects, are practically impossible to quantify. Such effects are often lost sight of in a purely quantitative analysis of the impact of foreign capital, an Indian critic claims:

> The significance of an overall assessment of the role of foreign
> capital, as indicated above, is often lost sight of in the elaborate
> micro-economic analysis of the contributions of foreign firms to
> capital formation, income and employment. If we abstract from the
> cost involved in the investment of foreign capital in India in terms
> of its effect on economic concentration and monopoly trends in India,
> and the pressures on the Indian economy for moving away from its
> declared objectives, it is possible to arrive at quantitative measure-
> ments of benefits of foreign capital. For instance, one could calcu-
> late the percentage contribution of private foreign firms to total ca-
> pital formation in the private business sector in India. Similarly,
> the contribution of the foreign sector to income and output, employ-
> ment, etc. may be worked out in quantitative terms. But it should
> be remembered that all these attempts at partial analysis do not enable
> us to arrive at a quantified measure of the net benefits or net costs
> to the Indian economy, emanating from the foreign sector. Any assess-
> ment of the role of foreign capital has to be based on an analysis of
> the impact of foreign capital in terms not only of its micro-economic
> aspects, but also, and more significantly, of its relevance to the
> overall direction and strategy of Indian economic development and
> the attainment of India's declared social objectives. [4]

---

1) Myrdal, G., op. cit., p. 31.
2) Little, I.M.D., and Mirrlees, J.A., op. cit., pp. 59, 219.
3) Cf. Meier, G.M., Leading Issues in Economic Development, Stanford 1970, p. 91.
4) Kurian, K.M., Impact of Foreign Capital on Indian Economy, New Delhi 1966, pp. 245-46.

The analysis of Swedish investments that is attempted here will include a fair amount of qualitative reasoning. But all quantifiable effects will, of course, be given full attention, as they may serve as indicators of the direction of unquantifiable effects with larger scope than their quantifiable parts. The aim is to give the total picture, even at the expense of analytical rigidity. The label "cost-benefit analysis" therefore seems rather pretentious. What I shall try to do is rather to present a number of the effects arising from the activities of the Swedish companies in India that may be of interest from a "development" angle.

Criteria. Many economists who have treated the impact of foreign private investment state that this impact is positive when the income accruing to the host country is larger than the income appropriated by the foreign investor. But when only private costs and benefits are taken into account, as is quite often the case, this criterion is, of course, only partial. The balance-of-payments effect and the employment effect are other partial criter which may be useful in special cases.

The best criterion by which to judge the direction of impact of foreign investment will naturally be an integrated criterion, embracing several of the most important effects.[1] As we are interested here in the possible total impact of the Swedish investments in India, an integrated criterion should be used, let us say, "long-term, socially progressive economic growth". Some such criterion is also at the basis of most of the policies and planning of the Indian Government.

All underdeveloped countries want long-term, self-sustaining growth, and it is therefore the long-term effects of foreign investment that are of most interest to them. The direct economic benefits of foreign enterprise are, as we have seen, often considered to be of less importance in the long run than the indirect contribution of technique and organization. To be beneficial foreign investment should affect growth, it should spur the development process over and above its initial addition to production. The social and economic structure should be changed, so that resources are combined in a better way and used more efficiently. What is important is the future use made of foreign investment and foreign aid - it is the indirect effects that are of decisive importance.

> Virtually all recipients of aid are attempting to establish a process of growth which can continue in the future without further assistance. The possibilities for success depend on the country's ability to change

---

[1] Chenery, H.B., The application of investment criteria, in Quarterly Journal of Economics, Vol. LXVII, 1953, p. 80.

its economic structure as it develops.Unless there is a rise in the savings rate or an improvement in the efficiency with which capital and human resources are used, the growth rate after aid has terminated will revert to the growth rate when it started, no matter how much aid and growth there has been in the intervening period. In other words, the prospects for achieving self-sustaining growth depend entirely on the indirect effects of assistance in changing the structure of the economy. [1]

The long-term, indirect effects are stressed also by Meier, when he concludes that foreign investment should be guided to those sectors where it will mobilize most additional national efforts: "Policies affecting the allocation of foreign capital should therefore look beyond merely the direct increase in income resulting from the investment and other such short-term criteria, to the broader and long-run possibilities - from the widening of investment opportunities to even the instigating of social and cultural transformations". [2] The rationale for encouraging foreign private investment therefore seems to be mainly the indirect benfits offered, which may result in the more efficient utilization of resources, improved institutions and attitudes, and increased national participation in the growth effort. But this dynamic perspective also tends to increase the importance of the indirect negative effects. [3] The indirect balance-of-payments costs often rise over time, and the negative political effects are essentially of a long-term nature.

The complexity of the total impact of foreign private investment in underdeveloped countries makes it impossible to reach a theoretical conclusion of universal applicability. The social framework differs from country to country, and the impact of different industries may show considerable variations. The theory only gives the instruments for empirical research, which has to be undertaken at the industry and company level. [4] The further discussion will for this reason be concentrated on the empirical effects at the company level.

The main categories of possible positive and negative effects of foreign private investment mentioned in Chapter 1 are shown in Chart 1. The be-

1) Chenery, H.B., Foreign assistance and economic development, in Adler, J.H. (ed.), op. cit., p. 274.
2) Meier, G.M., International Trade..., p. 114.
3) Södersten, B., op. cit., p. 464.
4) Hymer, S.H., op. cit., p. 187; Arndt, H.W., Overseas borrowing - the new model, in Economic Record, August 1957, p. 260; Johansson, H., Utländsk företagsetablering i Sverige, Uddevalla 1968, p. 20.

nefit from inflows of capital has a counterpart cost in capital repatration, and for the benefit from net profits there is a corresponding cost of dividen remittances. Benefits may also accrue in the form of new employment and positive consumer effects. The wage benefit is really a result of an advance calculation of oppotunity costs. External economies correspond to diseconomies, and there are sometimes also other types of indirect benefits and costs.

In Chart 1 the opportunity costs are depicted vertically to indicate that they in fact pervade all other aspects of foreign investment. In discussing the other benefits and costs, alternative events in the form of opportunity costs should always be taken into account. In the case of the Swedish companies. I shall argue in Chapter 9 that the Swedish investments have in fact replaced local production in the respective industries. Domestic producers had started their operations before the Swedish companies entered the market, and the immediate opportunity costs of the Swedish firms were therefore relatively high. But we have also to take into account the probable use of the resources thus disemployed by the Swedish investments. If these resources are put to productive use, the opportunity costs are reduced. Ideally, one should trace the alternative events throughout, but this would necessitate a general equilibrium approach, and I have chosen to limit myself to some type of partial analysis.[1]

In the following pages I shall discuss in more detail the effects mentioned in Chapter 1 and try to present relevant empirical material from the Swedis companies in India. My main aim is not to find out whether the Swedish firn are "good" or "bad" for development but to illustrate the types of effects, most of which are mentioned in the current literature, that I feel should be treated in an evaluation of foreign investment. The natural way to do this is to praise or criticize the activities of the Swedish companies, but it should be emphasized that I am not giving any personal credit or blame to the managements of the Swedish firms. All the effects treated are such as occur in the normal course of doing business.

The standard procedure in discussing the effects of foreign investment is to start with the profit benefits and then to mention in less detail the more elusive effects, like external economies. But as the indirect benefits - the "external economies in a wider sense" - are usually considered the main benefit of foreign investment, these types of effects merit priority treatment. I shall therefore study the external economies before the quantifiable effects.

---

1) Cf. pp. 260 ff.

CHART I

POSITIVE EFFECTS		NEGATIVE EFFECTS
Inflow of capital	o	Repatriation of capital
Net profits	p p o	Dividend remittances
Wage benefit	r	
Employment	t u	
Consumer benefits	n i	
External economies "in a narrow sense"	t y	External diseconomies "in a narrow sense"
External economies "in a wider sense"	c o	External diseconomies "in a wider sense"
Other indirect benefits	s t s	Other indirect costs

Chapter 2

INDIA AND FOREIGN INDUSTRY

In Chapter 1, the theoretical setting of the study was outlined. Before proceeding to the main subject of my study, the development effects of the Swedish investments, I think it necessary to make some preliminary remarks about the relevant Indian setting. I shall not give any general background information about India - "land and people" - that can be found in the standard official and private publications. A good comprehensive view of the overall economic situation will be found in Gunnar Myrdal's Asian Drama. Instead, the discussion in this chapter will be concentrated on industrial development in general, and special attention will be given to the role of foreign capital.

Industrial Development

Industry before independence

Before the British colonization, India produced handicraft products, especially textiles, of high quality. Indian chintz and Dacca muslin were well known and valued all over Europe. These luxury items were, however, of little economic importance. The majority of people in India occupied in handicraft manufacture lived in the countryside - the village artisans, who produced low-quality necessities for the people in the villages.

The urban luxury industry depended for its prosperity on the Indian princely courts and to some extent also on exports to Europe. When most of the princely courts disappeared with British rule, a major source of demand for the luxury production was suddenly snatched away. At the same time the European demand changed in the direction of machine-made cotton goods, instead of Indian-type silk fabrics. With declining demand, the urban artistic industry fell off very rapidly. [1] The disappearance in the early 19th century of most of the princely courts, and not the foreign

---

1. Edwardes, M., British India, London 1967, p. 89.

competition, was probably the main reason for the decay of urban manufacture, and the suddenness of the decline is thereby also explained.[1]

The quantitatively more important village handicrafts did not fall off as rapidly, but, on the other hand, they felt more the heavy pressure from foreign and later domestic industrial competition. Village tanners and dyers virtually disappeared, and only a minority of the many hand-loom weavers managed to survive by specializing in either very coarse or very fine textiles. The decline of handicrafts in India followed the earlier European pattern, with one important exception: European artisans thrown out of work by modern factories were absorbed in the new industries, but in India the industrialization process started too late to keep employment up, and the resulting distress for the Indian handicraft workers is well known.

The decay of the handicrafts was accelerated by the construction of the railways in the latter half of the 19th century. It seems that the railways were primarily used for military and commercial purposes, with the result that raw-material exports were encouraged rather than indigenous manufacturing industry.[2] At the same time the country was knit together, and the construction of railways was probably a prerequisite for more widespread industrialization at a later date.[3]

The first industries to be started in India followed the earlier trading pattern and were oriented outwards, producing for export. To replace the declining handicraft exports, the East India Company in the middle of the 19th century revived the old indigo production. When the Company's monopoly of the tea trade with China was lost in 1833, it started paying attention to proposals to start tea production in India. During the tea boom in the 1850's, many officers of the Company took to tea-growing for export purposes.[4]

---

1) Gagdil, D.R., The Industrial Evolution of India in Recent Times, London 1933, p. 42.
2) Myrdal, G., Asian Drama, p. 456.
3) Gadgil, D.R., op. cit., p. 196; Anstey, V., The Economic Development of India, London 1957, pp. 148, 153; The Oxford History of India, Oxford 1958, p. 709.
4) Details of the early industrial development in India can be found in, for example, Gadgil, D.R., op. cit.; Buchanan, D.H., The Development of Capitalist Enterprise in India, New York 1934; Dutt, R., The Economic Development of India, London 1957; Anstey, V., op. cit.; Griffiths, P., The British Impact on India, London 1952.

In the 1850´s, the basic legal framework for the emergence of large-scale industries was laid. The concept of a joint-stock company with limited liability was introduced in 1857, only one year after a similar law was passed in Britain. Indian legislation, up to the data of independence, followed closely the changes in the British common law, including company law.

The first cotton mill in India was erected in 1853. Cotton soon became the predominant factory industry, producing cotton yarn and later also cloth. The cotton industry was exceptional, in that it was financed mainly by Indian capital, although management was, to begin with, in British hands. But the two other main industries started before the First World War, jute and coal, were dominated by the British. The jute industry is heavily concentrated in Bengal, where the climatic conditions for growing raw jute are exceptionally favourable. Coal-mining started relatively early, but not until the late 19th century, when the railways both created the demand and solved the transport problem, did any significant expansion take place in the coal industry.

The early industrialization was concentrated in a few industries, and progress was not overly impressive. In 1881 there were in India 475 registered join-stock companies with a total paid-up capital of about Rs. 150 million. In 1911, 2251 companies had a capital of Rs. 650 million.[1]

When the First World War broke out, imports into India were heavily reduced. The absence of even light-engineering industries in the country made the situation very difficult for the existing industries and the railways and the lack of spare parts and machinery set definite limits to the expansion of industrial capacity and production. At the same time the war demand encouraged new industries, notably the cement industry. The major accomplishment of Indian entrepreneurship, the Tata iron and steel works, went into production just before the war, and war demands helped it through the first difficult period.

In the inter-war period, the established industries, except for the export industries, lived through the great depression without any major setbacks. Indigenous production of manufactures increased in the inter-war period from 30 to 40 per cent of the total offtake.[2] New consumer industries, like paper, matches and sugar, obtained some tariff protection and expanded considerably. But the engineering industry did not receive any

---

1) Sen, S.K., Studies in Industrial Policy and Development of India (1858-1914), Calcutta 1964, p. 138.
2) Kidron, M., op. cit., pp. 20-21.

protection, and the lack of both light and heavy capital goods was a serious bottleneck also during the Second World War.[1]

At the end of the Second World War, there were more than 20 000 factories in India. Despite the lack of capital equipment, many new important industries were started during the war, and with independence they obtained the protection needed for further development.[2] But the industrial structure was still heavily biased towards consumer industry and traditional fields; in 1946 the cotton and jute textile industries alone accounted for 45 per cent of the fixed capital in 29 major industries.[3]

Industrial policy. The industrial policy of the British colonial government was not very effective in encouraging the industrialization process. When Britain in the middle of the 19th century became a free trader, the British industry had already reached a relatively mature stage. At this stage the nascent Indian industry would have needed protection to withstand foreign competition, but instead, free trade was imposed on India, and the country became exposed to what has been called, by a vehement critic, the "savage whiplash of economic liberalism".[4] When it was found necessary to impose revenue duties on some goods imported into India, a countervailing excise was levied on Indian manufactures to ensure that the Indian industry would not get any protection.

During the First World War, the negative effects of India´s practically total dependence on imports for industrial goods became clearly visible, and after the war a policy of discriminating protection was introduced. But it was hedged in with so many restrictive conditions that it had little effect in promoting industrialization. In fact, new industries were virtually excluded

---

1) "Yet India´s second World War experience shows that surprisingly little growth in light engineering had taken place between the two world wars. Not until the outbreak of the second war were factories started for the manufacture of spinning ring frames and looms or even such simple items as pickers, bobbins, and starch, all of which are required by an industry which had been in operation since 1854" (Myers, C. A., Labor Problems in the Industrialization of India, Cambridge 1958, p. 16).
2) India. Fiscal Commission 1949-50, Report, Vol. I, Delhi 1950, p. 23.
3) Kidron, M., Foreign Investments in India, London 1965, p. 21.
4) Clairmonte, F., op. cit., p. 68.

from the scheme of protection. Between 1923 and 1939 only nine industries received protection, all of them being already firmly established. [1] In the words of the Fiscal Commission of 1949:

> Protection was not visualised as an instrument of general economic development, but was viewed as a means of enabling particular industries to withstand foreign competition, when they applied for protection. This resulted in a somewhat lopsided development. With such an approach, it was not possible for basic and key industries to develop. [2]

It is true that government spending stimulated several Indian industries, notably the coal, paper and woollen industries. But government support was also conspicuously absent from the vital iron, steel and machinery industries. [3] Numerous attempts to start viable steel works failed because of lack of government support. The Tatas were the first to get real support from the Indian Government, but they did not get any help from Britain - capital, machinery and management had to be obtained elsewhere. [4] The supply policy as concerned engineering goods and machinery was outright negative. [5] The Indian engineering industry had in colonial times to rely on private demand and occasional rush orders from the government for its precarious existence.

The Industrial Commission of 1918 suggested in the light of the war-time experience a more active government policy in the industrial field. But for various reasons these suggestions were not acted upon. [6] A more vigorous policy of industrial development was therefore not realized until after independence. The passive colonial policy has been summarized in rather critical terms by Myrdal as follows:

> Colonial policy was thus an intricate combination of overt and indirect suppression of indigenous manufacturing industry. Even potential supports, such as construction of social overhead capital and the introduction of modern commercial institutions, failed to stimulate industrialization because of the failure to recognize the specific needs of the South Asian economies. Often the effect was further to subordinate the colonies and keep them longer in the stage of 'hewers of wood and drawers of water', as mere appendages to the metropolitan economy. In sum, in the colonial context laissez-faire policies failed to trigger much in-

---

1) India. Fiscal Commission 1949-50, op. cit., p. 58.
2) Ibid., p. 50.
3) Ibid., pp. 46, 60 ff.
4) Ibid., p. 64.
5) Ibid., p. 77.
6) Hazari, R.K., op. cit., p. 13; Anstey, V., op. cit., pp. 220-21.

digenous industrialization. The doctrine of laissez-faire implied the absence of government aid and protection to manufacturing and to economic development generally, outside of the plantations and the extractive industries producing raw materials. Given this lack of positive industrial promotion and of serious efforts to reform the social system, the emergence of an expanding 'free economy' where private initiative would provide the dynamic impulse was rendered almost impossible. In conjunction with active support for the European enterprises in plantations, mining, forestry, and other extractive fields, laissez-faire passivity virtually guaranteed an absence of spontaneous industrialization. That some did occur is more to be wondered at than its relative dearth.

One should, moreover, qualify the common characterization of colonial economic policies, especially before the First World War, as laissez-faire. True, little or nothing was done to encourage industrialization, outside of the plantations and the extractive industries; but the influence of government was used to weight the scales with discriminatory measures that hindered industrialization and enhanced dependence on the production of raw materials for export. The puzzlement expressed by so many writers as to why India did not become industrialized after so many starts is therefore misplaced. [1]

Foreign capital and colonialism

Before independence, no reliable statistics were collected on the total size and industrial distribution of foreign capital. But the inflow of foreign private capital into India was for obvious reasons not very large during the depression in the 1930's or during the Second World War, and the overall distribution of foreign investment remained remarkably constant up to 1947. [2] The post-independence statistics, which will be treated later, are therefore a good indicator also of the foreign-investment situation during the first half of the 20th century.

According to one of the few estimates made before 1947, a total of Rs. 5750 million of foreign capital had been invested in India up to 1927. [3] Subtracting about Rs. 3600 million invested in the form of railway and government securities leaves some 2150 million invested in industry, which just about equals the total paid-up capital of all the joint-stock companies

1) Myrdal, G., op. cit., pp. 457-58.
2) Kidron, M., op. cit., p. 3.
3) Estimate of Dr. V.K.R.V. Rao, quoted in Kurian, K.M., Impact of Foreign Capital on Indian Economy, Delhi 1966, p. 42.

registered in India at the time. Another estimate from 1911 gives the industrial distribution of British private investments in India and Ceylon, exclusive also of government and railway securities (Table 1).

Table 1. Industrial distribution of British investments in 1911 in India and Ceylon.

Industry	Percentage of total British investment
Plantations (tea, rubber)	60
Utilities (tramways, electricity)	12
Oil	9
Mining	7
Finance (banks)	6
Industry and commerce	4
Shipping	3

Sources. The Economist, London, 21 June 1911, p. 1345, quoted in Islam, N., Foreign Capital and Development, Tokyo 1960, p. 84.

In India, tea was the main plantation industry, and the relatively small amount of British capital invested in manufacturing was heavily concentrated in jute. Coal was the main mining industry, very much dominated by British capital. Indian capital was prominent in cotton and, later, in steel and cement, but banking, shipping and foreign trade were very much foreign domains. Also the industries dominated later on by Indian capital were started by foreigners, and the largest companies in each industry were usually foreign.

> The pioneering enterprises in almost all the modern large-scale industries, not only in those like jute, plantations (tea, rubber, coffee), mining, public utilities, in which foreign enterprise and control remained predominant up to recent times but also in those industries like paper, leather, sugar, cement, in which the domestic enterprises rapidly grew and outnumbered the foreign enterprises, were started by foreign enterprise. Even in the iron and steel industry, which was the brightest monument to the Indian enterprise and capital, the early attempts and experiments, which did not, however emerge as commercial successes, were made by foreign enterprise, which succeeded in making pig-iron but not steel. [1]

---

1) Islam, N., op. cit., p. 170; Cf. pp. 172 ff.

The investment of foreign capital in India during the early years was greatly facilitated by the growth of the so-called managing-agency system. The financial houses in London and Liverpool in the 19th century were ready to supply capital to reliable British managements in India. But the number of British agents in India who knew the alien conditions, mostly merchants gradually taking to production, was relatively limited. To economize on the scarce resources, each agent therefore was employed to look after several enterprises.

The managing agents soon became independent and started promoting and financing new industries themselves, and as there were no laws controlling the manipulations of the managing agents, the managing-agency houses could relatively easily build up large industrial empires. In the late 1930's, some 60 foreign agency houses controlled more than 600 rupee companies and a number of sterling ones. [1] Indian entrepreneurs emulated the British agency system as a convenient system of unrestricted control with little capital. The abuses of the managing-agency system later led to restrictive legislation and the gradual abolition of the system.

The foreign managing agencies started with British capital and later added their own. But with the outbreak of the First World War, the supply of foreign finance was cut off, and the agencies then had to take in Indian capital for the wartime expansion. After the war, foreign investors remained shy, and the Indianization of the capital of the companies controlled by foreign agencies continued. Already in 1922, 60 per cent of the capital actually invested in jute was Indian, but only two jute mills were under Indian control. [2] Despite progressive Indianization of the capital, foreign agencies maintained up to 1947 control over major industries like jute, tea, coal, wool, shipping and general engineering. [3] Indian agency houses, on the other hand, controlled the expansion of the cotton, iron, sugar, cement and paper industries and gradually made some headway into the banking sector.

In 1948, the foreign managing agencies held, on an average, less than 15 per cent of the capital in their managed companies. Their control there-

---

1) Kidron, M., op. cit., p. 6. Cf. Kust, M.J., Foreign Enterprise in India, Bombay 1966, pp. 278 ff.
2) Islam, N., op. cit., p. 173.
3) Kidron, M., op. cit., pp. 4, 10, 11; Islam, N., op. cit., p. 172.

fore did not rest on ownership but rather on organization and backing from British interests, within and outside the country.[1] There were before independence also no restrictions on the inflow of foreign capital.[2] The organized and modern section of the Indian money market and foreign trade houses were in foreign hands and favoured foreign industry, and foreign companies could also count on preferential treatment by the Government.[3] It appears, for example, that foreign-dominated industries like the match industry were more readily given protection than industries controlled by Indians.[4]

Colonialism. Foreign investments in India during the colonial era were thus favoured more than Indian industry. But at the same time industrial development in general in India was discouraged in the interests of the "home manufacturers" in Great Britain.[5] The industrial policy of the colonial government and the scope and direction of the British industrial investments in India helped to turn India into a producer and exporter of mainly primary products. Industrial growth was slow and lopsided as a consequence, really, of the whole colonial system, of which the direct private investments were a part. It is impossible to isolate, for example, the effects of foreign investments in colonial India from the total invest-ment-cum-trade system of the colonial power.

---

1) "One broad conclusion emerges from this sketch of the foreign sector in British times. Its power did not rest primarily on ownership, al-though a virtual monopoly of a few key industries naturally helped. Had it done so, the heart of the system, the managing agencies, would have been lost well before the Second World War. Similarly, while its ability to provide certain technical and managerial skills was impor-tant, these were neither so complex nor so scarce after the First World War as to constitute an impregnable monopoly. This Indian capital was soon to demonstrate. The essence of its power lay rather in organi-zation - its self-sufficiency, its integrated and articulated character, its flexibility - and in being able to draft in outside resources in men, money, markets, or whatever, when necessary. In a larger context this power rested on a sympathetic government and a specific form of international economy which lay beyond its own area of control" (Kidron M., op. cit., p. 11).

2) India. Fiscal Commission 1949-50, op. cit., p. 49.

3) Kidron, M., op. cit., p. 12. Cf. Spencer, D.L., India, Mixed Enter-prise and Western Business, The Hague 1959, p. 30.

4) Ibid., p. 13. Cf. India. Fiscal Commission 1949-50, op. cit., p. 52.

5) See pp. 31 ff.

I cannot and need not analyse here the total impact of British rule in India, but the foreign investments during the colonial era must be seen in their overall context. The industrial development and foreign-investment policies of independent India are, of course, also related to and dependent on the historical development. I will therefore touch briefly on some points in the current discussion of the impact of colonial rule.

Britain was responsible for the unification of India and unwittingly created a national feeling. A uniform law and administrative system was diffused throughout the country, but at the same time the political institutions in the villages decayed. Famine relief, better health, and the transport system are British accomplishments. The early industries in India were started and promoted by the British, but the foreign industrial domination also stifled domestic initiatives and pre-empted industrial opportunities. The tariff, stores and industrial policies of the colonial government discouraged industrialization.

In the field of ideas, indigenous religious and cultural values may have suffered. But research and education were given a more practical turn, even though the educational system was imported directly from Britain without modifications. British companies were often unwilling to impart managerial and technical knowledge, and the Indianization of the administrative services was very gradual. [1] But the continuous presence of Englishmen in all positions must have had an effect, as regarded the transmission of know-how.

At the end of the colonial era, the total national output in India had increased substantially, as compared with Moghul times. But the population had also grown, and the food situation for the common man was probably unaltered. [2] As concerned clothing and housing, however, it seems likely that the situation for the average Indian was somewhat better at the end than at the beginning of the colonial period. [3]

---

1) Islam, N., op. cit., p. 183; Kust, M.J., op. cit., p. 10.
2) Strachey, J., The End of Empire, London 1959, p. 53; Anstey, V.,
   op. cit., p. 5.
3) Griffiths, P., op. cit., p. 477.

A complete judgment on the effects of British rule in India may be passed as an article of political faith. [1] As a scientific historical problem, it has not yet been fully treated. The outcome depends to a large extent on the alternative development assumed. In my view, John Strachey, many of whose ancestors were civil servants in India, gives an uncommon but excellent summary of the problem:

> It would indeed be easy to moralise over the history of imperialism, since that history includes some of the most ferocious events in the whole of human development: but it would not be useful. For example, the British empire in India was both iniquitous and beneficent: it was founded by violence, treachery and insatiable avarice, but also by incomparable daring and sustained resolution; it united India: it partitioned India: it industrialised India: it stunted India: it degraded India: it served India: it ravaged India: it created modern India: it was selfish and selfless, ruinous and constructive, glorious and monstrous. Such events cannot usefully be either celebrated or arraigned, but perhaps they can be understood. [2]

The foreign, mainly British, investments in India before independence thus largely had the same effects as the whole colonial system, of which they were an integral part. Whatever the sum of these effects may have been, the formal disruption of the colonial relations left independent India with a large foreign sector, which it became the task of the national government to harness and stimulate in accordance with the new national goals. Foreign investment after independence must be seen in a new light, but the residue of the historical relations which are still there should not be forgotten.

New objectives of industrial development

When India became independent in 1947, it was self-sufficient in textiles and sugar, and the production of jute, paper, coal, cement, steel and cigarettes was well established. But nearly 70 per cent of the industrial output consisted of consumer goods, and production of non-ferrous metals, electrical engineering goods, tractors, machinery, machine tools and

---

1) This was in fact done by the members of the Congress Party, who used to take a pledge on Independence Day, stating that "the British Government in India has not only deprived the Indian people of their freedom but has based itself on the exploitation of the masses, and has ruined India economically, politically, culturally and spiritually" (ibid., p. 359).
2) Strachey, J., op. cit., p. 13.

38

heavy chemicals was either non-existent or still in its infancy. One of the main objectives adopted by the national government was to change the industrial structure of the country.

In the first few years of independence, industrial progress was slow. The partition of India and the ensuing unrest resulted in declining industrial output. But order was gradually restored, and in 1951 India took the first step on the road to planned economic development with the inauguration of the First Five-year Plan. Although the industrial sector received only 5 per cent of the total public-sector outlay under the Plan, industrial production increased in the period 1951-1956 by 43 per cent. [1] During the period of the Second Plan, 1956-61, special emphasis was placed on industry, and as much as 24 per cent of the public-sector outlay was then spent on industry and minerals. Three steel plants in the public sector were commissioned, and there was considerable investment in basic metals, machine-building and other heavy industries. "If one were to pick a five-year period which really initiated the industrial revolution in India, one could name the period of the Second Five-Year Plan." [2]

At the same time, the period of the Second Plan saw India's first serious foreign-exchange crisis. The sterling balances accumulated during the Second World War, amounting to Rs. 17 billion in 1945-46, had by 1957 been run down, imports had to be severely curtailed, and India became increasingly dependent on foreign capital. During the Third Five-year Plan, industrial production continued to increase, but towards the end of the Plan it began to stagnate because of the crisis in agriculture in 1965-66. The Fourth Five-year Plan was postponed because of the economic crisis till 1969, and industrial production only slowly picked up momentum.

But as a whole the period of the first three Five-year Plans shows a remarkable achievement in the industrial field. In 1948 India could not even make a good pin or sewing needle, but now it can build its own atomic reactors. The traditional industries have developed at less than average pace, but new industries like engineering, chemicals and machine tools have grown rapidly. The share of output coming from consumer-goods industries has been halved during the period, from 70 to about 35 per cent. The changing structure of the economy is a result of the new national policies, but the policies and objectives have also changed in response to the economic developments.

---

1) Shah, N., op. cit., p. 12.
2) Ibid., p. 12.

Objectives and policies. The basic policies and objectives of the Indian Government have remained unchanged since 1947. The main objective is a welfare state with higher production, more employment, increased economic and social equality, less concentration of economic power and less foreign influence. These general aims are stated in the Constitution and are reiterated in numerous other official documents, and they are well diffused at least among the articulate elite. But the relative order of priority between the basic objectives is seldom made clear, although changes of stress are noticeable throughout the four Five-year Plans.

Before overall planning started in the 1950´s, special attention was given to industrial policy. The All-India Congress Committee of 1947, under the chairmanship of the late Prime Minister Jawaharlal Nehru, suggested that banking and insurance should be immediately nationalized and that certain key industries should in the future be reserved for the public sector, involving also the nationalization of existing key industries within five years. Private capital reacted strongly against these suggestions, the government called an Industrial Truce Conference, and the subsequent Industrial Policy Resolution issued in 1948 was much less socialistic than was expected; "its mildness took everyone by surprise".[1]

The 1948 Industrial Policy Resolution emphasized production rather than equitable distribution.[2] Nationalizations in key industries were postponed for at least 10 years, and it was stated that private enterprise, properly directed and regulated, had a valuable role to play. Special encouragement of cottage and small-scale industries was envisaged. All major industries were to be regulated in the national interest. The Industries (Development and Control) Act of 1951 later became the main instrument for this regulation. It was implemented through a comprehensive system of industrial licensing.

The first Five-year Plan gave top priority to agriculture, power supplies and irrigation. Increased production and employment were the central Plan objectives, and through the planning mechanism a simultaneous advance on all fronts was to be realized.[3] The Plan indicated a progressive widening of the public sector but no further nationalizations - the State was not to

1) Chopra, P., Uncertain India, Cambridge 1968, p. 108.
2) India. Industrial Policy Resolution 1948, quoted in India. Estimates Committee, Report 1967-68, Delhi 1967, p. 285.
3) India. Planning Commission, The First Five-Year Plan. A Summary, Delhi 1952, pp. 1 ff.

compete with private enterprise outside the sphere reserved for future development by the public sector. [1]

The second Five-year Plan was prepared at a time when the Leftwing group of the Congress Party was relatively influential. At the Avadi session of the Congress in 1955, it was resolved that "planning should take place with a view to the establishment of a socialistic pattern of society, where the principal means of production are under social ownership or control". [2] At about the same time some important nationalizations were carried out; air transport in 1953, the Imperial Bank in 1955, life insurance and the Kolar Gold Fields in 1956. The company law, the new Industrial Policy Resolution and the second Five-Year Plan of 1956 all bear the signs of the swing Left in Congress policy.

But the nationalizations were not motivated primarily on socialistic grounds, [3] and the "socialistic pattern of society" has in fact been shown to be just another slogan, with not much more specific meaning than the phrase "welfare state". But at the time when the "socialistic pattern of society" was accepted as the basic objective of the Second Five-year Plan, there was a marked stress on equality and the increased activity of the public sector. [4]

---

1) "The scope and need for industrial development are so great that it is best for the public sector to concentrate at this stage on the development of those industries in which private enterprise is unwilling or unable to put up the resources required and to undertake the necessary risks. Nationalisation of existing enterprises is of little advantage as most of the purposes in view can be served by judicious regulation" (ibid., p. 88).
2) Quoted in Kidron, M., op. cit., p. 131.
3) Kust, M.J., op. cit., p. 99; Kidron, M., op. cit., p. 133.
4) "These basic objectives have recently been summed up in the phrase ' socialistic pattern of society'. Essentially, this means that the primary criterion for determining the lines of advance must not be private profit but social gain and that the pattern of development and the structure of socio-economic relations should be so planned that they result not only in appreciable increases in national income and employment but also in greater equality in incomes and wealth. The benefits of economic development must accrue more and more to the relatively less privileged classes of society, and a milieu should be created in which the small man has chances of rising in life. For creating such an environment, the State has to take on heavy responsibilities. The public sector has to expand rapidly. It has to play a dominant role in shaping the entire pattern of investments..." (India. Planning Commission, Second Five-Year Plan, Summary, New Delhi 1956, p. 10.)

"...it is inevitable that the public sector must grow not only absolutely but also relatively to the private sector."[1]

The emphasis in the Second Plan was on large industrial projects in the public sector, and industrialization was given first priority. The new Industrial Policy Resolution of 1956, with "more teeth" in it than the 1948 resolution it replaced, increased the number of industries in the category in which the State would have the sole responsibility for further development ("Schedule A") and marked out 12 more major industries in which the State would "generally take the initiative in establishing new undertakings" but in which private enterprise would also be allowed ("Schedule B").[2] The support for cottage industries was re-emphasized.

The foreign-exchange crisis that occurred in the middle of the Second Five-year Plan tilted the balance of economic and social power in India in favour of the private sector, and the Third Five-year Plan was not as emphatic as the Second on a socialistic development. A "balanced advance" was recommended, and the need also of a less uneven regional economic development was stressed.

The increased emphasis on the private sector is continued in the Fourth Five-year Plan. "Expansion in industries in which required development could be ordinarily expected to take place in the cooperative or private sector is not envisaged in the public sector."[3] This is more an adjustment to reality than an ideological change; a growing public sector is obviously still desired. But the large public-sector plants have shown heavy losses, there is a general lack of resources for public purposes, and the pressure from a rapidly growing private sector for more public utilities reduces the scope for new public industrial initiatives.[4]

The private sector has continuously over-fulfilled the objectives stated in the Plans and accounts as a whole for more than 80 per cent of the national income.[5] The Indian Government has accepted that what it presides over is mainly a private-enterprise economy, and the market mechanism is being used to an increasing extent to achieve the results desired. From 1963 on-

1) Ibid., p. 11.
2) India. Industrial Policy Resolution 1956, quoted in India. Estimates Committee, Report 1967-68. op. cit., pp. 292 ff.
3) India. Planning Commission, Fourth Five-Year Plan 1969-74, Draft, Delhi 1969, p. 238.
4) Kidron, M., op. cit., pp. 146-47.
5) India. Planning Commission, Industrial Planning and Licensing Policy, Final Report, p. 13.

wards, price and distribution controls on several essential commodities have been removed, and many industries have been de-licensed, so that they can now develop free of government control. Since the industrial recession in the late 1960´s, when the former sellers´ market was suddenly converted into a buyers´ market, the Government has tried to stimulate demand and to increase through market incentives such things as industrial dispersal, decentralized decision-making, competitiveness and cost-consciousness.

At the same time as the private sector has been encouraged, the questions of equality and the concentration of economic power have been given increased attention. The Monopoly Inquiry Commission of 1965 found that 75 dominant business houses controlled nearly 50 per cent of the assets of all non-government and non-banking companies. In 1966 a gradual abolition of the managing-agency system was decided on, and the Fourth Plan emphasizes the social ends of planning.[1] All sizeable private Indian banks were nationalized in 1969, and in 1970, in response to the suggestions of the Industrial Licensing Policy Inquiry Committee, the largest business houses were prohibited from making further investments in other than large-scale undertakings and are now only encouraged within a narrow "core sector".

Policy implementation

The steps taken to restrict and control the activities of the big business sector were one major outcome of the examination of the licensing system made by the Industrial Licensing Policy Inquiry Committee. (Known as the Dutt Committee).[2] But the Committee also criticized severely the overall implementation of industrial objectives. The industrial licensing system introduced in 1951, that was to be the cornerstone of industrial-policy implementation, has apparently not fully served its purpose.

The idea was that the licensing system should regulate industrial development and canalize resources in accordance with the priorities and targets laid down in the Five-year Plans. But the priorities even of the broad Plan

---

1) "The broad objectives of planning could thus be defined as rapid economic development accompanied by continuous progress towards equality and social justice and the establishment of a social and economic democracy" (India. Planning Commission, Fourth Five-Year Plan, p. 5.)
2) India. Industrial Licensing Policy Inquiry Committee, Main Report, Delhi 1969.

objectives _inter se_ were never defined, and even less the relative priorities withing the industrial field. [1] Without any operationally defined industrial priorities, the licensing authorities could not discriminate properly between different applications for industrial licences. The relative scarcity of both foreign exchange and financial resources has a rule been under-estimated, with the result that too many industrial licences have been issued.

> The immediate result was that having an industrial licence became the crossing of only the first hurdle. It did not guarantee that the re-quired foreign - exchange import of capital goods would be available, financial assistance required would be provided or that the project would be assured of scarce domestic materials such as steel or ce-ment. This led to a wild scramble with constant pressure on the con-trolling mechanism and ultimately which of the capacities were actual-ly installed or not had no relationship with any order of priorities among the various industries which were included in the Plan. [2]

A major result of the _ad hoc_ system of licensing was that direct and in-direct favours were granted to the big business houses. Relatively to smaller businesses, the large houses obtained more licenses, earlier information about licensing-policy changes, more financial assistance and larger foreign-exchange allocations. They were also treated relatively leniently when they created capacities much beyond the original licences, and in some other cases they were directly favoured by the government. [3]

---

1) According to the Plans, the conflict between the major economic and social objectives was to be solved by a "balanced advance", but what was meant by a "balanced advance" was never defined. "In the short run, there may sometimes be a conflict between the economic and social objectives of developmental planning. The claims of economic and social equality and those of increased employment may have to be reconciled with the requirements of production. Experience of the working of the first two Plans suggests that on the whole the most satisfactory results are likely to be achieved by a balanced advance in all these directions. What constitutes a balanced advance will vary according to the needs and circumstances of the economy but, given the acceptance on the part of the community of the essential values or ends to be pursued, the processes of democracy and freedom of choice should be capable of throwing up the optimum to be aimed at in a given context" (India. Planning Commission, _Third Five-year Plan; A Draft Outline_, Delhi 1960, p. 3.

2) India. Industrial Licensing Policy Inquiry Committee, op. cit., pp. 100-101.

3) Ibid., pp. 29, 37, 63, 74, 179.

Smaller applicants, on the other hand, were often treated by the licensing authorities "in an unsympathetic manner".1)   The conclusion of the Dutt Committee is that "not only was no attempt made to use licensing to prevent the further growth of the larger industrial houses, but the process actually worked in their favour".2)

The licensing system also failed to realize the objective of a rapidly increasing State-owned industrial sector. The public sector has grown substantially over the Plan periods, but while the private sector has continuously over-fulfilled its objectives, the public sector has shown serious shortfalls in the very industries which were most crucial for further growth.3) This does not, of course, mean that the licensing system has been a total failure - part of the criticism voiced by the Dutt Committee is of a marginal character.

The categories of the Industrial Policy Resolution of 1956 have not been adhered to. Many of the industries reserved for the public sector ("Schedule A") have been opened up to private interests. As for "Schedule B", where the State would "generally take the initiative in establishing new undertakings", the licensing authorities have, when there has been a choice, repeatedly taken decisions in favour of the private sector. 'In short, the intention announced in the Industrial Policy Resolution regarding the future role of the State in the industries included in Schedule B was not reflected in the grant of licenses."4)   The licensing system also failed to prevent the growth of capacity in less essential industries, it did not reduce regional disparities, and it allowed for excessive import substitution and more foreign collaborations than were necessary.

Our conclusion, therefore, is that the licensing system was not properly organised for the purposes which it was expected to achieve; the authorities concerned were not clear about these objectives and no clear guidelines for their attainment were ever laid down. The result has been that the licensing system has not contributed adequately

---

1) Ibid., p. 56.
2) Ibid., p. 183. Cf. Myrdal, G., op. cit., pp. 926 ff.
3) Hazari, R.K., op. cit., p. 64.
4) India. Industrial Licensing Policy Inquiry Committee, op. cit., p. 106. Cf. p. 184; Kidron, M., op. cit., pp. 143-44; Myrdal, G., op. cit., p. 822. There may be some truth in the saying that "socialism operated in India only in fields which required high investment and low profitability" (Chopra, P., op. cit., p. 118).

to the attainment of the social and economic objectives of the Industrial Policy Resolutions and Plans.[1)]

This led to the situation described above, in which the public sector mainly has a passive role, adjusting to the demands of the private sector.

The Indian Government reacted to the report of the Dutt Committee by imposing the restrictions on the business houses already mentioned, and at the same time the exemption limit for licensing was raised considerably, so that no enterprise with assets below Rs. 10 million would have to apply for an industrial licence. Industrial licensing as a positive instrument will in the future be confined to a "core sector", consisting of basic industries for which detailed industry plans will be prepared.

Foreign Investment

Foreign capital after 1947

One of the first measures of the new administration was to collect data on industries in general, and also on foreign industry. The first official census of foreign capital was made in 1948 by the Reserve Bank of India, which has also been responsible for later surveys on foreign investment in India. The coverage of the 1948 and later surveys is nearly 100 per cent, and no one has ever questioned the integrity of the Reserve Bank. But the definitions used have sometimes been criticized, the main complaint being that the data on foreign investment do not include capital owned by foreign nationals who are residents in India but potential non-residents.[2)]

The distribution of foreign investment in 1948 between industries is shown in Table 2, column 2. The colonial pattern is evident: 24 per cent in plantations (mainly tea) and mining, 41 per cent in services and only 27 per cent in manufacture, heavily concentrated in the jute industry. The foreign stake in services in 1948 was concentrated in trade, finance, utilities and shipping – all typical areas of colonial investment.

---

1) India. Industrial Licensing Policy Inquiry Committee, op. cit., p. 184. Cf. pp. 103, 110, 123.
2) Subrahmanian, K.K., op. cit., p. vi; Kurian, M.K., op. cit., pp. 67 ff.

The changes in the industrial distribution of foreign capital from 1948 to 1967, as shown in Table 2, are dramatic. Manufacturing accounted for 50 per cent in 1967, as against only half that proportion in 1948. Petroleum investments, half of which are in refineries, have also shown a relative increase, while the proportions of plantations and services have dwindled. Within the services sector, trade and finance have shown a relative decrease. In the now dominant manufacturing sector, the accent has shifted from lighter, consumer-goods industries, typified by textile and cigarette manufacture, to heavier, producer-goods industries, like chemicals, metal products, transport equipment and electrical goods.

Table 2. Outstanding foreign business investments in 1948 and 1967, industrywise

	Value 1967 (Rs. million)	Percentage 1948	Percentage 1967
Plantations and mining	1,392	24	9
Petroleum	2,066	8	14
Manufacturing	7,380	27	50
Services	3,976	41	27
Total	14,824	100	100

Sources. India. Ministry of Finance, Pocket Book of Economic Information, Delhi 1970, p. 82; Reserve Bank of India, India's Foreign Liabilities and Assets 1961, Survey Report, Bombay 1964, p. 71.

In the colonial era, British investments naturally had a predominant position. In the 1948 survey, 81 per cent of the outstanding foreign private investment was British.[1] Since then, investments from the United States have increased substantially, and the tightened import restrictions have led to investments also from other western countries. In 1967, 44 per cent of the outstanding investments were British, 25 per cent were from the United States, and the remainder was shared between other countries and international institutions.[2]

In 1948, foreign branches accounted for more than half the total foreign investment, and the remainder was in foreign-controlled Indian companies. The branch form of investment is heavily concentrated in the plantations,

---

1) Reserve Bank of India, India's Foreign Liabilities..., p. 75.
2) India. Ministry of Finance, op. cit., p. 81.

petroleum and services sectors, where in 1967 still some 90 per cent of branch investment was found.[1] Within these particular sectors, the branch is also the predominant form of foreign investment, especially in the plantations sector, where there are practically no foreign-controlled Indian companies at all.[2]

The sectors in which branch investments are most prominent are on the whole stagnant. Branches have also been special targets for government scrutiny, and over the years, branches have therefore declined relatively to foreign-controlled rupee companies (see Table 3). But the most dramatic change of investment form is the upsurge in later years of portfolio investments, which were negligible in the 1950´s but were in 1967 the predominant form of foreign investment in the private sector.[3] From 1961 to 1967, portfolio investment increased its share from 21 to 53 per cent (see Table 3). Portfolio investments in India come mainly from official sources, with large loans, for example, to private iron and steel companies from the United States and the World Bank. Portfolio "investment" from smaller countries usually takes the form of supplier credits.

Table 3. Outstanding direct and portfolio investments in 1961 and 1967

		Percentage 1961		Percentage 1967
Direct investments				
Branches	41		19	
Foreign-controlled Indian companies	38	79	28	48
Portfolio investments		21		53
		100		100

Sources. India. Ministry of Finance, Pocket Book of Economic Information, Delhi 1970, p. 84; Reserve Bank of India, India´s Foreign Liabilities and Assets 1961, Survey Report, Bombay 1964, p. 73.

In 1947, foreign capital was still predominant in, for example, tea, jute, coal and shipping. But Indianization of the capital in companies controlled

1) Ibid., p. 84.
2) Kurian, M.K., op. cit., p. 100.
3) India. Ministry of Finance, op. cit., p. 84.

by foreign managing agencies started quite early, and Indian businessmen gradually also obtained effective control of formerly foreign-controlled firms. During the Second World War, there was plenty of money available for industrial finance - many banks had liquidity ratios exceeding 80 per cent and the government paid in advance - and some Indian industrial families became very rich at this time. They used their money to buy up British firms, willingly sold at the prevailing high prices. The uncertain political situation probably accelerated the rate of Indian take-overs.[1] To begin with, the new government gave its tacit support to indigenous business versus foreign.

Disinvestment by foreign interests reached its peak in 1949-50. The unstable situation and the socialistic tendencies of the Congress government kept the fresh inflow of foreign capital low until the mid-fifties. Up to 1955, petroleum investments on concessionary terms dominated the picture, but since then the larger part of foreign investment has been in manufactures.

On the foreign-exchange crisis in 1957-58 followed a more positive attitude on the part of the Indian Government towards foreign capital. At the same time new forms of investment gradually emerged. Very few branches have been established in later years and then only in consultancy engineering and the like. Subsidiaries, which were responsible for most of the investment in the early 1950's, have to an increasing extent been supplemented by investments with minority foreign-capital participation, combined with technical-collaboration agreements.[2]

Also the pure technical-collaboration agreements, without any foreign financial participation, increased rapidly from the late 1950's.[3] A foreign collaboration agreement became for Indian firms a weapon of competition, both on the market and in relation to the government. The government was favourable to new technology being imported in this way, especially if also the foreign-exchange component of a new project was paid by the foreign

---

1) Wiggins, G.A., Private Foreign Investment in the Development of India since 1900, M.Sc. (Econ.) thesis, unpublished, London 1956, pp. 25, 34 ff.
2) Reserve Bank of India, Foreign Collaboration in Indian Industry, Bombay 1968, p. 41.
3) In 1948-67 the accumulated approved collaboration agreements numbered 3100, of which, however, at least half have expired.

collaborator, and a foreign trade-mark gives in the extremely xenophile Indian market an important edge over indigenous competitors.[1] In the late 1950´s foreign investment,and Indian companies with fresh foreign collaborations,started off a boom which was very much afflicted with"collaborationitis".

Foreign exchange and foreign control

The magnitudes of the monetary effects of foreign investment on the Indian balance of payments since independence are shown in Table 4. In 1948-66 there was a total deficit of the order of Rs. 2000 million. Other calculations show a larger deficit.[2] The inflow in kind has regularly been larger than the cash inflow, except in the last few years, when cash receipts have shown a steep rise. Investment in kind is sometimes less valuable than cash inflows.[3]

Table 4. Net foreign-exchange inflow from private sources abroad into Indian private sector, 1948-66

	Inflow/outflow 1948-66 (Rs. million)
Cash inflow	3033
Non-cash inflow	2955
Capital repatriation	-2359
Investment-income outflow	-5596
	-1967

Sources. India. Ministry of Finance, op. cit., p. 85; Reserve Bank of
        India, Bulletin, January 1967, p. 5; Reserve Bank of India, India´s
        Balance of Payments 1948-49 to 1961-62, Bombay 1963, p. 59;
        Reserve Bank of India, Foreign Collaboration in Indian Industry,
        Bombay 1968, p. 9; Kidron, M., op. cit., p. 306.

1) Cf. p. 252.
2) Kidron, M., op. cit., p. 310.
3) "The real inflow of imported resources through kind investment should
   be placed far below than what has been shown by the book values because of tie-up-purchases, mark-up prices, use of clandestine capital
   and other restrictive practices associated with capital goods import
   through kind investment" (Subrahmanian, K.K., op. cit., p. 95).

Data for the years 1963-66 are for the financial years 1963-64 etc. Revalued assets, which were of importance up to 1956, are not included in the foreign-exchange inflow, neither are re-invested earnings (cf. p. 204; Myrdal, G. , op. cit. , p. 623). The respective inflows and outflows are, of course, not casually related, the outflows mostly being connected with older investments than the inflows. The time and price distributions of the foreign-exchange flows have not been taken into consideration.

The British disinvestments resulted in relatively high figures of capital repatriation in 1948-53, and there was a later peak in 1958-59, caused by large capital repatriations by the petroleum companies. The outflow of investment income has been relatively steady, which is probably due to the fact that most foreign companies follow a policy of keeping dividends constant and instead letting re-investments fluctuate.[1] The indirect foreign-exchange contribution of foreign companies in India through imports and exports has traditionally been positive, largely because of substantial tea and jute exports by old British firms, but the shift towards investment in manufacturing industry serving the local Indian market later turned the foreign sector's export surplus into a deficit.[2]

Foreign control. The data on foreign investments in India are very seldom related to any industrial totals, and it is therefore difficult to determine the relative share of foreign industry in India. The best measure I have found of the importance of foreign industry is that at least 34 per cent of the total industrial output in 1965 came from foreign branches and foreign-controlled rupee companies. I say at least, because in all probability the figure is an understatement.

The branches included in the above percentage calculation represent 91 per cent and thus not all the branches in the organized sector, and the foreign-controlled rupee companies included represent only 71 per cent of the paid-up capital in all such companies in the organized sector. The total output figure for foreign companies is therefore somewhat understated. But the figure for total output, to which the outputs of these sample foreign investments are related to reach the 34 per cent figure, includes 98 per cent of all factories with more than 10 workers and also includes the public-sector companies.[3] The total figure is therefore on the low side, and a more

---

1) Cf. pp. 226,236.
2) Kidron, M., op. cit., p. 311.
3) Reserve Bank of India, Bulletin, June 1968, pp. 1, 7, 13; India. Central Statistical Organisation, Annual Survey of Industries 1965, Volume 1, Delhi 1969, pp. xiii ff., 9.

correct figure of foreign-controlled industrial output in India might be in the range of 40-45 per cent. But all we can say with certainty is that forei firms controlled at least 34 per cent of the total output in 1965.

A study by the Reserve Bank of India on foreign collaboration makes a mor limited comparison between public limited companies with foreign majority and minority capital participation and the total capital employed in 1964 in selected public limited companies and concludes that 37 per cent of the total capital is employed in companies with foreign financial participation.[1] Similarly, the profits of the foreign-participation companies made up 39 per cent of the toal profits.[2]

Foreign control and influence is, of course, also possible in the case of purely technical collaborations without financial participation. More than half the new industrial projects in 1964-66 for which data are available had foreign collaboration, and the number seems to be rising.[3] "...it is now virtually impossible for an Indian firm to start up or expand without presenting a scheme for foreign collaboration."[4]

Qualitatively, the foreign companies in India have a prominent position. The Government tries to guide fresh foreign capital into new, usually technology-intensive sectors. Apart from foreign branches in plantations and older foreign-controlled companies in consumer industries like soap, cigarettes, soft drinks, matches and biscuits, foreign investment is nowadays mostly found in petroleum, rubber goods, chemicals, medicines, electrical machinery and other new industries. Foreign companies are normally also relatively large.[5]

By definition, all foreign branches and subsidiaries are foreign-controlled. The foreign subsidiaries established in India before 1947 were mostly 100

1) Reserve Bank of India, Foreign Collaboration in Indian Industry, Bombay 1968, pp. 22, 51. The selected public limited companies cover (including foreign companies) 70 per cent of all public limited companies. Cf. Kidron, M., op. cit., p. 186, where foreigncontrolled assets are estimated at about 40 per cent of the total assets in the organized private sector).
2) Reserve Bank of India, Foreign Collaboration..., pp. 16, 22, 45, 51.
3) India. Planning Commission, Industrial Planning and Licensing Policy, Final Report, Delhi 1967, p. 42.
4) Kidron, M., op. cit., p. 262. Cf. Kurian, K.M., op. cit., p. 109.
5) Unfortunately, no readily available data exist on the relative share of foreign investments in different industries. Cf. Reserve Bank of India, Foreign Collaboration..., pp. 22, 51; Kidron, M., op. cit., pp. 186 ff.

per cent foreign-owned, but because of the restrictive policies of the independent government, most subsidiaries established after 1947 have had
a majority of less than 75 per cent. In 1956-64, only seven companies were
allowed to enter with full ownership. [1]

Apart from branches and subsidiaries, the Reserve Bank also collects information pertaining to minority capital participations. A 25-per-cent
foreign ownership is considered by the Reserve Bank to be a controlling
interest. In 1963-64, the average foreign share of minority participations
was 28 per cent, which means that many of these companies must have
been foreign-controlled, according to the Reserve Bank definition. [2] Relatively many minority participations have a foreign share of 40-50 per
cent and in a number of these cases a de facto majority ownership is
effected through additional shares being held by nominees or by Indian
employees. [3] Control through minority participation can also be secured by rationing share allotments, whereby a wide dispersal of local
ownership is ensured. [4]

All minority participations are, of course, not foreign-controlled. In a
number of cases, the foreign company takes a relatively small equity as
payment for machinery and know-how without any intention of exercising
control. On the other hand, many of the purely technical collaborations
are in reality controlled by the foreign collaborator, particularly in the
technology-intensive industries.

Policies towards foreign capital

As could be expected, the British colonial policy was quite friendly towards
foreign private capital. The Fiscal Commission of 1922 and the External
Capital Committee of 1925 recommended "that no obstacles be raised to
the free inflow of foreign capital", and only in the cases in which foreign
companies were subsidized outright were any restrictions proposed, and
then very mild ones: a subsidized foreign company was to register in India
as a rupee company, was to afford facilities for training Indian apprentices,
and a "reasonable proportion" of its directorate was to be Indian. [5] A

---

1) Reserve Bank of India, Foreign Collaboration..., p. 14.
2) Ibid., p. 43.
3) Kidron, M., op. cit., p. 286.
4) Ibid., p. 286; India. Industrial Licensing Policy Inquiry Committee,
   op. cit., p. 138; Kust, M.J., op. cit., p. 147.
5) India. Fiscal Commission, Report 1922, quoted in India. Fiscal Commission 1949-50, op. cit., p. 49; India. External Capital Committee,
   Report, Calcutta 1925. Cf. p. 65.

proposal about safeguards for Indian control was brushed aside as an "extreme suggestion".[1]

The early Congress policy towards foreign capital was as negative as the early statements of the Congress government on the role of the private sector.[2] The National Planning Committee recommended in 1945 that foreign capital should be withdrawn from key industries and prevented from entering them in the future, and in 1946 the Congress-dominated interim government declared:

> It seems to us preferable that the goods which the country cannot produce at present but would be in a position to produce later on should continue to be imported from other countries rather than that their local manufacture should be started or expanded by foreign firms. In the course of time it will be possible to restrict or discontinue foreign imports, but foreign vested interests once created would be difficult to dislodge.[3]

In the Industrial Policy Resolution of 1948 it was stated that legislation would be introduced for the regulation of foreign capital.[4] But the 1948 resolution was on the whole much milder than earlier policy statements, and in 1949 also the demand for special legislation on foreign investment was withdrawn. The 1949 statement of the Prime Minister in Parliament is the basic statement on the policy towards foreign investment, and is still valid.[5]

The 1949 statement says that foreign capital can, as a supplement to Indian capital, provide additional savings and technical knowledge. Foreign capital is promised non-discriminatory treatment and free remittance facilities for both profits and capital. "Vital importance" is attached to the employment and training of Indians also for the highest posts in the foreign companies. The "51-per-cent rule" of Indian control is reiterated, with a cautious reservation attached:

> Government have stated before that as a rule the major interest, ownership and effective control of an undertaking should be in Indian hands.

---

1) India. External Capital Committee, op. cit., p. 10.
2) P. 40.
3) Quoted in Kidron, M., op. cit., pp. 68-69.
4) India. Industrial Policy Resolution 1948, reprinted in India, Estimates Committee, Report 1967-68, p. 291.
5) India. Prime Minister's Statement in Parliament 1949, quoted in India. Ministry of Finance, Pocket Book of Economic Information, pp. 282 ff.

54

They have also stated that power will be taken to deal with exceptional cases in a manner calculated to serve the national interest. Obviously there can be no hard and fast rule in this matter. Government will not object to foreign capital having control of a concern for a limited period, if it is found to be in the national interest and each individual case will be dealt with on its merits.[1]

The 1949 statement does not provide any guidelines as to the specific sectors in which foreign capital would be welcome. But the general policy has been to allow only such foreign financial or technical collaborations as are in line with the targets of the Five-year Plans, bringing new technology that is not forthcoming indigenously. "The normal policy of the government is to restrict foreign collaboration to those cases which bring technical know-how into the country, such as is not adequately available indigenously for developing new lines of production or where domestic capital is inadequate or not forthcoming."[2] Foreign investment is normally not allowed in purely financial, commercial or trading enterprises, and foreign companies with an assembly type of production are required to substitute gradually indigenous supplies for imports.

The 1949 rule has in the main been followed, in the sense that formal majority ownership, if not effective control, has mostly been in Indian hands. But a number of foreign majority-owned companies were also allowed into the country in the 1950´s, in cases in which the technology was considered very difficult and when it was a question of a high-priority industrial field, where little progress had been made to date. When majority ownership has been approved, it has usually been limited to 60 per cent, and the government sometimes insists that half the Indian participation should be made available to the public.[3]

The promise in the 1949 statement of non-discriminatory treatment of fo-

---

1) Ibid., p. 283.
2) Reserve Bank of India, Foreign Collaboration..., p. 2. Cf. the following passage in the First Five-year Plan:"The broad principle to be followed is that foreign investment should be permitted in spheres where new lines of production are to be developed or where special type of experience and skill are required or where the volume of domestic production is small in relation to demand, and there is not reasonable expectation of the indigenous industry being able to expand at the desired rate" (India, Planning Commission, The First Five-Year Plan p. 92).
3) Kust, M.J., op. cit., p. 145.

reign capital has been kept, and the implicit discrimination that takes place in the form of tax concessions etc. is mostly of a positive nature.[1] The promised free-remittance facilities have also been made available, although substantial capital repatriations sometimes meet with difficulties on account of "the Government's known reluctance to allow the repatriation of a large block of capital".[2]

The foreign-exchange crisis of 1957-58 led to an increased emphasis on foreign financial collaboration as a means of easing the foreign-exchange situation.[3] The crisis also made it easier for foreign investors to obtain majority capital participation. To the former, unofficial, technology criterion for allowing foreign majority ownership were added two new ones: when the foreign-exchange requirements of a project exceeded 50 per cent of the proposed equity, and when a substantial proportion of the production was to be exported. The foreign equity for initial imports was to be a maximum,[4] but there were tendencies at the time towards an even more liberal policy, allowing foreign equity for capital-goods imports as a minimum.[5]

In a Government press note of May 8, 1961, the 1949 demand that the "major interest, ownership and effective control of an undertaking should be in Indian hands" was reduced to the feebler demand that an Indian majority would be "generally welcome". After the Chinese war in 1962 the foreign-exchange situation became even more serious. The Indian Investment Centre was established in 1961 to stimulate foreign investment, the formal procedures for processing foreign collaborations were streamlined, and

---

1) Kust, M.J., op. cit., p. 111; Reserve Bank of India, Foreign Collaboration..., p. 2.
2) Kidron, M., op. cit., p. 257. Cf. Kumarasundaram, S., Foreign collaborations and Indian balance of payments, in Hazari, R.K. (ed.), Foreign Collaboration, Bombay 1968, p. 206.
3) India. Industrial Licensing Policy Inquiry Committee, op. cit., p. 137.
4) Kust, M.J., op. cit., p. 143.
5) "The cost of imported capital equipment is allowed as a minimum to be financed in the form of foreign equity participation and/or loans. Over and above this minimum, majority control must, to the extent possible, be in Indian hands. In suitable cases, and provided arrangements are made by which Indian participants can exert effective influence on the company, particularly in the matter of development of Indian expertise and know-how, foreign investment as bulk of the capital structure is allowed" (Reserve Bank of India, Foreign Collaboration..., p. 2, based in part on a government press note of August 15, 1958, Cf. Kidron, M., op. cit., p. 268).

the Finance Minister stated in 1963 that "I think the stage has come when we would be justified in opening the doors even wider to private foreign investment..."1)

Later in the 1960's, the policy towards private foreign investment took more definite shape and became at the same time a little more strict. The factors usually mentioned as being of importance for the approval or disapproval of foreign collaboration were as follows:

1. Whether capacity in the particular field of industry is required to be developed, having regard to the Plan targets;

2. Whether the technology involved is not indigenously available;

3. Whether the import of capital goods involved is of such a high order that without the collaboration proposal the implementation of the scheme would involve an avoidable drain on the foreign-exchange resources of the country;

4. Whether the approval of the collaboration will jeopardize the industries already existing in that particular field or in associated fields of industry;

5. Whether the proposal would involve any undue exploitation of foreign patents, trade-marks and brand names etc.;

6. Whether the manufacturing scheme proposed fits in with our policy both in respect of availability of raw materials and components;

7. Whether the products to be manufactured are exportable and if so whether the collaboration will accelerate or increase our export potential. 2)

The criteria for allowing majority foreign participation were also explicitly formulated. A foreign majority was to be considered only when one or both of the following criteria were satisfied:

1. The main constristion of the project is in a field of technology where the country has made little progress and where a great deal of additional development is necessary;

---

1) Krishnamachari, T.T., Inaugural speech at the All-India Economic Conference, December 1963 (mimeographed).
2) India. Estimates Committee, Report 1967-68, p. 234. Cf. Economic Times, March 31, Bombay 1969.

2. The amount of foreign exchange is such that, unless the foreigner
is allowed to have a majority share-holding, the country will have to
find a substantial amount of the foreign exchange for the project, no
alternative methods of long-term finance being practicable.[1]

In 1968, the government issued an "illustrative" list in which industries
were grouped in three categories: cases in which financial and technical
collaboration might be permitted, cases in which only technical collaboration would be allowed, and cases in which no foreign collaboration at all
would be permitted. [2]   If a foreign majority were allowed, it would mostly
be a majority of not more than 60 per cent, and older companies with highe
majority percentages would be expected to come down to 60 per cent when
they applied for a licence for substantial expansion. The terms of collaboration agreements with regard to royalties and fees was also standardized.[3]

In 1969-70, a further tightening of the foreign-investment policy could be
noticed. The Fourth Five-year Plan states that foreign collaboration should
only be resorted to for meeting a "critical gap", foreign collaboration in
producing consumer goods should not be allowed at all, and in fields in whic
indigenous enterprise was not established but would be forthcoming within
a short time, no foreign collaboration should be permitted. In 1970, following the recommendations of the Dutt Committee, it was decided that foreign
investment would in the future be encouraged only in a "core sector", consisting of industries like fertilizers, non-ferrous metals and heavy
machinery - the sector in which also the large business houeses would be
permitted to invest. [4]

Foreign investment and priorities

Foreign investment after 1947 has, on the whole, been channelled into prior
ty industrial fields. Investment in plantations and other colonial types of industry has stagnated, while foreign participation in the intermediate and
heavy manufacturing sectors has increased substantially. The policy of Indianization has also been successfully implemented, although the transfer

---

1) Economic Times, March 31, Bombay 1969.
2) India. Government Press Note, November 1968.
3) See p. 238.
4) India. Planning Commission, Fourth Five-Year Plan..., p. 241;
   India. Industrial Licensing Policy Inquiry Committee, op. cit., p.
   190.

of skills supposed to follow on Indianization may not always have materialized. [1)]

The first exception from the Indian Government's policies towards foreign investment came as early as 1951, when the first oil-refinery agreements were concluded with Stanvac and Burma Shell. The agreements were extremely favourable to the foreign firms, granting exemption from the Industries Act, tax concessions, duty exemptions and a guarantee against nationalization and other measures of Indian control. The refinery agreements have stood out as an early failure of the Government to implement its stated foreign-investment policies. [2)]

The major criticism of the implementation of the foreign-investment policies is that industrial licensing, particularly after the foreign-exchange crisis in 1957-58, has been far too much geared to short-term balance-of - payments considerations. "With the continuous uncertainty regarding what foreign exchange would be available and especially since 1962 with the greatly increasing demands of defence, a pragmatic approach developed of undertaking whatever could be undertaken, which would not immediately burden the country with foreign payments." [3)] This short-sighted "foreign-exchange fetishism" is criticized by Kidron as follows:

> Out of it all there evolves a foreign-exchange fetishism, some of whose illogic has to be seen to be believed. The growing dependence on foreign resources and, even more, the growing resignation to such dependence, have affected the whole tenor of the Government's approach to foreign private capital: if in the first decade of Independence the official attitude was governed by considerations of control and economic power, it has since then been progressively determined by narrow balance-of-payments considerations with rather self-defeating consequences in further concessions to the private sector, to foreign investors, further dependence on aid, further delays in public-sector projects, and so on. [4)]

The short-term, balance-of-payments approach adopted - not in policy declarations as much as in practice - combined with the sellers' market creat-

---

1) "It is frequently argued in support of private capital imports that they graft much-needed managerial and technical skills onto Indian industry at little or no extra cost. The evidence, however, points the other way" (Kidron, M., op. cit., p. 312; cf. p. 161).
2) Ibid., pp. 90, 267 ff.; Mehta, B., Oil and Self-reliance, Delhi 1965.
3) India. Industrial Licensing Policy Inquiry Committee, op. cit., p. 123.
4) Kidron, M., op. cit., p. 316.

ed by the import restrictions, led to indiscriminate import substitution and approval of foreign collaborations also in low-priority industries. "This approach overlooked the indirect burden on the country's foreign-exchange resources and the direct burden on other scarce materials for production of items which were not of high priority in the scheme of economic development."[1] Because of the competitive advantage of having foreign brand names on the Indian market, many collaborations were applied for and sometimes approved, irrespective of the Plan priorities.

The Dutt Committee found 202 approved foreign-collaboration agreements in low-priority consumer-goods industries, distributed between 70 product groups, including

> ... toys, sports goods, spectacle hinges, snap fasteners, ball-point pens, vacuum flasks, crockery, lipsticks and other cosmetics, toothpaste and ready-made garments. Not only are collaborations permitted in such cases, but even repetitive collaborations are allowed ... they are also permitted to be renewed, so that the outflow of foreign payments continues over long periods of time. Such renewals have been permitted in cases like domestic refrigerators, thermometers, steel furniture, toilet soap and sewing thread. [2]

Two of the policy principles enumerated on page 57 state that foreign collaboration should normally not be allowed when the technology involved is indigenously available or when the approval of the collaboration would jeopardize industries already existing in the field. But in certain industrial fields new collaborations have been allowed, although one or more similar collaboration agreements had already been approved. The Dutt Dommittee found repetitive collaborations in 58 per cent of the product groups it had examined. The worst example was the textile finishing industry, where 56 foreign collaborations of a similar nature had been approved.[3]

Repetitive collaborations are costly. Each new collaboration entails foreign-exchange costs for technical fees, foreign technicians and imported capital equipment. The import of different varieties of the same type of know-how also produces diseconomies of scale, because the materials and components going into the finished product must be produced in separate lots to conform to the different specifications. The lack of standardization also makes indigenous adaption of foreign technology more difficult.[4]

---

1) India. Industrial Licensing Policy Inquiry Committee, op. cit., p. 137.
2) Ibid,, p. 130.
3) Ibid., pp. 124-25.
4) Ibid., p. 130.

Foreign collaboration has also been approved in industries already well established in the country without foreign affiliation. "Foreign or foreign associated concerns were permitted to establish capacities in industries where and when they had no special contribution to make, to the disadvantage of indigenous manufacture and technical know-how."[1] The Dutt Committee published an "illustrative list" of 73 products that were being manufactured both by companies with foreign collaboration and by companies without such affiliation.[2] The Committee complains that little has been done to encourage genuinely Indian parties, and it also emphasizes the danger that foreign subsidiaries in India are unduly favoured, because of their brand names and other advantages, by the progressive de-licensing of industries now taking place.

Implementation of the foreign-investment policy has been deficient also on other counts. Foreign investments have, more than the rest of the private sector, been concentrated geographically in the already industrialized areas, and foreign and indigenous private interests have also been permitted to encroach on the industrial sectors reserved for government enterprise.[3]

The number of minority participations, many of which are controlled from abroad, has increased substantially since 1956.[4] The more or less official relaxations, as regards foreign majority participation, in the late 1950´s are reflected in the fact that 45 per cent of all majority-owned subsidiaries established in 1948-64 were commissioned in 1956-60. Foreign majorities may have been justified in some cases, but it would be difficult to justify the licences granted to companies like Horlick and Nestlé, which obtained 83 and 90 per cent majority participations respectively for the production of milk products and baby foods.[5]

Summary. The 19th century saw both the decay of the Indian handicraft industry and the first steps towards the building up of modern industries. Except for cotton, the first industries and plantations were dominated by the British. Despite booming demand during the two World Wars, Indian industrial progress was not overly impressive, and in 1947 the economy was still very much a colonial type of economy.

---

1) Ibid., p. 184.
2) Ibid., p. 132.
3) India. Industrial Planning and Licensing Policy, op. cit., pp. 4-5; Subrahmanian, K.K., op. cit., p. 54; Kidron, M., op. cit., p. 158.
4) Cf. p. 53.
5) Reserve Bank of India, Foreign Collaboration..., p. 14; Kust, M.J. op. cit., p. 150.

During the last 20 years the national government has brought about an impressive large-scale industrialization, but it has failed to implement particularly its socialistic objectives. The public sector has grown only slowly, and policy measures are increasingly being realized through indirect influence on the predominant private sector. The licensing system has permitted a conspicuous growth of the largest private business houses, and to obviate this and other inadequacies, the government has of late reorganized the licensing system.

The coming of independence led to foreign disinvestment, but since the 1950´s there has been a relatively steady inflow of foreign capital. Most of it goes to technology-intensive industries in the manufacturing sector, Branch investment has stagnated, while minority financial and technical collaborations have shown a continuous increase. More than one-third of the industrial output in India is under foreign control.

The colonial policy towards foreign investment was non-restrictive. In 1949, the Indian Prime Minister emphasized the Indianization of staff and effective national control. The implementation of the foreign-investment policies has been deficient in several respects, and short-term, balance-of-payments considerations have predominated over the long-term goals. At the end of the 1960´s, a trend towards more restrictive foreign-investment policies could be noted.

Chapter 3

SWEDISH COMPANIES

After the preliminaries in Chapter 1 and 2, I shall start out here on my main mission - to illustrate the development impact of some Swedish companies in India. A common procedure will generally be followed: for each type of effects the theoretical benefits and costs mentioned in Chapter 1 will be elaborated on a little. They will then be discussed in the general Indian context, and finally some relevant empirical material available on the Swedish companies will be presented.

But first I shall introduce the Swedish companies by giving short summaries of background data on each company.[1] The companies chosen for treatment are all the majority-owned Swedish subsidiaries in India, six in all. Apart from these companies, there are another 35 Swedish technical and/or financial collaborations in the country.[2] Of the six majority companies, the Western India Match Company, WIMCO, is nearly as large as all the other subsidiaries taken together, and in the following pages I shall often treat WIMCO separately and the other five majority companies as a group.

The Swedish Companies and Their Environment

Swedish Match and WIMCO

The Western India Match Company, WIMCO, is a subsidiary of the Swedish Match Company, STAB, which boasts that every seventh match produced in the world comes from a company associated with Swedish Match. The concern was even more dominant in the 1920's, when under its bold leader, Ivar Kreuger, it was well on its way towards a world monopoly in matches.

---

1. A more detailed presentation of the companies will be found in the set of case histories mentioned on page 8.
2. Forstenius, E., Swedish Collaborations in India, Swedish Embassy, New Delhi 1970 (mimeographed).

Up to 1922 the Indian match market was covered by imports from Sweden and Japan. In 1922, a revenue duty on imports of more than 100 per cent was imposed, which gave a strong impetus to indigenous industry, and many new factories were established. In 1927, there were in India 27 large-size factories and an unknown but much larger number of so-called cottage factories, working on a small scale, exclusively with manual labour.[1]

When the revenue duty was imposed, Swedish Match was providing a large share of the Indian match imports, and the concern would have preferred to continue to export from Sweden instead of starting production in India. But with the high duty on matches, Swedish Match was compelled to invest in order to be able to compete successfully on the Indian market. WIMCO was formed in 1923, and in 1927 controlled 40 per cent of the Indian match market. After some shuffling and reshuffling of factories, WIMCO ended up with five match factories in present-day India: in Ambernath (north of Bombay), Calcutta, Madras, Bareilly (east of New Delhi) and Dhubri in the state of Assam (see the map on p. 73). The Dhubri factory was formally constituted as a separate company, the Assam Match Company, AMCO but it will be treated here as an integral part of WIMCO.

In the 1920's the colonial government introduced a limited scheme of protection for Indian industries, and in 1927 a Tariff Board was set up to see if the protection given by the revenue duty to the match industry was merited. In this connection many allegations against Swedish Match and WIMCO mostly emanating from their competitors, were taken up for discussion. The Tariff Board found that WIMCO/Swedish Match had been guilty of dumping imported matches and of lowering the reputation of indigenous matches by unfair propaganda, but it did not find any substance in the allegations of deliberate monopolistic tendencies and actions.

The general opinion of the Tariff Board was that the indigenous match companies had a long-term relative advantage and a better cost situation than both WIMCO and Swedish Match, and there was therefore no reason to fear any possible monopolistic tendencies shown by the foreign concern. The Board still recommended continued protection, because of the dumping by Swedish Match and because of the consumers' prejudice against Indian matches that had been created. The Board's optimism did not embrace the indigenous cottage industry - it was conceded that the cottage industry had favourable employment effects, but in the Board's opinion the cottage labour was sweated and the manufacturing conditions were unhealthy.

---

1) India. Tariff Board, Report of the Indian Tariff Board regarding the grant of protection to the match industry, Calcutta 1928; India. Tariff Board, Match Industry, Vol. I-IV, Calcutta 1928.

As we have seen, the Tariff Board was not of the opinion that WIMCO had so far tried to establish a monopoly in the Indian match market. But, to prevent future negative monopolistic effects, the Board proposed that WIMCO should express its capital in rupees, offer some share capital for subscription by Indians and take on a reasonable number of Indian directors. All these things WIMCO did eventually do, but these measures did not turn out to be very efficient checks on the formation of a monopoly.

After the Tariff Board inquiry was over, a period of cut-throat competition started. A considerable over-capacity had been built up in the match industry, and many companies were eventually forced to close down. Conditions did not improve when the government introduced a match excise in 1934, which raised the consumer price of matches. The price war was won in the end by WIMCO - at the cost of low profits throughout the 1930's - and after the struggle there remained, besides WIMCO, only one large competitor, Esavi, in Calcutta. Esavi has stayed on but has not offered WIMCO any serious competition.

The Indian match companies did not leave the market without protest. But the government favoured WIMCO, and when in 1938 WIMCO sold half its share capital to Indian investors, this was evidently considered by the government as a sufficient concession to the critics. The only real competition that remained came from a few cottage factories that had managed to stay on in a small region in South India, where conditions for match manufacture on a cottage scale were particularly favourable. The number of factories in this region increased from 5 in 1933 to 90 in 1949.

The Second World War was a very profitable period for the match manufacturers as well as for other industries. Import difficulties forced WIMCO to start the production of glue for match-boxes and labels and also of potassium chlorate, a chemical that is the main constituent of the heads of matches.

With independence, the government's policy with regard to the match industry underwent a definite change. The cottage industry was given precedence at the expense of WIMCO, first with excise rebates and then in the form of a virtual ban on the expansion of WIMCO's production. The rationale for this was mainly the great employment potential of the cottage sector - with the same aggregate production as WIMCO it nowadays employs some 20,000 people full-time and more than 300,000 part-time, while WIMCO has only about 10,000 employees.

Despite the restrictive formal policies, the government has in practice been quite lenient towards WIMCO and allowed the company both to re-equip its factories and to realize a continuous increase in production with a retained market share into the late 1950's. In return, WIMCO has maintained voluntary price control throughout its country-wide sales network, consisting of 400 depots and 20,000 wholesalers. It was not until the 1960's that the cottage industry managed to get more than half the match market, and then probably less because of government support than because of its own increased competitiveness, both as concerned quality and marketing ability.

The slower expansion of sales of ordinary matches in the 1960's resulted in lower profits for WIMCO, and the situation was aggravated by perhaps a little too generous dividend-distribution policy. To make up for the market share lost to the cottage industry on ordinary matches, WIMCO has begun to offer in urban markets special and more profitable productions like booklet and wax matches. The acute shortage of match timber has also led the company to experiment with cardboard boxes. A change-over to cardboard boxes would make WIMCO's old machines definitely obsolete and generate large import needs for the replacement of machinery. The management hopes that in the wake of a new technology also other rationalizations may be carried out, in order to change WIMCO's old methods of administration and organization.

The lower profits and stagnation on ordinary matches have also lead to increased attention being paid to other products than matches. The increasing import difficulties have resulted in progressive import substitution and vertical integration within the company. For example, in 1942 the production of potassium chlorate for the head composition was substituted for imports, a salt works was opened in 1964 to produce eventually the raw material for potassium chlorate, and in 1970 a small factory was to be commissioned for the production of magnetite electrodes, that are used extensively in chlorate production.

In 1958 a paper mill for the production of paper for match boxes and wrapping was opened, and WIMCO has also invested in a pulp mill to get supplies for the paper factory. The new products have primarily been taken up for import-substitution purposes, but in the 1960's production and outside sales have been stepped up with the explicit aim of increasing total profits. In 1969 the new products generated one-third of the total profits. WIMCO has also started production of some new types of chlorates, and further diversifications are to be expected, perhaps also on the distribution side, where WIMCO has a country-wide distribution network that could be used also for other products than matches.

The new Swedish companies

The other five majority-owned companies, which I shall here call the new Swedish companies, all started production in the 1960´s. They represent the modern, technology-intensive type of investment: Vulcan-Laval (dairy machinery), Atlas Copco (compressors), Sandvik (hard-metal products), SKF (ball-bearings) and SF (air-treatment equipment).[1] Except for SF in Calcutta, all the new Swedish companies are located in the city of Poona, south-east of Bombay (see maps on p. 73-74). The main reason for investment for all the companies was the increasing import restrictions introduced by the Indian Government oafter the foreign-exchange crisis in 1957-58. The new Swedish companies had to choose between investing in India or losing entirely their established market.

Vulcan-Laval. The new Swedish companies are all straightforward investments by highly specialized international concerns, except for Vulcan-Laval. The "Laval" part of the name shows the connection with Alfa-Laval, a Swedish concern specializing in equipment for food production. Alfa-Laval formed in 1961 an Indian subsidiary, Alfa-Laval (India), and Vulcan-Laval is the result of a merger between this company and Vulcan Trading, a subsidiary of Swedish Match/WIMCO.

Vulcan Trading was established in the 1930´s by the managing director of WIMCO as an import agency in India for Swedish products. With the growth of Indian industry, the imports gradually shifted to more sophisticated products. In the mid-fifties, Vulcan Trading took on agencies for Atlas Copco, Sandvik and Alfa-Laval, and these soon grew in relative importance. Atlas-Copco and Sandvik products alone represented in 1961-62 some 70 per cent of the total earnings of Vulcan Trading.

But, as the import restrictions were further tightened, several Swedish companies started negotiations on their own with the Indian Government about local production, and Vulcan Trading then clearly saw that it would not have any future as a pure trading company. It had either to face liquidation or to try to transform itself from an import agency into a manufacturing company. But the question was then what to manufacture. The solution finally proposed was that Vulcan Trading should start a general machine shop, where machinery work for Alfa-Laval (India) and subcontracting for the other Swedish investments would be done. Vulcan Trading would keep its sole selling agency, at least for the Atlas Copco and Alfa-Laval products.

---

1) SKF stands for Svenska Kullager Fabriken and SF for Svenska Fläkt-fabriken.

Vulcan Trading bought a large piece of land in Poona and then sold parts of it to Atlas Copco and Sandvik. Everything was fine until Atlas Copco cancelled the sole selling agreement with Vulcan Trading and took over the sales side themselves. Vulcan Trading then had to take on less profitable Indian agencies to keep up its turnover. On top of this, the cooperation between Vulcan Trading and Alfa-Laval (India) in the manufacture of Alfa-Laval products broke down, and both companies went into the red.

After some negotiations, it was decided in 1965 that Vulcan Trading and Alfa-Laval (India) should merge to form a new company, Vulcan-Laval, which would concentrate on the Alfa-Laval type of products. But as Alfa-Laval was not very interested in India any longer, the majority holding in Vulcan-Laval went instead to STAB (Swedish Match), the parent company of both Vulcan Trading and WIMCO. The share capital was, to begin with, 99 per cent foreign-owned, but in 1969 the Indian Government forced Vulcan-Laval to sell out 25 per cent of the shares to the Indian public.

After a low mark in 1966, the production of Vulcan-Laval started to increase, and there have since not been any further losses. A slow but steady turnover increase has been achieved, despite the gradual dropping of Indian trading agencies. Some 75 per cent of the total sales go to the food-processing industry. The government is an important buyer on the dairy side, and Vulcan-Laval tries to diversify into other products not covered by government price and other controls. There are two important competitors in the dairy field, and the other products manufactured by Vulcan-Laval are also sold in competition with Indian firms.

In 1969, some 80 per cent of Vulcan-Laval's products were still of the Alfa-Laval type. A large number of the equipments and plants produced are specielly made for each customer, and turnkey contracts are quite common. Vulcan-Laval therefore has to maintain a sizeable engineering and drawing department. The company is gradually abandoning the concentration on Alfa-Laval products and is on its way to becoming a general engineering company with some concentration on food-processing technology. Vulcan-Laval has entered into new collaboration agreements with several independent Swedish firms for new products, and a Swedish packaging subsidiary of Vulcan-Laval's majority owner, STAB, will provide technical know-how for cigar-making and tube-filling machines.

Atlas Copco. The Atlas Copco group has a world-wide reputation in compressed-air technology, centred on products like air compressors and rock drills. The background of the Indian company has already been given in connection with Vulcan-Laval. Production of certain compressors and rock drills started in 1962 at the factory in Poona. Atlas Copco was relatively late in applying for a manufacturing licence and therefore received consent for quite a small production, but, on the other hand, it was allowed 100-per-cent foreign ownership, which is very unusual.

The production of compressors and rock drills is essentially of an assembly type. Components are bought from sub-suppliers or imported and then assembled. The initial investment of Atlas Copco was therefore relatively low, and production and profits very soon reached a satisfactory level. The main bottleneck has been imports and the small initial licence obtained, but relatively high exports in later years have at least temporarily solved these problems.

The greater part of the sales goes to the mining and construction sectors, and 70 per cent of Atlas Copco´s production was in 1968 bought by the public sector. Atlas Copco is also a sales agent for drill steels and drill bits manufactured by Sandvik. Compressor, drill and Sandvik drill steels are sold as one unit, which gives Atlas Copco a certain edge over its competitors. The company is very prominent within its limited market range, in spite of the general over-capacity in the industry.

Sandvik Asia. The Sandvik group has some 15 per cent of the world market in hard-metal products, and it is also well known for its special steels. Hard metal is a popular name for tungsten carbide, a tungsten alloy which is used instead of diamonds for the cutting of steel, for example.

The Sandvik factory in India started manufacturing drill steels (sold by Atlas Copco) in 1961 and tungsten carbide and products thereof in 1963. Tungsten ore is imported, transformed chemically into tungsten carbide and then formed into bits for various uses. Sandvik´s production is of a heavy type, and the investment in plant and equipment is higher than for Atlas Copco and Vulcan-Laval.

The engineering industry is Sandvik´s best customer, and demand is growing. Production and profits have risen continuously, and the Swedish parent company, which owns 60 per cent of the shares, gets both handsome dividends and high royalties from its Indian subsidiary.

SKF. The SKF concern is the largest ball-bearing manufacturer in the world, catering for some 25 per cent of the world market. The Indian subsidiary started production in 1965, after a delay of several years, due to legal difficulties in the acquisition of land for the factory site in Poona. When SKF started manufacture in India, ball-bearing production had been going on in the country for 15 years, and the bearing market was therefore already competitive when SKF entered it.

SKF has invested much more money than the other new Swedish companies, reflecting the very capital-intensive character of bearing production. In 1969 some 700 people were employed, which is only marginally more than the other Swedish firms, despite their much smaller investments. SKF is also somewhat over-invested, as regards factory and staff buildings.

SKF continuously diversifies its bearing production, and a small number of textile-machinery parts is also produced. The market share of SKF has shown a steady increase and in 1969 was about 20 per cent. Ninety-five per cent of the sales go to the private sector, mainly to the automobile industry. Sales are handled by a separate sales company, which was established in India in branch form as early as 1933. The profit trend has followed the increase in sales, and in 1970 SKF was the most profitable bearing company in India.

SF. The SF concern started as a subsidiary to a Swedish heavy electrical company, ASEA, but is now an independent company, with 16 subsidiaries outside Sweden. The Indian subsidiary started production in 1962 in Calcutta. It is the smallest of the Swedish companies in India and its shares are not quoted on the stock exchange.

SF is a general engineering company, of the same type as Valcan-Laval, specializing in air treatment. The manufacture is technology-intensive and no homogeneous products can be singled out. SF designs and installs specially made humidifiers, ventilating plants, dryers, etc. for large-scale industries like the textile and cement industries. SF has several competitor for each type of plant, but there is no other company in India specializing in air treatment only, and competition is therefore product-based rather than technology-based. Sales and profits have been satisfactory.

Location

After this brief presentation of the Swedish companies, I shall now proceed to analyze a number of their possible effects on development, starting with something very tangible - the actual location of the Swedish companies and the effects thereof. In this context the "external economies in a narrow sense" will be treated. After that I shall discuss employment effects and a number of "external economies in a wider sense" connected with employment and recruitment. The main reason for treating these and other types of external economies before more measurable effects like profits and outflows is that the external economies, particularly the "external economies in a wider sense", are usually considered to be the main benefit of foreign investment and therefore merit priority treatment.

70

The location of an industry affects the Indian national objective of equality: a project in a poor part of the country is better than an identical project in a rich part, because the employment and income generated then benefits a generally poorer section of the population.[1] Besides, public expenditure for utilities, roads, etc. and general external diseconomies like congestion are usually lower outside the already industrialized areas.

The colonial government in India paid little attention to questions of industrial location, even though some attempts were made to induce new industries not to establish themselves in the most congested cities. One of the main purposes of the industrial licensing system introduced in the early 1950's was to ensure that new industries were located in accordance with the government's regional priorities. But no serious attempts were made to identify formally which regions should have priority, partly because all the Indian states naturally wanted to be considered "backward" in this sense.[2] The licensing system therefore failed to accomplish fully the desired industrial dispersal.

In spite of the fact that the industrial licensing system has not been of much help, some positive steps have been taken to promote industrial dispersal, particularly in late years. A few large public-sector projects have been located in the under-developed areas of the country, and a tax-incentive scheme has been introduced, in which capital-gains tax is waived on sales of property in connection with the transfer of an industry from a congested area.[3] Quite a few backward Indian States have also started schemes of their own to encourage industrial development - land, basic facilities and concessions are offered to prospective investors.

The Swedish companies have generally had the same motives for their location in India as Indian firms in general, but it may be that the foreign investors have given a little more weight to the availability of land, good communications and good climate.[4] If I may speculate, the difference, as concerns land, may be explained by the fact that foreigners may have

---

1) Little, I.M.D., and Mirrlees, J.A., op. cit., pp. 43-44.
2) "... the licensing system as a whole did not do much to reduce regional disparities in industrial development. We also find that taking into account the districtwise distribution of all industrial licenses, not only the more industrialised States but the highly industrialised areas in these States got a very large number of licenses" (India. Industrial Licensing Policy Inquiry Committee, op. cit.,p. 110).
3) India. Planning Commission, Fourth Five-year Plan, pp. 27 and 34.
4) Poona Metropolitan Regional Planning Board, Industries in the Poona Region 1964-65, unpublished, p. 116.

Swedish foreign investments 1965

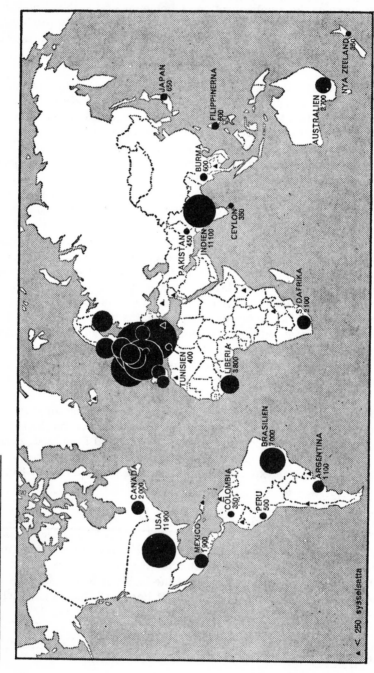

Source. Lund, H., Svenska företags investeringar i utlandet, Stockholm 1967, p. 37. The figures indicate number of employees in each country.

WIMCO FACTORIES

Map Showing Industrial Locations in and around Poona

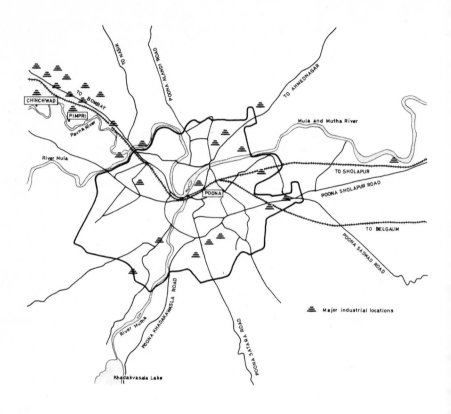

more difficulties in acquiring land than Indian investors, and the stress on good communications and climate may be traced to the fact that the Swedish decision-makers are actually foreigners with different standards than Indian investors.

The WIMCO factories were from the beginning spread out over the country, mainly because it was considered necessary to be near the main markets and sources of raw materials.[1] The location of most of the new Swedish companies in Poona was partly due to the fact that Vulcan-Laval had acquired a large plot of land there, but there were also other reasons.

WIMCO. The location of WIMCO's factories was largely in consonance with the government's priorities. WIMCO wanted to have its main factory in western India and was then asked to start a factory in Ambernath (north of Bombay), which was to become a new industrial centre that would relieve the already congested city of Bombay. WIMCO followed this advice, which has proved to be very costly. Not until very lately did the Ambernath area become industrialized, and over the years this has meant extra overhead costs for WIMCO, on top of the already high transport costs. These high overhead costs have in part resulted in positive social effects - for example, WIMCO was forced in Ambernath to train local labour more or less alone, which made it easier for new industries to start in the area at a later date.

The WIMCO factory in Calcutta to some extent accentuated the industrial congestion in this centre. It was erected by the Hoogly River in the vicinity of a pottery factory and several jute and paper mills. The Madras factory was more of a pioneer, as there were at the time only six industries in the town and none at all in the faraway location chosen by WIMCO.[2]

The factories in Dhubri and Bareilly (see map on p. 73) are both situated in remote places. When WIMCO started production in Dhubri, there was not much of a town, just a small village at a railway-river reloading point. WIMCO is still the only large-scale industry in Dhubri and the third largest industry in Assam, after tea and oil. Looking back, the company thinks that it would have done much better if the factory had been located in the Assam capital, Gauhati, where there are more supporting facilities than in Dhubri. The Bareilly factory, finally, was preceded by only one industry, a turpentine factory. Today, there are several big industries and a vigorous small-scale sector at Bareilly.

---

1) See map on p. 73.
2) As a result of the distant location and labour demands, the Madras Government had to construct a new railway station near the factory, Wimconagar.

It is not known who it was who actually took the decision to locate factories at such remote places as Dhubri and Bareilly. It was a doubtful decision from the business point of view, but a measure well in line with present policies of industrial dispersal. The Madras and Ambernath factories were, to begin with, also located in non-urban areas, but today they contribute to the industrial congestion in the respective regions. The Calcutta factory has always had an unhappy location from the dispersal point of view.

The future locational policy of WIMCO is clearly against the Government's priorities. The factories in Calcutta, Madras, Bareilly and Dhubri have from the business point of view locational drawbacks of a political and physical character. But Ambernath has relatively good communications with nearby Bombay and lies in Maharashtra, which is a politically stable (=conservative) state. WIMCO's new chlorate factories are located there, the experiments with cardboard are being conducted there, and the magnetite factory and other new investments will probably also be concentrated in Ambernath. But Ambernath has become a congested area, and it would therefore be much better for the country if WIMCO decided instead to expand in Dhubri or Bareilly, for example.

Swedish companies in Poona

No less than four Swedish companies (Vulcan-Laval, Sandvik, Atlas Copco and SKF) are located in Poona, and the problems of this region will therefore be treated in some detail. Poona is an old educational, administrative and military centre, situated at an altitude of 1800 ft. on the Deccan plateau, some 120 miles south-east of Bombay. Communications with Bombay are, relatively speaking, good, both by road and rail. A population of one million lives in a dry and stable climate.

The character of the region is rapidly changing with industrialization, but 63 per cent of the area is still used for agriculture. [1] Before 1946 industrial development was slow or non-existent, and the dominant industry was a Government ordnance factory. In 1946 the Kirloskar brothers put up, a diesel-engine factory in Poona, marking the start of an influx of modern industry. The development was stimulated by curbs on industrial investment within the greater Bombay area, and reached its climax in 1961-63, when 196 new factories started production. [2]

---

1) Diwan, G.R., Working Paper on the Poona Metropolitan Region, Poona 1968, p. 5 (mimeographed).
2) Sabade, B.R. Poona, the New Industrial City, no date, p. 3 (mimeographed).

There are roughly 9,000 factories employing 900,000 workers in Maharashtra. Poona had in the late 1960's 900 factories employing 90,000 workers, which means that Poona is responsible for one-tenth of the industrialization in Maharashtra. Poona is nowadays considered a congested area. [1] The social (government) cost per newly employed worker in Poona is less than in Bombay but much higher than in still younger industrial towns like Nasik. The Union Government incentives for industrial dispersal are therefore available for industries in Poona, and the Maharashtra Government has started an incentive scheme of its own to encourage dispersal from Poona.

The problem is aggravated by the fact that industrialization has been unplanned and irregular. The area along the Bombay-Poona road was found most attractive, because of the good rail and road communications, and a ribbon development of industries is therefore to be found in the Pimpri-Chinchwad area north-east of Poona (see map on p. 74). This area should ideally accommodate its industries on 1,500 acres and sustain a population of 0.25 million but in reality industry takes up 4,000 acres and sustained in 1968 a population of 0.7 million. [2] The industrial output in Pimpri-Chinchwad is double the output in Poona City. [3]

The overall explosive industrial growth in the Poona region has caused many problems. Although the main expansion areas have been Pimpri and Chinchwad, the workers still settle in Poona City. One reason for this has been that housing has not been provided along with employment opportunities in the expansion areas. The slum population in Poona City in 1968 was three times as large as in 1960.

An allied problem is the growth of commuter traffic between the city of Poona and Pimpri-Chinchwad which causes serious traffic congestion on the Bombay-Poona road. No less than 65 per cent of the workers in the factories in the area are commuters. [4]

There are also not enough housing facilities in the area, and the shortage of organized drainage and water supply has caused river pollution and created a "major health problem in the Pimpri-Chinchwad area". [5] The

---

1) A regional planning committee, called the Gadgil Committee after its famous chairman, in 1966 recommended that in 1991 about 5,400 acres should be used for industrial production in Poona. In 1968 already 7,600 acres were committed to such production. Cf. Diwan, G.R., op. cit., p. 9.
2) According to the Gadgil Committee, cf. Diwan, G.R., op. cit., p. 9.
3) Poona Metropolitan Regional Planning Board, op. cit., p. 189.
4) Diwan, G.R., op. cit., p. 9.
5) Diwan, G.R., op. cit., p. 24.

industrial development in Pimpri-Chinchwad has been irregular and un-
authorized, mainly because there have not been any local authorities with
adequate power. A planning board for the Poona region was not instituted
until 1967.

The Swedish companies in Poona are all situated along the Bombay-Poona
road - Vulcan-Laval, Atlas Copco and Sandvik near Pimpri between the .
railway and the road and SKF further north at Chinchwad. The location of
the Swedish firms in the Poona region is contrary to present policies of
dispersal, and the location within the region at Pimpri-Chinchwad further
aggravates the congestion problem.

Responsibility for this detrimental location lies not so much with the Swedish companies as with the Maharashtra authorities. In the early sixties,
industries were invited to go to Poona, and most of the industrial development in Pimpri-Chinchwad was sponsored by the Maharashtra Industrial
Development Corporation. Questions as to who took the initiative apart,
the Swedish companies in Poona followed the general tendency of foreign
investment to establish itself in already industrialized areas. [1] Indian
new investment is also concentrated in industrialized areas but not to the
same extent as foreign industry.

Infrastructure and physical environment

Infrastructure. The Government may have direct costs for foreign investment in the form of extra concessions and investments in infrastructure.[2]
We have then to make some assumption as to what should be considered as
"extra". What should be the proper sphere for Government and what shoul
the private companies be expected to provide themselves? I shall assume
here that the Government is supposed to provide transport facilities up to
the factory area for all new companies, and also public utilities (power an
water). If the price of the utilities provided is lower than the social cost o
providing it, any private production of, for example, power constitutes a
social gain to the extent of the difference between the social value and the
official price of power.

---

1) In 1959-1966 almost 90 per cent of the investment of foreign companie
went to the three most developed states in India (India. Planning Commission, Industrial Planning and Licensing Policy, Final Report, Bor
bay 1967, p. 48).
2) See p. 17. Tax concessions will be treated later. The various locational concessions now offered to prospective investors by many State
were not available to the Swedish companies at the time of investment

All the Swedish companies (except for SF in Calcutta) are located near rail-way lines. The companies in Poona have their sites along the main Bombay-Poona line, which has made it unnecessary to construct separate tracks to the Swedish factories. The WIMCO factories are dependent on the railway for timber transport and they all have separate tracks inside the factory areas. It is not known exactly who paid for these extra tracks, but it seems probable that the Government paid about half the cost of the WIMCO rail-way sidings, which at present price levels would be something like Rs. 1 million.

The WIMCO factories have also built a few roads, the cost of which has sometimes been shared with other companies or with the Government. Most of the roads outside the factory areas have now been handed over to the ma-nicipalities concerned at zero price, which means that the municipalities have saved the construction cost, amounting to, say, a total of Rs. 200,000 at present prices. By handing over the roads, the factories save future maintenance costs. The new Swedish companies are situated very near good roads, except for SKF, which has spent Rs. 25,000 on a road and two bridges between SKF and the railway. The annual maintenance cost of this road, de-frayed by SKF, amounts to Rs. 10,000.

The WIMCO factories started at a time when public utilities were practi-cally non-existent, and they still produce most of the water and electricity they need themselves. The change-over to public supply is slow because of the greater risk of failure of the public utilities. The new Swedish com-panies use only the public supply, although some wells for drinking water have been drilled. SKF has paid Rs. 125,000 for a well and Rs. 175,000 for a generator set, which is used to supplement the public electricity supply in periods of shortage.

Public utilities in India are generally priced somewhat too low, and the water and electricity production of the Swedish companies is therefore to some extent a social gain.[1] With the same kind of reasoning, the outside roads built by the Swedish firms have gradually become socially produc-tive. It is, on the other hand, probable that part of the costs of special railway tracks for the match factories should be considered as a social cost. All in all, it is probable that the costs incurred by the Swedish companies for investments in infrastructure have to some extent exceeded the social costs.

But we also have to discuss the alternative events. In Chapter 9 the oppor-tunity costs and alternative events are treated in some detail. In short, it

---

1) Streeten, P.P. and Lipton, M. (eds.), The Crisis of Indian Planning, London 1968, p. 75.

is likely that the resources "released" by the WIMCO investment have not been used very productively, but part of the resources disemployed by the new Swedish investments have probably been used for new industrial investment. In so far as the released resources are used in a productive way, corresponding benefits and costs in connection with infrastructure will arise. If there is such alternative investment, the Swedish companies have the social cost of using additional supplies of public utilities offered at too low a price. This cost is probably larger than the possible benefits arising from the construction by the companies of roads, wells, etc. This goes for the new Swedish companies. The case of WIMCO, on the other hand, seems to be indeterminate.

Effects on physical environment. Generally speaking, the problems of smoke, smells and pollution have only very recently become topical in the developed countries, and even less attention is paid to such problems in underdeveloped countries. The negative environmental effects of this kind are called in my terminology "external diseconomies in a narrow sense".

In India, the Poona region is relatively advanced, and some environmental effects have been included in an industrial survey of Poona. According to the survey, 12 per cent of the factories in Poona emit mildly offensive smoke, and 12 per cent also have mildly offensive effluents.[1] In comparison, none of the Swedish factories in Poona has any offensive effects on the environment. In fact, the only factory where such effects are possible is the SKF factory, which uses some offensive acids in its galvanization department. But the company claims to have the best cleansing apparatus in India, and it also claims that, even without cleansing, the waste water let out into the river is cleaner than the river itself.

The timber waste from WIMCO's match factories is either sold or used in the boilers. The smoke from the boilers is at times mildly offensive but is let out through high chimneys. At the Calcutta factory some chemical effluents are let out into the Hooghly River, but mostly such effluents are disposed of on WIMCO's own land, sometimes after cleansing in septic tanks.

There are also positive effects on the physical environment - external economies instead of diseconomies. For example, great care has been taken over the years to plant gardens, hedges, etc. around the WIMCO factory buildings. All the Swedish factories are kept clean, and especially SF has tried to make the environments as agreeable as possible.

---

1) Poona Metropolitan Regional Planning Board, op. cit., p. 100.

The Swedish firms in Poona offer a pleasant sight along the Bombay-Poona road and have nice buildings and gardens. This is partly by mistake; all the Swedish companies in Poona have over-invested in buildings. Sandvik pays Rs. 60,000 per year for "aesthetic" painting alone. According to the Poona Planning Board, only 15 per cent of the factories in the region have gardens.[1] The Swedish companies seem to pay more attention to environmental effects than the average Indian company and the net impact of the Swedish investments in this respect is probably positive.

Production and Priorities

Swedish companies and priorities

The demand for foreign exchange, savings and skills of the type brought in by foreign private investment is much in excess of supply in most underdeveloped countries. These countries have therefore tried to channel the not very abundant and relatively costly foreign investment into priority sectors that are crucial for development.

In India, the public sector **is** given priority over the private sector. The domains wholly reserved for the public sector are enumerated in "Schedule A" of the Industrial Policy Resolution of 1956 and comprise arms, steel, electricity, metal-processing, transport, etc.[2] Within the private sector, cottage and village industries are given most support. Small-scale and medium-sized industries are preferred to larger industries, and large-scale Indian companies are preferred to foreign. When there is a choice, foreign companies are thus in this sense given the lowest priority.[3]

In 1947 the sectorwise distribution of industrial investment in India was very lopsided - 70 per cent of the industrial output consisted of consumer goods. The First Plan therefore gave first priority to industries producing capital goods, so that a viable industrial base for further development could be created. Not until the Fourth Plan was this policy somewhat relaxed and consumer-goods industries given more leeway.

---

1) Poona Metropolitan Regional Planning Board, op. cit., p. 215. In the draft industrial survey produced by the Board, three out of seven photographs are of Swedish companies.
2) See p. 42.
3) Cf. pp. 182 ff.

The distribution of foreign manufacturing investments in India before 1947 accentuated the predominance of the consumer-goods industries. Since 1947, the policy has normally been to keep foreign investments away from non-priority sectors like consumer goods. The illustrative lists issued in 1968 by the Government to indicate where foreign equity investment would be welcome included only one consumer-goods industry (watch-making).[1] The "core sector" of the new licensing policy of 1970, to which foreign investment is in the future to be restricted, does not include any consumer-goods industries. Foreign investment since 1947 has, on the whole, been channelled into priority sectors, but there are also a number of examples of foreign investment being found in low-priority consumer-goods industries.[2]

Swedish companies. "Schedule A" of the Industrial Policy Resolution of 1956 enumerates the industries that are exclusively reserved for public undertakings.[3] The schedule includes the "mining and processing of copper, lead, zinc, tin, molybdenum and wolfram". As the first part of the production process in Sandvik is the processing of wolfram, the company seems to be established contrary to the Government's priorities. But Sandvik was actually invited by the Indian Government, and therefore either the policy schedule must offer special interpretations or the Government has made one of its many exceptions.

The success of WIMCO works against the policy of giving first priority within the private sector to cottage industry. As regards other priorities it has to be remembered that WIMCO was established long before there was any industrial policy or foreign collaboration policy in India.

If a highly mechanized, domestic match industry had been allowed to start production at all in India after Independence, it is probable that it would have been given opportunities to expand along with the general increase in demand. Matches are consumer goods but are considered to be essential consumer goods. But it is highly improbable that any foreign investment in the match industry would have been approved after 1947. Besides, the luxury matches and cardboard varieties that WIMCO is introducing on urban markets cannot even be classified as essential consumer goods.

Most of WIMCO's new products (paper, chlorates) and the products from the other Swedish companies arrived on the market during the Third Five-

1) India. Government Press Note, November 1968.
2) Cf. pp. 60-61.
3) India. Industrial Policy Resolution 1956, New Delhi 1956. Reprinted in India. Estimates Committee, Report, 1967-68, p. 299.

year Plan. A proper point of reference is therefore the priorities of this Plan (the priorities have not changed much during the Plans). New investments were envisaged primarily in the heavy engineering and machine-building industries, and second priority was given to major producer goods, like aluminium, mineral oils and basic chemicals and intermediates.

The chlorates produced by WIMCO, especially the sodium chlorate, can be classified as basic chemicals, together with the salt from WIMCO´s salt works, and this production is therefore well in accordance with the priorities of the Government. This is not true of the medium-quality match paper produced by WIMCO, which must be given priority on a par with the final product, matches.

The new Swedish investments all belong to the light-engineering sector. This is not included in the basic priorities of the Third Five-year Plan, but the new Swedish companies all serve important industries and their products could not be classified as consumer goods. Vulcan-Laval sells dairy machinery that is important for agricultural production, Sandvik manufactures cutting tools for heavy industry, Atlas Copco supplies compressors to the industrial and construction sectors, SKF´s bearings are in use everywhere in industry and transport, and SF produces equipment which is necessary in, for example, the cement and textile industries.

As all the Swedish companies I am discussing here are foreign-majority-owned, it could be argued that all of them must have priority, as foreign-majority holdings are allowed. But this is not a reliable priority criterion.[1] In another sense, however, they all have priority. In 1966 a list was drawn up, comprising 59 industries that were to be favoured in the allocation of import licences. All the Swedish companies are in this category. The list was compiled on the basis of three criteria: the importance of the industry to the national economy (Vulcan-Laval, Sandvik, Atlas Copco, SKF, SF), the significance of the industry for the export effort, and whether or not it produced an essential item of mass consumption (WIMCO).[2]

There is another list of priority industries, made for purposes of taxation, which includes only 28 producer-goods industries of special importance. The industries on this list are given special rebates on income tax and favourable conditions of depreciation allowance.[3] Only Sandvik and SKF are in this category, presumably because of their importance for heavy industry.

---

1) See p. 61.
2) India. Estimates Committee, Report 1967-68, op. cit., p. 165.
3) India. Ministry of Finance, Pocket Book of Economic Information, Delhi 1970, p. 306.

Industrial linkages

The "external economies in a narrow sense", as I have defined them here, include the physical external economies and industrial linkages.[1] The industrial-linkage effects may be of two kinds. A "forward linkage" is the market relation between a buyer and a seller, seen from the seller's point of view. By breaking technological bottlenecks or providing cheap products, a new foreign investment can stimulate additional domestic investment. A corresponding "backward linkage" is realized by the demand of a new investment for the products of other industries.[2] The immediate result of the linkage effects is that profits are raised for customers and suppliers of the new industry, and the main characteristic of the linkages is in fact that they work through the market mechanism.

The linkage effects have been discussed extensively in the literature on cost-benefit analysis and economic development, and the possible difference between "technological" and "pecuniary" effects has been a major issue.[3] I shall not enter into the controversy here, because the linkage effects are not a specific feature of the Swedish investments but a mere consequence of a company's position in the industrial structure. The linkage effects of the Swedish companies are to some extent cancelled out by corresponding linkages emanating from those Indian firms that the Swedish companies are likely to have replaced.[4] Here I shall only illustrate the linkage effects by examples from the Swedish companies.

WIMCO has some demand effects of a non-industrial character. For example, the demand for matchwood from the Dhubri match factory gives the timber-felling contractors an annual profit of Rs. 2 million, a sum that is probably not used for industrial investment. More industrial-like are the splint factories in South India, which are supported by the demand from WIMCO and the cottage match factories.

The vertical integration in WIMCO that is made possible by the large size of the company tends to reduce the possible stimulating effects of backward linkages. Instead of encouraging domestic investment in the form of a chlo-

1) See p. 14.
2) See Meier, G.M., The International..., p. 142.
3) Scitovsky, T., Two concepts of external economies, in Arrow, K.J. and Scitovsky, T. (eds.), Readings in Welfare Economics, London 1969, p. 242; McKean, R.K., Efficiency in Government through Systems Analysis, New York 1958, p. 136; Prest, A.R. and Turvey, R., op. cit., pp. 160 ff.; Little, I.M.D. and Mirrlees, J.A., op. cit., pp. 211 ff.
4) Cf. pp. 260 ff.

rate factory, WIMCO invested itself. Instead of buying the salt for the chlorate factory from outside, WIMCO will eventually produce it within the company. On the other hand, a backward linkage is effected when WIMCO substitutes for imports by investing, together with other firms, in a domestic pulp mill.

The production of Atlas Copco is essentially of an assembly type, with consequent strong backward-linkage effects. A rock drill manufactured by Atlas Copco consist of about 1,000 separate parts, most of which are purchased from other companies in India. Vulcan-Laval buys large quantities of steel from the big public-sector steel plants and also things like milk cans, electrical wire and mild-steel fabricates from some 200 small-scale suppliers. The number of small-scale industries in Poona has increased substantially as a result of the investment of the Swedish companies and other large industries in the area.[1]

The productions of SKF, Sandvik and SF are of a more basic type, in which purchases of components are small. SKF and SF buy large quantities of steel (mostly imported), which is then shaped according to specifications. Sandvik imports tungsten ore, which is processed and sold with few accessories. Hence, the Swedish companies have, on the whole, not very strong "backward-linkage" effects, and, as might be expected, the backward-linkages with any individual Swedish company have not been so strong as to induce domestic companies to make substantial new investments.

The forward-linkage effects produced by foreign investment are sometimes held to be of special importance in underdeveloped countries, where there are so many specific scarcities. New investments may drastically reduce costs for other industries by breaking bottlenecks in production.[2]   To illustrate the possible extent of such effects due to products sold by the Swedish companies, the total sales in 1968 of the Swedish firms are shown in Table 5, together with the distribution of sales in the public and private sectors.

---

1) Poona Metropolitan Regional Planning Board, op. cit., p. 105.
2) Meier, G. M., The International Economics of Development, op. cit., p. 142.

Table 5. Total market sales of the Swedish companies in 1968 and percentage distribution of sales in the public and private sectors.

	Sales in 1968 (Rs. million)	Public sector (per cent)	Private sector (per cent)
WIMCO			
Matches	231.7	5	95
Paper	8.7	5	95
Potassium chlorate	4.4	0	100
Sodium chlorate	1.9	0	100
Salt	1.6	0	100
Vulcan-Laval	24.6	50	50
Atlas Copco	30.5	70	30
Sandvik	26.2	40	60
SKF	36.0	5	95
SF	12.5	30	70
	378.1		

Sources. Company statistics. The Percentage distributions in sectors are rough estimates (very rough for WIMCO). The sales figures do not include internal sales. The sales figure for Atlas Copco includes Rs. 11.1 million of Sandvik products.

The forward-linkage effects from WIMCO´s main production line, matches, are, of course, nil, as matches are consumer goods. The WIMCO paper sold outside is mainly used for packaging purposes and has probably not stimulated any new investments or production. The potassium chlorate is sold mainly to the cottage industries, which use it for their match production The sodium chlorate may, by its domestic availability, stimulate fresh investments in the bleaching industry. The sales of salt save money for the industrial consumers, who do not have to clean the salt as before.

Vulcan-Laval sells mainly to the food-processing industries making dairy products, frozen foods, and beverages. The availability of Vulcan-Laval bottling plants and other products may be a stimulus to the setting up of dairies, breweries, etc. Most of the production goes to the dairy field, but low-priority industries like Coca-Cola are also big customers. Atlas Copco sells to the mining and construction sectors, to industry and also to some extent to agriculture. A large part of its sales goes to the public sector and, like the other Swedish companies, Atlas Copco tries to expand relatively more on the private-sector side, where there is no social control and no difficulties with terms of payment.[1]

The compressed-air equipment from Atlas Copco could be a technological stimulus to industrial development, and this is also true of the products of Sandvik and SKF. The low backward linkages of Sandvik and SKF correspond to high forward-linkage effects. Tipped tungsten-carbide tools and SKF bearings are used by all industries, including heavy industry. Finally the equipment manufactured by SF is often a necessary complement to industrial establishments in the textile, tea and other industries.

Summary. The firms included in this analysis are all the Swedish majority-owned companies in India. The largest of them is WIMCO, which was established in 1923. It soon captured a large part of the Indian match market. The Tariff Board of 1928 acquitted WIMCO of charges of monopolization, but soon afterwards all but a few cottage factories in the south were forced out of the market by the competitive pressure from WIMCO. Since 1947 the Government has supported the cottage industry, but not until in the 1960's did sales by the cottage industry outpace WIMCO's match sales. The new Swedish companies are, with one exception, located in Poona. They all produce modern light-engineering goods.

Foreign companies tend to some extent to establish themselves, more than Indian companies, in already industrialized areas, and at least the new Swedish firms conform to this tendency. The WIMCO factories, to begin with, built some roads and provided their own power and water supplies, but the new Swedish firms are dependent on the public supply, which is normally somewhat underpriced. The Swedish companies seem to give more attention to positive and negative environmental effects than Indian firms.

The product groups of the Swedish investments fit in rather well with the Indian industrial priorities. As concerns the linkage aspect, Atlas Copco is located in the middle of an industrial chain with strong backward and forward linkages, and Sandvik and SKF have strong forward-linkage effects.

---

1) The Indian Government departments are notorious for their slow payment.

Chapter 4

EMPLOYMENT

In presenting the different facets of the activities of the Swedish companies
I now move on to the subject of employment and recruitment. An evident
benefit of foreign investment is that it can increase total employment. One
factor that influences the amount of new employment created is the technology chosen - a relatively labour-intensive technique may be more useful
in the Indian context than a capital-intensive one. In connection with the
employment effects, I shall treat the employment and recruitment policies
of the Swedish companies."Progressive" policies in these respects can yiel
external spread effects of value for development.

Employment and Productivity

Employment and turnover

If foreign investment is not substituted for domestic investment, the employment created is a positive effect. When labour employed in the foreign
investment is drawn from other occupations, the employment effects are
of an indirect nature. The employment objective espoused by most underdeveloped countries is often a mixture of two objectives, a genuine employment objective and the desire to promote a more equitable distribution of
income by increasing the number of wage-earners.[1]

The right to work and the right to receive unemployment assistance are
included in the Indian Constitution, but the ordinary Indian has neither.
Increased employment opportunities have been an important objective in
all the Five-year Plans.[2] To begin with, much was hoped for from the

---

1) See p. 12.
2) The First Plan maintained that "fuller utilization of the idle manpower
   in the country must necessarily be the major objective of policy", and
   in the Second Plan it is stated that "in the context of prevailing unemployment, the absorption of labour becomes an important objective in
   itself" (India. Planning Commission, First Five-year Plan, op.cit.,
   p. 8, and Second Five-year Plan, op. cit., p. 12).

coming industrialization of the country, but later it was realized that the immediate employment effects from industrialization would be small. The planners appear to have accepted this and, on a general level, increased production is sometimes given equal or more stress than the employment objective.[1]

Employment in the manufacturing sector in India, inclusive of small-scale industries, actually declined in 1966-68 and in 1968 was 4.4 million, embracing some 8 per cent of the population. Relatively speaking, there was a larger percentage employed in industry in 1901 than in 1961.[2] It is quite probable that the total effect of industrialization in the short run is a net reduction of employment. This is particularly relevant as regards industries in the modern sector, to which nearly all foreign investments belong; the production of large-scale, modern industries is often substituted for small-scale production with a larger employment potential.[3]

In Table 6 are given some employment data for the Swedish companies. Employment in the WIMCO factories has not grown siginificantly over the last few years, while the quantitatively less important employment in the new Swedish firms has shown a faster growth. Employment in WIMCO has in fact been stagnant since just after the Second World War - maximum employment was reached in 1952.

Apart from the employees in the factories, WIMCO employs people in wood extraction. In Assam alone, more than a thousand people are employed, on an average, for six months of the year in matchwood extraction. But WIMCO tries to rationalize its extraction activities and also the work in the factories. In fact, a ban has been placed on new recruitment, and the average growth of employment during the last few years of 2 per cent is in reality undesired. The reason for this is that the factories are "overpopulated". It is estimated that, if WIMCO could start afresh, with the machines actually installed, only half as many people as there are now would be needed. With the new cardboard technology the demand for labour will be even less. In contrast to WIMCO, the employment in the new Swedish companies has grown at the relatively high rate of 12 per cent per year.

---

1) "The principal means to enlarging employment opportunities is to get the economy to move as fast as possible with the maximum dispersal of productive activity throughout the country" (India. Planning Commission, Fourth Five-year Plan, op. cit., p. 344).
2) India. Planning Commission, Fourth Five-year Plan, op. cit., p. 343; Pant, S.C., Indian Labour Problems, Allahabad 1965, p. 10.
3) Myrdal, G., Asian Drama, pp. 1172 ff.

Table 6. Total employment in 1968 in Swedish companies and growth rate of employment in 1965-68

Company	Total employment 1968 (bracket showing average)		Average growth rate of employment 1965-68 (per cent)	
WIMCO				
Factory 1	2,132		-1	
Factory 2	2,055		2	
Factory 3	2,011	1,809	-2	2
Factory 4	1,404		6	
Factory 5	1,443		3	
Vulcan-Laval	589		15	
Atlas Copco	416		8	
Sandvik	555	525	22	12
SKF	675		5	
SF	390		8	
	11,670			

Sources. Company statistics. The figures for WIMCO have been supplied by the factories themselves when available. The five WIMCO factories are as follows: Ambernath, Madras, Calcutta, Dhubri, Bareilly. Non-match workers are included. Figures for Vulcan-Laval are available only up to 1967.

The figures of employment and growth of employment in the Swedish companies are not the whole story. As will be shown later, most of the new recruits in the Swedish companies were already employed at the time of recruitment.[1] The Swedish firms therefore do not have any direct employment effects. But indirectly, people get employment in a chain reaction throughout the industrial structure, and the ultimate effect is probably that permanently unemployed or underemployed people get more employment.

But, as I said before, it is likely that the Swedish companies´ production is substituted for the production of Indian firms.[2] With the same production techniques, these Indian firms would - as I shall argue later - probably have less efficient organizations and therefore have relatively more people

1) See p. 105.
2) Cf. pp. 260 ff.

employed than the Swedish companies. But the resources released when the Swedish companies substitute for domestic production are probably also put to a relatively labour-intensive use. The net employment effect of the Swedish firms is therefore likely to be small and probably positive.

This is not true of WIMCO. The present alternative to WIMCO is production by the cottage factories.[1] The cottage match industry has a large employment potential, which is probably far larger than the possible alternative uses of the resources released by the investment and production of WIMCO. Each job in WIMCO is worth 30-40 jobs in the cottage industry, and the net employment effects of WIMCO are therefore likely to be extremely negative.

Turnover. The rate of turnover of labour and the rate of absenteeism may both be measures of the stability of the work force. High rates (low stability) may be a sign of bad industrial relations and discontent with the work situation, and the low rates generally associated with foreign companies may then signify good industrial relations, which may yield external effects of positive value for development. But this is all speculation. The turnover rate, for example, is influenced by many factors and no certain conclusions can be drawn from high or low rates.

Historically the turnover of labour has been very high in Indian industry. In the 1940's, the work force in the mills in industrial centres changed almost completely in a year and a half.[2] WIMCO also had trouble in the early years: "We often find difficulty in keeping labour. Even in a place like Ambernath, because they want to live in the town. At Dhubri, for instance, we find we cannot retain our labour."[3]

But in recent years low turnover figures have been more frequent. The only official statistics available are from the textile industry in Maharashtra and Gujarat, and they depict a turnover less than half the rate in the textile industry in the USA.[4] The main reason for this is, of course, the discrepancy between supply and demand for labour in India. Under present conditions, the employees typically attach tremendous importance to tenure of employment.

---

1) Cf. pp. 65-66.
2) Jathar, G.B., and Beri, S.G., Indian Economics, Bombay 1949, p. II:100.
3) India. Tariff Board, Match Industry..., Vol. III. op. cit., p. 140.
4) Myers, C.A., Labour Problems in the Industrialization of India, Cambridge 1958, p. 47.

91

The labour turnover in the Swedish companies is shown in Table 7. The average annual turnover is 8.5 per cent, which compares favourably with 17.8 per cent in the cotton textile industry in Maharashtra. A high turnover means relatively higher labour costs for the company in question, and the rational thing to do is then to try to press down the turnover rate. This is also done in the Swedish companies generally, but in one special sense WIMCO tries to get a higher turnover. It has trouble in getting rid of old and inefficient labour. "The sad thing is that people do not leave us". It is hailed as a triumph by the top management when a WIMCO factory succeeds in fixing a lower retirement age or in getting rid of its employees in some other way. To simply fire permanently employed people is practically impossible in India. [1)

Table 7. Labour turnover in the Swedish companies in 1964-68 (severance rate as a percentage).

	Average annual labour turnover (per cent) 1964-68	
WIMCO		
Factory 1	6.2	
Factory 2	4.1	5.3
Factory 3	3.1	
Factory 4	8.4	
Factory 5	4.8	
Vulcan Laval	2.7	
Atlas Copco	0.9	
Sandvik	14.7	9.8
SKF	27.2	
SF	3.6	
Cotton textile industry in Maharashtra (1963-67)	17.8	

Sources. Company statistics. Maharashtra figure from India. Labour Bureau, Indian Labour Statistics 1969, Simla 1969, p. 174. The turnover figure for Vulcan-Laval is available only for the year 1966 (2.66 %). The turnover rate is calculated as the ratio of the number leaving in a year to the total number employed. For factories 1-5, see Table 6, p. 90.

1) Cf. p. 101.

Atlas Copco is a relatively small company with, it seems, a positive atmosphere, and active steps are taken to bring down the rate of turnover. This may explain the extraordinarily low turnover rate for this company. SKF has the highest rate, which is partly due to the fact that many temporary workers were taken on in the first few years, and, according to plan, most of these temporary workers were subsequently fired. About half the average rate of turnover for the Swedish companies consists of such "involuntary quittings". The second dominant reason for leaving is better wage and job prospects. Other important reasons are indebtedness (a lump-sum payment is made on retirement from service), illness and family reasons.[1]

Productivity

The Indian planners have two, sometimes conflicting goals, that should both to some extent be fulfilled: more employment and higher productivity. "Productivity" usually means "labour productivity", which is not self-evident. It may be argued that productivity should be measured in relation to the scarce factor in the economy, which in India is foreign exchange rather than labour. The conclusion to be drawn from figures of increasing "labour productivity" is, of course, not always that labour has become more efficient but that other inputs, like capital, may have increased and resulted in higher output.

Modern industries can increase labour productivity by drawing labour from low-productivity occupations and by improving the skills and abilities of their employees. Labour productivity is generally low in underdeveloped countries. The traditional opinion of the normal productivity of Indian labour is well expressed by the Factory Commission of 1908:

> While the Indian factory worker may work hard for a comparatively short period, his natural inclination is to spread the work he has to do over a long period of time, working in a leisurely manner throughout and taking intervals of rest whenever he feels disinclined for further exertion.[2]

The exigences of modern industry have probably increased the productivity pressure on the Indian workers, but, relatively speaking, their productivity still seems to be low: "...the intensity, skill and diligence with which

---

1) Cf. Vaid, K.N. op. cit., p. 43.
2) India. Factory Commission 1908, quoted in Jathar, G.B. and Beri, S.G., Indian Economics, op. cit., p. 96.

the labor force works when it is working are, as a rule, low and do not generally show much improvement... in most of the cases in which relevant comparisons can be drawn, it appears that output per worker falls substantially below the norms in Western countries."[1] The reasons for lower efficiency have often been stated: institutions, attitudes, climate, malnutrition, physical factors, etc.

Comparisons of productivity in terms of racial differences or "natural inclinations" are relatively rare nowadays and are at least not typical of the managements in the Swedish companies. Their estimates of the productivity of Indian labour in comparison with European - capital equipment being the same - average about 60 per cent but are always given with reser vations as regards causes and with the rider that "under equal conditions, equal productivity". Prominent causes are stated to be lack of working tradition, climate, health and education. An example of a rather special cause of low labour productivity is the fact that the lower quality of the wood used in match production means lower utilization of machines and added need for workers to clean away wood waste.

While the workers get relatively high productivity ratings by the management in the Swedish companies, the productivity of staff is generally considered very low, as compared with Europe. "Really, I think they are lazy" "That's where all the money goes", and "Clerical staff are just bad orators are not uncommon expressions illustrating the low rating of office productivity. One Swedish company with sister companies all over the world has the lowest office productivity of all the companies in its concern. Capital-equipment differences are not included in these estimates, but an important reason for low staff productivity is probably the lack of office machinery - not computers but simple machines for book-keeping, electrical calculators, etc. The Indian Government normally does not allow the domestic sale of such equipment, presumably in order to maintain employment.

The predominant reason assigned for low staff productivity is bad organization, i.e. the cause of low staff productivity in the Swedish companies is mainly inefficient management. This has been demonstrated in the case of Atlas Copco. In 1968 the company opened a new branch office in Hyderabad with six people employed, who were doing exactly the same work as 35 employees in other, older, branch offices. Atlas Copco and Vulcan Laval have had numbers of old and inefficient personnel since the time of

---

1) Myrdal, G., op. cit., pp. 1140, 1141; Cf. India. Fiscal Commission 1949-50, op. cit. p. 233.

Vulcan Trading, which is also the main reason for the high percentage of staff in these companies. [1]

According to the shaky averages in Table 8, the productivity of labour (measured as sales per worker) in the Swedish companies is growing at the same rate as in other industries in India. Productivity figures before 1965 are available for WIMCO and they tally with the present trend. The figures for the growth of physical productivity in the last column also corroborate roughly the sales per worker figures. The low productivity figures for Vulcan-Laval are probably connected with the re-organization of the company, and the high figures of increase for SKF are partly explained by the fact that the company started the production of bearings as late as 1965. The figures of workers' productivity in SF are probably uninformative, as the sales figure in this company mainly depends on the efforts of non-workers.

Productivity data are difficult to interpret, and sales per worker and especially sales per non-worker are very crude measures. Therefore no certain conclusions can be drawn. But, according to Table 8, it seems that the Swedish firms do not differ much from other industries in India, as concerns the growth of productivity per worker but that office productivity possibly grows somewhat faster in the Swedish companies. Again, this is subject to many reservations.

Outside India, no relevant comparisons can be made, except as concerns physical productivity. On an average, a WIMCO match worker in 1968 needed 4.1 hours to produce 1000 match boxes, while a Swedish worker only spent 0.7 hours making the same quantity. [2] This comparison is not surprising, taking into account the differences in capital equipment. But it may be noted that also several of the new Swedish companies are already definitely lagging behind their contemporary European sister companies in productivity and quality, which must, of course, have consequences for the future abilities of the Swedish firms to compete in the world market. The European companies constantly renew their machinery, while the companies in India are allowed to import new machines only in very special cases.

The Swedish companies all try to raise labour productivity. The "cheap-

---

1) See Table 8, p. 96. Atlas Copco handles the sales of Sandvik drilling products, which accounts for some of its large number of staff. The technical nature of the production in Sandvik and SF is one reason for the relatively high figures of non-workers for these companies.

2) STAB, Matchco News, 1968:3, p. 18.

Table 8. Percentage of non-workers, sales per worker and growth of productivity in the Swedish companies in 1965-68

	Percentage of non-workers 1968	Sales per worker 1968 (Rs.1000´s)	Average growth of sales per worker (per cent) 1965-68	Average growth of sales per non-worker (per cent) 1965	Average growth of production per man-hour (per cent) 1965-6
WIMCO					
Factory 1	15	30	8.4	0.3	5.5 ⎫
Factory 2	12				1.7 ⎪
Factory 3	12				4.5 ⎬ 3.0
Factory 4	16				0.0 ⎪
Factory 5	9				3.1 ⎭
Vulcan-Laval	62	252	-5.3 ⎫	-16.3 ⎫	⎰ (11.3)
Atlas Copco	66	218	13.0 ⎪	5.7 ⎪	⎱ (11.0)
Sandvik	50	95	9.8 ⎬ 8.8	12.3 ⎬ 11.9	
SKF	33	79	35.2 ⎪	37.0 ⎪	73.5
SF	64	139	-8.9 ⎭	4.4 ⎭	
Poona (1964-65)	25	18			
All India (1964 and 1961-64)	14	17	8.7	-4.5	

Sources. India. National Commission on Labour, Statistics of Selected
 Manufacturing Industries, Delhi 1968, pp. 2-3; Poona Metropolitan Regional Planning Board, op. cit. , pp. 194 and 199; company
 statistics. Data on value added are unfortunately not available.
 When at variance, WIMCO factory statistics have been preferred
 to head-office statistics. Non-workers in the head office are not
 included. Factories 1-5 are as enumerated in Table 6, p. 90.
 The productivity of non-workers at Vulcan-Laval covers factory
 staff only. Employees in the SKF sales company are not included.
 The all-India figure covers 98 % of all factories employing 50 or
 more workers with the aid of power and 100 or more workers
 without power. Figures of production in the last column relate
 to number of matches, compressors, rock drills and bearings.
 Figures for Atlas Copco and to some extent also for SKF in the
 last column contain estimates and extrapolations.

labour policy" of earlier times, when managers were more or less indifferent to the number of workers they employed, as wages and productivity
were both very low, has today been reversed. Labour is no longer considered cheap, and the Swedish companies try to rationalize as much as possible.
It is considered better to pay more to few workers than to pay little to many
- it is more economical to try to raise the productivity of existing labour
by paying higher wages than to employ cheap but less efficient labour. Moves towards higher productivity are generally viewed with suspicion by the
workers, who fear that employment will be reduced or that the management
will take all the fruits of increased exertions by the workers.

Choice of technology

In the current discussion on underemployment in underdeveloped countries,
a basic argument is that well-populated countries like India should preferably
use labour-intensive techniques. The goal of increased employment could
thereby be achieved and at the same time the distribution of incomes would
become more equal.[1]   But this increased employment is not always the
primary reason adduced for the use of labour-intensive techniques. Instead,
the theory of factor proportions and comparative advantage is applied, which
says that production is maximized if the scarce factor in the economy is
well rationed. If the scarce factor in India is capital, then capital should
be economized and more of the relatively abundant factor (labour) should
be used.[2]

The argument is thus that, if capital-saving techniques are used, capital
is economized, and as capital is the bottleneck to growth, output is thereby
also maximized. Growing output is beneficial and also a prerequisite for
a long-term increase in employment opportunities.

Against this basic argument in favour of labour-intensive techniques, se-

1) That is, more equal within the segment of society in which profits and
   wage incomes exist. Part of the population is left even further behind
   by an increase in factory wages.
2) "... no technique should be chosen just because it gives employment.
   The object of the operation is not to be able to count up the largest total of statistical employment but to increase production. (It is misleading to state the question in terms of labour-intensive techniques.
   The advantage of handicrafts lies in being capital-saving, not in being
   labour-using.)" (Robinson, J., Economic Philosophy, p. 122, quoted
   in Pant, S.C., op. cit., p. 246) Cf. Sen, A.K., Choice of Techniques
   in a Labour Surplus Economy, in Meier, G.M., Leading Issues...,
   pp. 349 ff.

veral arguments for capital-intensive techniques have been put forward.
The assumption that capital is the main bottleneck to development may be
wrong. If, instead, skills constitute the scarce factor, it might be bett،
to start large capital-intensive industries, where more efficient use can
be made of the scarce skills than in smaller companies. [1]

Even if capital is the main bottleneck, as compared with labour, labour-
intensive techniques are not, in absolute terms, necessarily identical with
capital-saving techniques. In a famous study, Dhar and Lydall have shown
that, when labour-intensive small-scale industries are somewhat mechanized, they tend to use not only more labour per unit of output than large
industries but also more capital per unit of output. [2]   Their study has weak-
nesses, but it leads Gunnar Myrdal to the following conclusion: "...the capital-saving argument does not seem to carry much weight as a general
reason for supporting small-scale industry". [3]

Another argument based on the assumption that capital is the scarce resource is that profits in the usually large capital-intensive industries are
more likely to be re-invested than profits in labour-intensive industries.
The proponents of capital-intensive industries also argue that labour-intensive industries cannot succeed in making top-quality goods, that their
long-run costs of production are higher, and that capital-intensive units
are more likely to export and thereby break the foreign-exchange bottleneck, with the result that production and also employment may rise more
than proportionately. Modern capital-intensive plants can also give more
"prestige".

Even if it is conceded that in India labour-intensive techniques are better
than capital-intensive, the possibilities of substitution are small, at least
in one direction. More capital-intensive production is often possible, but
change to more labour-intensive techniques is in most cases very difficult. [4]
The new machines now made in the industrialized countries are all sophisticated and capital-intensive, and most of the older machines have already
been scrapped. The application of labour-intensive technologies in countries
like India would therefore require a research effort on the company level
which is not likely to be forthcoming. Even if it were, the objective of
higher employment might still not be achieved in this way, as the modern

1) A drawback is that most employees remain unskilled, and development
   might then be retarded by lack of mass involvement and training. Cf.
   Myrdal, G., op. cit., p. 1171.
2) Dhar, P.N. and Lydall, H.F., The Role of Small Enterprises in Indian
   Economic Development, Bombay 1961.
3) Myrdal, G., op. cit., p. 1223.
4) Rosen, G., op. cit., pp. 123-24.

sector is such a small proportion of total industry. "Even if highly labor-intensive techniques were adopted in South Asia´s modern industrial sector, there would be little change in the proportion of the total labor force it absorbed."[1]

Still, there might be scope for labour-intensive techniques in some fields. Even if the production process in itself is capital-intensive, it may be possible to substitute labour for machines in internal transport, handling, packaging, etc. Construction work is often quoted as a sector where there are possibilities of substitution. Imported second-hand equipment that is more labour-using than the latest machines might be of advantage if the Indian Government were not (often with good reason) so very suspicious of it. It is possible that "too capital-intensive" industries are started because of artificially low rates of interest, because of artifically pegged high wages and because the investors want to safeguard themselves against labour troubles (less labour usually means less probability of trouble).[2]

In this matter the Indian Government has taken the long-range view and, with some reservations, has preferred more production and employment in the future to present employment:

Sustained programmes over a period of years for the rapid development of agriculture and expansion of modern industries will be the only solution to the problem of unemployment. In the transitional stage, it is necessary to maintain and indeed to promote labour-intensive methods of production to the fullest extent, so long as this does not lead to a smaller aggregate production in the economy. This policy was accepted in the Second Plan and will have to be continued in the Third and subsequent plans.[3]

One would expect WIMCO to be relatively labour-intensive in production and the new Swedish investments to be more capital-intensive. This is also the picture that emerges from Table 9, and the percentages of non-workers in Table 8 (p. 96) point in the same direction. Compared with other companies in India, WIMCO has invested somewhat less capital per worker than the average. But the new Swedish companies are extremely capitalintensive when compared with the average Indian company. There is a slight difference between Vulcan-Laval, Atlas Copco, and SF, which have more assembly and precision work, in contrast to the single-product, more capital-intensive production in Sandvik and SKF.

---

1) Myrdal, G., op. cit., p. 1172.
2) Cf. p. 119; Rosen, G., op. cit., p. 122.
3) India. Planning Commission, Third Five-year Plan, op. cit., p. 85.

Table 9. Capital employed per worker in the Swedish companies in 1968

	Capital per worker 1968 (Rs. 1000´s)	
WIMCO	17	
Vulcan Laval	101	
Atlas Copco	68	127
Sandvik	203	
SKF	190	
SF	74	
Poona (1964-65)	11	
All India (1965)	19	

Sources. See Table 8, p. 96, and India. Central Statistical Organization, Annual Survey of industries 1965, p. 9. Capital employed = total liabilities less provision for losses. Capital per worker figures for Poona are defined as total investment per production worker.

The Swedish companies have normally the same type of technology as their respective parent companies. WIMCO´s match technology, however, is now behind the match technology in Europe, where cardboard has been substituted for wood. But the paper and chlorate in WIMCO are both highly mechanized and eventually the salt manufacture will be so too. The new Swedish firms have essentially the same machines as their parent companies, although automation is not always carried as far as in Sweden.

The reason for the somewhat lower technological intensity in the Swedish companies in India, compared with the parent companies in Sweden, is usually not that labour is cheaper. The main reason is that the Indian market is too small to support factories on the large scale that is needed for further automation. The degree of mechanization thus depends more on the size of the market and the production unit than on wage levels.[1]

The actual possibilities of substituting labour for machines are small in the Swedish firms. It is mostly either physically impossible or economically not feasible, in spite of the fact that costs per hour for machines are sometimes a hundred times the cost of labour. It has also happened that Swedish companies have imported more moderna machines than were

1) Cf. Sveriges Allmänna Exportförening, Svenska produktionsinvesterin̲g ar i Latinamerika, Stockholm 1970, p. 32.

strictly warranted economically, in order to minimize the need for labour and thereby to avoid difficulties in dismissing workers and to reduce the risks of labour trouble. The Swedish companies seem to use techniques that are as capital-intensive as possible in the small Indian market. Relatively labourintensive techniques are used only for certain kinds of transport and in some types of materials-handling.

Rationalization. The conflict between the long-term objective of increased productivity and the short-term employment needs comes to the fore in connection with the rationalization issue. In India, both organized and unorganized labour are opposed to rationalization, on the grounds that it only means increased workloads and less employment. The gains from rationalization are allegedly wholly expropriated by the management.[1]

The industrial legislation introduced after Independence has generally been favourable to labour. The main legislation in this context is the Industrial Disputes Act of 1947, in which several measures were introduced to increase the job security of workers. It is now extremely difficult for a company in India to fire a worker, and every dismissal must be preceded by elaborate proceedings, charge sheets, enquiries, etc. According to a personnel officer in a Swedish company, "the recent amendments to the Industrial Disputes Act show a trend towards making the job security practically absolute". If in very special cases a company is allowed to dismiss any workers, it has to follow a "last-in-first-out" principle, which further emphasizes the older workers´ property rights to their jobs.[2]

The Indian Government has adopted a policy of "rationalization without tears", which means that no one is normally to be deprived of his job because of rationalization measures. Subject to certain safeguards and the guaranteed job security, the Government has thus accepted the principle of rationalization.

Of the Swedish companies, only WIMCO has had serious trouble with rationalization. The new Swedish firms are not in immediate need of new machines, and they can expand fast enough to absorb any surplus of labour created by rationalization. Their main problem in this context is rather

---

1) Pant, S.C., op. cit., p. 242.
2) "The attention to the workers´ property rights in the factory job is evident in the elaborate regulations concerning dismissal and the difficulty factories have in firing a permanent worker merely on the grounds of inefficiency" (Lambert, R.D., Workers, Factories and Social Change in India, Princeton 1963, p. 92).

to get rid of undesirable workers (workers alleged to be inefficient, agitators, thieves, etc.).

WIMCO started match production in the early twenties, using manual processes. To begin with, its new factories were run on double shifts. As more machines were brought in, less labour was required, and the surplus workers were dismissed. In Ambernath only, some 1,200 workers were fired when the second shift was abolished in 1926. After Independence, dismissal has become much more difficult, and WIMCO has had to rely mainly on "natural wastage", the retirement or death of workers, to bring down employment. The pace of rationalization and technical development depends, it is said, very much on the actual rate of "natural wastage". Fortunately for WIMCO, this rate is at present relatively high.

The trade unions in the WIMCO factories are clearly against rationalization. When in the 1960´s the Government´s excise banderols were no longer to be put on the match boxes, several machines were taken away and some 50 workers in each match factory were made redundant and could also legally be dismissed. But the trade unions said no. The factories thus had to keep the banderol workers, but some of the factories managed to get, in exchange, a consent from the union that some minor rationalizations would be allowed, and in one case a fixing of the retirement age was permitted. This type of negotiation is not uncommon. Another match factory once got permission to fix the retirement age at 60 years in exchange for a gratuity scheme and the introduction of an employment preference for sons of retired workers.

Recruitment

Work-force characteristics

The impact of foreign investment in connection with education, attitudes, living standards etc, is primarily something which affects the situation of the employees. To ascertain such effects in the case of the Swedish companies, we therefore have to look at their work forces.

Geographically, some 80-90 per cent of new recruits to the Swedish companies come from the State in which the company is located. Some of the WIMCO factories, though, had in the early years much recruitment from outside the State. The factory at Ambernath had in the beginning difficulties in attracting labour, and in the first years only 10 per cent of the employees came from the State, "...the reason being that Ambernath is a lonely place".[1]

Gradually employment took its normal channels also at Ambernath. But in 1935-36 there was a strike and the factory was closed for 60 days. The company then succeeded in bringing in strike-breakers, poor people from another State, Andra Pradesh. Their sons were later employed in the factory, with the result that some 35 per cent of the present work force at Ambernath stem from Andra Pradesh.

The Calcutta factory employs some 30 per cent East Bengalis (the greater part of East Bengal is now in Pakistan). During the Hindu-Muslim riots in Bengal in 1952, practically all WIMCO's 600 Muslim employees fled to Pakistan. They were replaced by East Bengali Hindu refugees. The Calcutta factory also has some 20 per cent Bihari people employed, as has the Dhubri factory. The reason stated for this is that the Biharis are big and hefty and do not mind lifting heavy burdens or carrying things on their heads, something which a Bengali is said to refuse to do. The Biharis are therefore considered very useful in loading, transport, etc.

As we have seen, WIMCO has a relatively labour-intensive technique, compared with other companies in the large-scale sector, and substantial quantities of unskilled workers are employed. The level of literacy and education in the WIMCO factories is therefore usually the same as or somewhat lower than in the respective areas. The new Swedish companies, on the other hand, employ much skilled labour and many technicians and therefore require more educated people. In the Poona area about half the population is literate, but nearly all the workers in the new Swedish companies are literate.[2] Most skilled workers in the Swedish firms in Poona have matriculated.

The distribution of employees by age and marital status also shows a difference between the older WIMCO factories and the new Swedish firms. The WIMCO workers are 40-45 years old and mostly married, while the workers in the new Swedish companies are, on an average, 26 years old and therefore not married to the same extent as in WIMCO.

Previous employment. The main economic benefit from foreign investment has been presented here as total product minus costs of material, labour, etc. Labour costs should then be calculated as opportunity costs. If the wages actually paid out to new employees exceed their marginal productivity in previous occupations, private cost exceeds social cost, and the

---

1) India. Tariff Board, Match Industry, Vol. III, op. cit.,p. 184.
2) Diwan, G.R., op. cit., p. 32 (12).

difference can be regarded as a national gain. If the newly employed had no previous occupation and the company in question does not substitute for others, there will, of course, be a positive employment effect.

The traditional example of industrial impact in this context is the farmer who is suddenly taken from his plough and thrown into factory employment. His marginal productivity in agriculture was zero or near zero, and the main part of his wages can therefore be added to the benefits from the company in question. The company then also has to carry the initial "burden of socialization", of training and adjusting the farmer to modern industrial work.

A few earlier studies show that the notion of a direct transfer from agriculture to modern industry is often unrealistic. "We can immediately dismiss the notion that we are dealing with a peasant workforce", says R.D. Lambert, who has conducted a sociological study on the workforce in the modern industries in Poona.[1] In his sample only 3 per cent of the worker had ever been engaged in farming. The corresponding figure for a very new industrial centre in agricultural surroundings was 9 per cent.[2]

Hence, the new workers have normally not been farmers. As might be expected, many of them are unemployed at the time of recruitment (many come direct from school or from an industrial training institute) - some 37 per cent of a total of 821 workers in Lambert's study. But the majority have had some form of previous employment, and here I quote Lambert again:

> The job histories of the workers present a truly remarkable spread of employers. There were in all 431 different employers mentioned. Here is a partial list just to give some of the flavor of the range of previous employers: ink factories, domestic service, oil mills, cinema houses and studios, sugar factories, newspapers, laundries, tea companies, hospitals, public works departments, banks, police, military, railways, schools, grocery stores, hydro-electric supply companies, dispensaries, buslines, hotels, stone-cutters, air-lines, bidi works, bakeries, docks, pan shops, soap factories, tongawallas, cycle marts, law journals, pleaders, ayurvedic medicine factories, tin makers, fire brigades, lumber companies, and telephone exchanges. All of these have been mentioned more than once, and the full range is even broader.[3]

---

1) Lambert, R.D., Workers Factories and Social Change in India, Princeton 1963.
2) Vaid, K.N., The New Worker, New Delhi 1968, p. 41.
3) Lambert, R.D., op. cit., p. 61.

It is not surprising that the new Swedish companies, most of which are located in Poona, follow roughly the pattern of the Lambert study. Some 15 per cent only of the employees in the new Swedish firms come from farmers' families, but even in these cases they have mostly been to school for a long time and have not actually worked on the land.[1] It has to be remembered that most workers in the new Swedish companies are very young. The majority of them had been employed before, mostly in big factories but also in small industries, petty trade, etc., in conformity with the Lambert pattern.

The WIMCO factories that are now located in industrialized areas (Ambernath, Calcutta, Madras) largely get their workers from the same type of sources as the new Swedish companies, while the more isolated factories (Dhubri, Bareilly) still recruit relatively many sons of farmers and even actual farmers. In the beginning, all the WIMCO factories recruited almost exclusively farmers, as no other workers were available. A common characteristic of the workforce in all the Swedish companies is that the farmers and descendants of farmers now employed are all settled in the respective factory areas. They sometimes have a piece of land to which they will return on retirement, but generally they visit their villages only intermittently at week-ends. They have thus taken to factory life for good and will not go back to the land after a few years of factory work.[2]

The fact that the Swedish companies tend to recruit people who are already employed means that the direct employment effects are small, but indirectly people will get employment in the places of those who move over to the Swedish firms.[3] The task of socialization, of introducing people to industrial work, is largely passed on to other, smaller establishments. Only the WIMCO factories in the early years carried this burden in respect of the farmers employed in the initial stage. The question of wages and the effects thereof will be taken up in the next chapter.

Recruitment policies

Some of the possible external economies from foreign investment are con-

---

1) The present study does not include detailed sociological research on the factory employees. Most of the percentages presented here are therefore estimates with sometimes a very low degree of precision, made by personnel officers, trade-union leaders, etc. Double-checking makes the figures more reliable, but it is still only the general trend that can be considered certain.
2) Cf. p. 174.
3) Cf. p. 90 ff.

nected with recruitment. Foreign firms may by their recruitment practices indirectly influence the labour market and the recruitment policies of other industries in a direction conducive to economic growth. Recruitment in underdeveloped countries is often highly personal and influenced by status criteria, while the labour market in industrialized countries is usually more "depersonalized", giving primary importance to qualities like skills and experience.

Employment policy. If skills and experience are of first importance, it means that preference in recruitment is given to these qualities and not to other qualities, i.e. there will be less discrimination between applicants on grounds irrelevant to the job. A prohibition against the State discriminating in such a way is to be found in the Indian Constitution, in which it is forbidden to "discriminate against any citizen on grounds only of religion, race, caste, sex, place of birth or any of them".[1]

It can safely be said that the Swedish companies do not discriminate in recruitment in respect of religion, race or caste. It does happen that some personnel officer may show preference for his own community, but these are exceptions. Several Swedish firms have a policy of mixing communities especially in the offices, to avoid communal strife. Women are discriminated against for special reasons,[2] while no one is preferred just because he was born at a certain place.

Sometimes knowledge of the English language, for example, is required and also certain levels of education, but these qualities must be regarded as being included in "skill and experience". The Swedish companies pride themselves on not letting education be "over-prized", as is said to be common in other firms.[3] Youth, however, cannot be included in "skill and experience", but most of the Swedish companies discriminate against older people. Thirty-five years is a common upper limit for recruitment. One of the Swedish firms justifies its preference for quite young people with the argument that younger people find it easier to adjust to the specialized production and high tempo in the company: "The lazy habit is difficult to get out of".

Most of the WIMCO factories have in recent years given in to trade-union demands that preference should be given in recruitment to the sons and relatives of the workers. This practice is found also in some Government offices and serves as a sort of old-age pension to retired employees. At

---

1) The Constitution of India, Allahabad 1968, p. 4.
2) See pp. 110 ff.
3) Cf. Lambert, R.D., op. cit., pp. 129 and 166.

the same time it conserves the traditional opinion that the job is a kind of property owned by the worker.[1] Of the new Swedish companies, some have the opposite policy of giving preference to non-related people. If the applicant knows too many employees in the company or any of the directors, he is disqualified. Likewise, proposals from Government officals to employ their sons and relatives are usually turned down.

Recruitment channels. Before the First World War the resistance to movement out of the agricultural sector in India was considerable and factories had difficulties in getting workers. A system of recruitment through intermediaries was then adopted. The "jobber" recruited gangs of workers by harsh methods. Later the supply of potential factory workers grew, but the jobber stayed on and in many cases he controlled both the supply of and the demand for labour.

Workers had to bribe the jobber to get work, which meant that financial strength was more important than skill and experience in securing a job. The next stage was a system of direct recruitment, in which vacancies were notified at the factory gate and/or directly to the workers already employed, whose friends and relatives then stood a better-than-average chance of getting a job.

The most modern form of recruitment is of an indirect type, through employment exchanges and newspaper advertisements. The existing employment exchanges in India were taken over by the State in the mid-fifties, and some years later notification of vacancies was made compulsory. But these measures did not lead to a "depersonalizing" of the labour market through a switch-over to formal recruitment mechanisms. The employment exchanges are usually notified after an employee has actually been taken on. They have many "bogus" registrations and in the last few years their activity has also shown tendencies to stagnation.[2]

Instead, the direct and informal ways of recruitment are still used. The "jobber" is on his way out and money is not needed any more, but the di-

---

1) Cf. p. 101.
2) India. Labour Bureau. Indian Labour Statistics 1969, Simla 1969, p. 49. Cf. Pant, S.C., op. cit., p. 26. The slow change-over to formal mechanisms is also noted by Lambert in the study mentioned above: "The use of formal mechanisms is one way of impersonalizing the labor market, a process which in the West was deemed to be essential to the full growth of an industrial system. It is clear... that this process has not proceeded very far in India, in these factories at least" (Lambert, R.D., op. cit., p.71).

rect way of recruiting workers at the gate or through the employees is still prevalent. In a study from a new industrial center, Kota, it is learned that 88 per cent of the workers got their jobs through informal channels.[1] In the same study, 61 per cent of the workers were of the opinion that what mattered most in getting a job was general social contacts and contacts "with those who matter in the company". The same answer was given by 50 per cent of the employees in the Lambert study.[2]

In Table 10 are presented the scanty data available on recruitment practices in the Swedish companies. The recruitment channels are enumerated with the most formal first and the most informal last. Several channels can be used at the same time and the data are incomplete, but the general picture is that direct, informal channels of recruitment are most important also in the Swedish firms. A trend towards the greater utilization of formal recruitment channels may perhaps be discerned in the case of the new Swedish companies, but no certain conclusions can be drawn.

The Swedish companies have to notify vacancies to the employment exchanges and they try to help the exchanges to get high placement figures by always notifying, but this notification is in practically all cases given after the actual recruitment. The common opinion of those responsible for recruitment in the Swedish firms is that the persons offered by the employment exchanges are second- or third-rate people.

Advertisements are generally used only to get staff and skilled workers, but it also happens that all jobs are advertised. Vulcan-Laval, for example, shows a very high percentage of advertised jobs, but in reality most workers in this company come through the employees. The news immediately goes around when a post is vacant.

Most companies in India receive written applications all the time, and in some of the Swedish firms these applications are used for recruitment purposes. Such recruitment gives a fairly wide range of choice and thus a fair possibility that the right man will get the job.

Direct recruitment was necessary for the WIMCO factories in the early years. In Dhubri the first personnel officer had to go from door to door, canvassing for workers. Direct recruitment is still the most common form of recruitment in WIMCO, but there is no need for canvassing any longer. The workers always have names to propose, and a large pool of casual and temporary workers is a good basis for recruitment. The preference given

---

1) Vaid, K.N., The New Worker, New Delhi 1968, p. 74.
2) Vaid, K.N., op. cit., p. 72; Lambert, R.D., op. cit., p. 76.

	Indirect channels				Direct channels		
	Employment exchange	Newspaper advertise- ment	Written appli- cation	Indi- rect, total	Through workers	Hand- picking	Direct, total
WIMCO							
Factory 1	5			5	80		80
Factory 2	30	20	50	100			0
Factory 3	0	1		1		99	99
Factory 4	5			5	95		95
Factory 5	1	1		2		95	95
Vulcan-Laval	5	90		95	5		5
Atlas Copco					95		95
Sandvik	5	60	5	70		10	10
SKF		40	60	100			0
SF	5	1		6		94	94
Poona	2	2	22	26			
Kota	2	10		12	70	18	88
U.K.	11	4	52	67			

Sources. Company statistics; Lambert, R.D., op. cit., p. 71, for Poona
and U.K. figures; Vaid, K.N., op. cit., p. 74 for Kota figures.
The figures do not add up to 100 %. The percentages are in no way
exact. "Through workers" includes recruitment through notice
boards in the factory or at the gate. "Hand-picking" includes recruitment from a temporary pool.

to sons of workers in the WIMCO factories also contributes to high figures
for direct recruitment.

As a rule, nobody is given a permanent post directly but has to serve a
minimum of 3-6 months as a "temporary". The Swedish companies follow
the rule "slow to hire, slow to fire", more or less by compulsion. They
are forced by law to be "slow to fire" and therefore a new worker is employed as a "temporary" for quite some time, while the company finds out
all about him and his past. Once he is made "permanent", it is very difficult for the company to fire him.

Women and casual labour

Two of the first Directive Principles of State Policy embodied in the Indian Constitution are concerned with the employment of women: "The State shall in particular, direct its policy towards securing (a) that the citizens, men and women equally, have the right to an adequate means of livelihood; ... (d) that there is equal pay for equal work for both men and women".[1]

The proportion of women workers to the total female population of India has increased during the last few decades, but the proportion of women workers in factories to the total factory workers has constantly decreased. In 1967 women workers constituted less than 10 per cent of factory worker. Women tend to get mostly unskilled jobs and jobs in sweated industries.[3]

One obvious reason for the decreasing employment of women in factories is the legislation enacted to protect them, which has raised the cost to the employers of employing women. Women cannot work in shifts, as they are forbidden to work at night, and there are restrictions on their total number of work hours and overtime. The employment of women is forbidden in hazardous and unhealthy work, such as carrying heavy loads or working underground.[4]

Women are also not popular, as they are sometimes absent for childbirth and child care. Sometimes the employers have to pay maternity benefit, and where more than a certain number of women are employed, t company has to provide crèches, separate toilets, etc., all of which raise the cost of employing women. The enforcement of the principle of equal pay for women and men further raises the cost.[5] Finally, the employment of women is decreasing, because women are mostly found in the type of unskilled jobs that are the first to disappear with mechanization.

In the beginning, the WIMCO factories used much female labour for box-filling and other manual jobs. Women were thought to be superior to men in certain manual jobs because of their greater finger dexterity. In 1927, women constituted 16 per cent of the total work force in WIMCO. But then

1) The Constitution of India, Allahabad 1968, p. 12.
2) India. Labour Bureau. Indian Labour Statistics 1969, p. 39. Cf. Pant S.C., op. cit., pp. 385 ff.
3) Pant, S.C., op. cit., p. 387.
4) Pant, S.C., op. cit., p. 392.
5) The principle of equal pay is not always enforced and it has even happ ed that Government industrial tribunals have awarded lower pay for women on the ground that wages for women have always been somewhat lower than for men. Cf. Pant, S.C., op. cit., p. 207.

it was realised that machines were even more nimble than women, and it was considered better to have men tending the machines. In 1942 the employment of women had decreased to 2 per cent and this year the recruitment of women workers was stopped altogether.

Children were also employed in the beginning in the WIMCO factories. They constituted some 3 per cent of the total work force in 1927 but only 0.4 per cent in 1942. Since 1942 no children have been employed in the WIMCO factories. The employment of children in India is essentially a thing of the past; in 1961 only 3,000 children were employed in Indian factories.[1]

In the work-force sample in Poona made by Lambert, women constituted only 3.4 per cent, and all of them were in unskilled occupations. There is a general shortage of women in the Poona area, but this is not assigned by Lambert as a reason for the low percentage of women workers. The reason is rather the scarcity of good jobs for women: "There is little evidence of scarcity of female labour if the jobs were available, and particularly if their pay were equal to that of males."[2]

Both the WIMCO factories and the new Swedish companies have at present very few women employed (Table 11). The women in the WIMCO factories are mostly those still left of the women workers recruited before 1942. The SKF has some women cleaners and the few other women in the new Swedish firms are employed in secretarial and other office capacities. It has to be remembered here that office jobs like typing, which in Europe are almost exclusively done by women, are in India just as exclusively reserved for men. The employment of female typists by the new Swedish companies could be regarded as part of their "westernizing" effects.[3]

The reason most often given for the low percentage of women employed is that the statutory obligations make it too costly to employ women. Creches, toilets and special transport have to be provided and maternity benefit has to be paid. Some new Swedish companies also mention as reasons that women are more often absent, that they do not have the required strength and that it is immoral to employ women as long as there is unemployment among men.

---

1) Pant, S.C., op. cit., p. 402.
2) Lambert, R.D., op. cit., pp. 26 and 83. Cf. Diwan, G.R., op. cit., p. 33 (13).
3) See pp. 177 ff.

Table 11. Women employed in the Swedish companies in 1968

	Number of women employed in 1968	Women employed as percentage of total work force in 1968
WIMCO		
Factory 1	17	0.8
Factory 2	11	0.5
Factory 3	1	0.0
Factory 4	-	-
Factory 5	-	-
Vulcan-Laval	9	1.5
Atlas Copco	42	10.1
Sandvik	Not available	Not available
SKF	8	1.2
SF	13	3.3

Sources. Company statistics.

The attitudes to the opposite sex are sometimes illuminating. Some representative opinions of the management cadre in the Swedish companies are that, in comparison with men in India, women are:

faster at punching cards, good at manual packing, better at concentrating, more often absent, good for secretarial, follow-up, confidential and repetitive jobs, more nimble, less responsible, less imaginative, more interested, more loyal, more content, more interested in getting married, seldom frustrated, not aspiring, more busy with kids and the family, more willing to work overtime, more cooperative, better at typing fast, better at fixing small things like flowers, more satisfied in a low position, less punctual, better at routine and assembly work, more diligent and more careful.

The picture that emerges from the above quotation is that of the "typical secretary" of European business lore. Such opinions among the management of Swedish companies may increase the employment of women as secretaries, with the western prejudices against women retained. At the same time the employment of women as workers may suffer. But as there is in any case an economic disincentive on account of the statutory obligations in recruiting women workers and as there are plenty of men available, the "secretarial" image of women found in the Swedish companies may have the short-term positive effect that, totally speaking, more women will be employed in the Swedish firms than in comparable Indian companies.

Casual labour. A common feature of the dock industry in the industrialized countries is the casual-labour market, where workers are employed on a day-to-day basis. In India, this system is in operation in the manufacturing industries too. The main reason for the existence of such a system is the generally high rate of absenteeism, which creates a market for temporary labour.

At the gate of almost every factory, people crowd in the morning to get a casual job that day. They are paid less than permanent workers, they have practically no statutory rights and they are usually not members of any trade union. Many employers exploit this situation by paying them very low wages and by constantly keeping a large part of their labour force as casuals. In this way they circumvent the existing legislation, which practically forbids the firing of permanent workers. The Government therefore is reported to have a law in the offing that forbids companies to employ casual labour altogether.

It is sometimes difficult to distinguish between casual and temporary workers. In principle, temporary workers are taken on probation on permanent vacancies, while casual labour is only employed for casual work for a few days. In practice, the two categories blend: temporary workers are used on non-permanent vacancies and casuals may work in the same company for years. In Table 12 the two categories are therefore combined and the percentage of non-permanent labour to the total work force is calculated.

The basis for the calculations may differ slightly from company to company, but the general picture is that the Swedish companies have relatively more permanent workers than the average. This may be more expensive in the short run, but in the long run the labour force thereby probably becomes more efficient. It is a recurring demand from the workers that temporary and casual labour should be made permanent as soon as possible. A positive attitude on the part of the management in this matter therefore helps to create a more content and more efficient work force.

According to law, an employee who has worked in a company continuosly for 6 months must be made permanent. This law, like many other laws in India, is constantly evaded. Many companies fire their temporary and casual employees one day and employ them the next and thereby their "continuous" employment is broken. The Swedish companies have fewer non-permanent workers than other companies and cannot therefore use this loophole in the law to the same extent as other companies, but cases do occur.

Table 12. Average number of non-permanent labour in the Swedish companies in 1968 as percentage of total employment

WIMCO		
Factory 1	12	
Factory 2	16	
Factory 3	6	11
Factory 4	17	
Factory 5	6	
Vulcan-Laval	10	
Atlas Copco	2	
Sandvik	8	7
SKF	14	
SF	0	
Telco		22
Poona (1957)		16
Engineering industry		
(1958-59)		16

Sources. Employers' Federation of India, Handbook of Labour Statistics
1968, Bombay 1968, p. 15, for the engineering-industry figure;
Lambert, R.D., op. cit., for the Poona figure. Other figures
are from company statistics, including the percentage for Telco,
a big Indian company in Poona.

The new Swedish companies have, as can be seen in Table 12, fewer non-
permanent workers than WIMCO. The casual workers in the new Swedish
firms are mostly employed for a few days at a stretch for truly "casual"
work, while their temporary workers stay on and are made permanent
after about a year. It has also happened that casual workers have been
made permanent, especially in store departments and the like.

In WIMCO, the non-permanent force is dominated by casual workers, who
are sometimes employed for a very long time at a stretch (though not formally, as the company would then be obliged to make them permanent).[1]

[1] Before 1948 workers had no rights at all and the distinction between
permanent and casual labour is therefore without importance for this
period - anyone could be fired at short notice. The percentage of
casual labour in WIMCO is said to have been constant over the years.
In 1927, 17 per cent of the employees in WIMCO were registered as
"coolies". (India. Tariff Board, Match Industry, Vol. III, op. cit.,
p. 21).

The preference in recruitment for the relatives of workers accentuates the difficulties for the non-related casuals, as they have then to wait still longer to become permanent. The average time before a casual has become permanent in the WIMCO factories has been 3-4 years.

Mobility and promotion

The long-term development objective of rising levels of income is often expressed by saying that there should be a general increase in productivity. When transferred to the factory floor, this general statement usually means that the productivity of labour should be raised. This can be done through mechanization but also through better organization of the work, which increases the efficiency of the employees.

I have already treated some facets of labour efficiency and possible influences from foreign investment. In this section I shall take up the question of labour mobility and promotion. The general idea is that, if there are many possibilities of movement between different jobs in a factory and if promotion is actively favoured, the employees have a greater chance of getting the particular job in which they will be most productive. They will then also find it worth while trying to improve their job situation and their work, i.e. they will adopt an attitude that will lead to higher productivity.

Promotion is the same thing as vertical mobility, and horizontal mobility is then mobility between jobs and occupational classes within the same wage or skill level. Lambert found that workers in Poona did not care much about occupational mobility, but that they cared very much about the retention of their job.[1] A certain minimum effort was put in to satisfy the employer but not more than that. The job was seen as a property, and the employees tried to safeguard this property by claiming a special designation and a minute job specification for their particular job. Their ideal was the "pigeon-hole" structure found in the older textile industry.

In the Swedish companies, the attitudes of the employees and their organisations seem to be the same as in the Lambert study but the response from the management is different. WIMCO had to begin with an elaborate set-up of occupations: machine-men, helpers, transporters, turners, carpenters, fitters and so on. The management now tries to reduce the number of designations, but without much success. The result is that workers are unwilling to move horizontally and unwilling to do work which is not specified in their job description.

---

1) Lambert, R.D., op. cit. pp. 180 ff.

But the new Swedish companies (except perhaps SKF) have not repeated WIMCO's mistake, and the workers are called "operators", "sheet-metal workers" and other non-committal designations. The only major division used is 6-7 categories of skill. The transfer of a worker from one department to another and minor changes in the nature of the job are therefore easier than in WIMCO, although they are often resisted by the workers. The SF has even gone so far as to abolish also the categories of skill, which is quite an unique achievement in the Indian context.

Neither WIMCO nor the new Swedish companies are able to overcome the immobility between broader occupational classes. Workers do not become clerks, clerks do not become supervisors, supervisors do not become workers, etc. A striking feature is the extremely static nature of the clerk category. An elaborate, guild-like system of designations and grades governs the status hierarchy in the offices. Salary is sometimes considered less important than grade, and it has happened in at least one Swedish firm that typists who have been given some clerical work (high status) have refused to do any more typing (low status). The conditions found by Lambert seem to prevail also in the Swedish companies:

> The general picture, then, is static. Turnover is low. The clerks have more seniority than the factory average in every company. Upward mobility is slight. Only six out of the eighty clerks in the sample had current clerical designations different from the ones they had when they entered the firm. Insulation from the rest of the workforce is relatively complete. In the factory, clerks represent the petty literati class with all of the status and role consequences that that term implies.[1]

Promotion. Promotion or vertical mobility is considered very important by the Indian planners.[2] One type of vertical mobility is relatively rare in Indian industry, especially among clerks, namely, the movement from one factory to a higher position in another factory. The implication is that there are people who would like to leave their organization but who stay on and dislike their job rather than take a risk. The result is presumably lower productivity.

---

1) Lambert, R.D., op. cit., p. 129.
2) "Vertical mobility of labour is thus no less important than horizontal mobility, for nothing is more destructive of hope and more inhibitive of effort than a feeling that the accident of birth or of a poor start in life is likely to come in the way of a capable person rising in life in terms of economic and social status" (India. Planning Commission, The Fourth Five-year Plan, op. cit., p. 3).

A company may be called "progressive" if it tries to utilize the innate capabilities of its employees by encouraging promotion within the company. Older Indian companies have recruited most of their skilled labour and supervisors from outside without giving their own workers the chance.[1]. The Swedish companies are all to some extent trying to promote their own employees; one company even states that it often has to persuade its employees to seek promotion. The response among the employees to such unusual measures is said to be weak, and in particular the workers generally do not show any active interest in promotion. Lambert has found the same characteristic: "Clearly, the bulk of the workers are 'fatalistic', at least so far as upward mobility in their factories is concerned."[2]

The employees in the Swedish companies are given preference in promotion only when they have roughly the same formal merits as outsiders. Several Swedish firms have earlier promoted workers to be supervisors without giving them enough training. This has created certain problems, as these supervisors have then not had the training necessary for an adjustment to new techniques. A certain theoretical level is therefore demanded now for the supervisory posts, which means that more workers are excluded from promotion. This is apparently accepted by the workers, and on the whole the trade unions assert that they are satisfied with the promotion policies of the Swedish firms.

Summary. The ultimate effect of the new Swedish companies on employment is likely to be small but positive. WIMCO, on the other hand, competes with the extremely labour-intensive cottage industry and has therefore probably very negative effects on employment. The Swedish companies have lower-than-average rates of labour turnover.

The Swedish companies are very capital-intensive in the Indian context. WIMCO is an exception, if compared with the average large-scale industry, but in comparison with the cottage industry WIMCO is, of course, very capital-intensive. The possibilities of substituting labour for capital are generally small and have not been actively examined by the Swedish companies.

The workers in the Swedish firms are normally recruited from and settled in the factory areas. Most of them come from other companies, and very few have ever been farmers. The Swedish companies appear to some extent to use more formalized recruitment channels than Indian firms, and their employment policies are less discriminatory, for example, as con-

---

1) Lambert, R.D., op. cit.,p. 137.
2) Lambert, R.D., op. cit., p. 184.

cerns women and casual labour. The Swedish companies are trying to increase the occupational mobility of their employees and they are also promoting higher productivity in other ways, but the employees are from past experience usually suspicious and opposed to changes.

Chapter 5

LABOUR CONDITIONS

In the preceding chapter I discussed problems of employment, recruitment and productivity in connection with the Swedish companies. In this context it is natural to treat questions concerning wages, welfare, social security and standards of living.

Wages

"Whether they worked in a big plant or in a small mill, in a public-sector undertaking or in a private enterprise, in an assembly shed or in a workshop, they wanted higher wages more than anything else".[1] In India, the factory workers give first importance to higher wages, and rising income in the form of wages is also a major national objective.

Rising wages without a concomitant increase in labour productivity may cause disturbances,[2] but higher wages can also increase labour productivity by allowing higher nutrition standards etc.[3] Higher real wages may also imply lower profits and income for the capitalists and thereby less savings available for investment.[4]

The Indian Government has not followed a clear and consistent wage policy. The most concrete thing said in the Plans about wages is a reference to

1) Vaid, K.N., The New Worker, New Delhi 1968, p. 111.
2) Examples from Puerto Rico and Mauritius show that negative employment effects have followed from isolated wage increases. Meade, J.E., Efficiency, Equality and the Ownership of Property, Cambridge 1964; Reynolds, L.G., Wages and Employment in Labour-Surpolus Economy, in The American Economic Review, 1965:1.
3) Myrdal, G., op. cit., p. 747.
4) Capitalists are not always prudent savers. In many underdeveloped countries they spend a considerable part of their income on luxury consumption and non-productive investments in, for example, urban residential housing. Ibid., p. 747.

the principles of wage determination recommended by the Committee of
Fair Wages.[1]

The "fair" wage is only one of several wage concepts in the Indian discussi
Soon after Independence, legislation was passed on "minimum" wages in
different occupations. The Constitution calls for a "living" wage which,
according to the Committee on Fair Wages, should be higher than the "mi
nimum" wage, so as to allow "not merely physical subsistence but for the
maintenance of health and decency, a measure of frugal comfort and some
insurance against the more important misfortunes".[2] The "fair" wage
would presumably be somewhere between the "minimum" and the "living"
wage. The lower limit of the "fair" wage is the "minimum" wage and the
upper limit is set by the capacity of the industry to pay.

According to the Committee on Fair Wages, the capacity of the industry
to pay should be related to specific industries in specific regions - the industry-cum-region formula for wage-fixing, which has since been followed
practically everywhere in India. The Committee pointed out that the level
of wages should be fixed so as to "enable industry to maintain production
with efficiency", and the fair wages should "not be so out of line with wage
in other industries as to cause movement of labour and consequent industrial unrest". The Committee concluded that "rates of wages fixed as a
result of proper collective bargaining" were good approximations to the
"fair" wage.

As for the effects of foreign investment, I have already discussed the
notion that the social costs of labour are lower than the private costs when
labour is drawn from low-productivity occupations. The difference between
the productivity of labour in a foreign industry and in former occupations
could be regarded as a social gain when it shows up in higher wages.[3] It
is of interest here to see if foreign companies pay better wages than indigenous companies.

---

1) India. Ministry of Labour, Report of the Committee on Fair Wages,
   New Delhi 1963 (1949).
2) Ibid., p. 34.
3) The social costs for the actual transfer of labour are probably low in
   the new industrial areas but not in regions where labour is drawn directly from agriculture.

Wage levels in the Swedish companies

In 1927, a worker in WIMCO had an average total wage of about Rs. 35 per
month in Ambernath and Calcutta and Rs. 25 per month in Dhubri.[1] The
average wage in other match factories was at the time about Rs. 30 per
month - less in the country and more in the cities.[2]

WIMCO probably continued to pay an average wage up to Independence. In
1939, an unskilled worker in Ambernath got Rs. 40 per month. which illu-
strates the fact that wages did not rise very much during the colonial period. Since Independence, the policy of the Government has been more favourable towards wage increases, and trade unions have had greater chances of influencing wages. As a result, the general nominal wage level, already boosted by the wartime inflation, increased appreciably. The WIMCO
factory in Bareilly in 1952 paid an average wage of Rs. 150 per month.
Foreign companies - especially old and reputedly rich companies like
WIMCO - have been expected to pay more than Indian companies. WIMCO
has several times been directed by industrial tribunals to raise its wages
on the ground that the company could afford it.

The wage levels in the Swedish companies in 1965 are shown in Table 13.
According to this table, all the Swedish firms, except for SF, paid above
the all-India average of Rs. 1,854 in 1964.[3] The WIMCO factories paid
their workers on an average Rs. 3,000 per year, while a worker in the
new Swedish companies earned Rs. 2,250 per year. The difference between
WIMCO and the new Swedish companies can largely be explained by the fact
that there is some seniority in the Indian wage structure which gives older
companies higher wages. Also, Poona is a new industrial area, and in such
areas wages are regularly lower than in older industrial areas.

The earnings of "other than workers" show wide variations, but the more
technology-intensive nature of the new Swedish companies shows in the
higher average wages for these companies,as compared with WIMCO and
the average Indian companies. A maximum is reached by SF, with an average wage for "other than workers" of Rs. 10,870 per year. SF pays its
engineers on an average Rs. 1,600 per month, and the nature of the compa-
ny´s manufacture requires a sizeable engineering staff.

---

1) India. Tariff Board, Match Industry, Vol. III, op. cit., p. 21.
2) India. Tariff Board, Match Industry, Vol. I, II, op. cit., passim.
3) The all-India average for 1965 was only marginally higher than the
   1964 figure. India.Central Statistical Organization, Annual Survey of
   Industries 1965, Calcutta 1969, p.9.

Table 13. Wage levels in the Swedish companies in 1965

Company	Area	Average annual earnings of workers, 1965 (Rs.)	Average annual earnings of other than workers, 1965 (Rs.)
WIMCO			
Factory 1,	Maharashtra	3,580 ⎫	5,720 ⎫
Factory 2,	Tamil Nadu (Madras)	2,560 ⎪	6,000 ⎪
Factory 3,	West Bengal	2,720 ⎬ 2,970	- ⎬ 6,100
Factory 4,	Assam	2,120 ⎪	5,410 ⎪
Factory 5,	Uttar Pradesh	(3,890) ⎭	(7,440) ⎭
Vulcan-Laval,	Maharashtra	2,320 ⎫	6,050 ⎫
Atlas Copco,	Maharashtra	2,570 ⎪	8,150 ⎪
Sandvik,	Maharashtra	2,360 ⎬ 2,250	8,050 ⎬ 7,970
SKF (1966),	Maharashtra	2,250 ⎪	6,720 ⎪
SF,	West Bengal	1,750 ⎭	10,870 ⎭
All industries, all India (1964)		1,854	4,160
Cotton textiles, Maharashtra (1964)		2,648	5,320
Cotton textiles, Tamilnadu (1964)		2,212	4,860
Cotton textiles, West Bengal (1964)		1,723	3,820
Cotton textiles, Uttar Pradesh (1964)		2,066	4,730
Sweden, match worker 1968		26,700	

Sources. India. National Commission on Labour, Statistics of Selected Manufacturing Industries; Delhi 1968, for all 1964 figures; STAB, Matchco News, 1968:3, p. 18, for the Swedish figure; company statistics. Figures for WIMCO include, as always, figures for the sister company AMCO (= Factory 4). Figures for earnings include the money value of benefits and privileges. The division between workers and other than workers is according to the definitions in the Annual Survey of Industries (ASI). As in the ASI presentation, the money value of benefits for WIMCO has been allocated proportionately between salaries and wages (the ensuing divergences from the actual figures are probably insignificant). Benefits for Atlas Copco workers are calculated on the staff percentage. Figures for Vulcan-Laval and SF include factory employees only. As SKF actually started production in 1965, the figure for this year is not representative and has been replaced by the 1966 figure. Figures for Sweden have been converted at the rate of Rs 1 to Sw. Cr. 0.7.

West Bengal (Calcutta) traditionally has a lower general wage level than
Maharashtra (Bombay), a relation that holds good also between comparable
companies in Table 13. Wide variations in wage levels between industries
and geographical areas are in fact typical of India.[1] Comparisons with
an all-India average are therefore not always very informative. Instead,
one should look at specific industries in specific areas as is done in Table
13. Compared with the cotton textile industries in the respective areas,
wage levels in the Swedish companies are not uniformly higher.

Table 13 is based on the statistics compiled for the Annual Survey of Industries. Another and more up-to-date set of wage statistics is collected by
the Labour Bureau. Annual earnings for all employees earning less than
Rs. 400 per month are compiled, and it is presumed that this category
largely coincides with the worker category.[2] I have obtained corresponding statistics from a few Swedish companies and the result is presented in
Table 14.

Table 14. Average annual earnings for employees earning less than Rs.
400 per month in 1967

	Average annual earnings for employees earning less than Rs. 400 per month in 1967
WIMCO, Factory 5 (Uttar Pradesh)	2.443
Sandvik (1965-66, Maharashtra)	2.360
SF (West Bengal)	2.445
All industries, all India	2.232
Textile industry, Uttar Pradesh	2.014
Machinery industry, Maharashtra (1966)	2.457
Machinery industry, West Bengal	2.131

Sources: India. Labour Bureau, Indian Labour Statistics 1969, Simla
1969; company statistics. The figures include the money value
of concessions.

---

1) Pant, S.C., op. cit., p. 208. Pant finds a maximum ratio between
the highest and the lowest industrial wage of 15.5.
2) To keep pace with inflation and rising wages, the upper limit has been
changed from Rs. 200 per month to Rs. 400 per month and further
changes are expected.

The figure of average earnings for workers in the Bareilly factory in Uttar Pradesh given in this table is probably more reliable than the very high figure in Table 13. But the factory still pays best in its area and, according to Table 14, also better than the average textile factory in Uttar Pradesh. Table 14 also shows that, compared with other machinery industry, Sandvik pays somewhat lower and SF somewhat higher wages. It seems resonable that Sandvik, located in Poona, should have a lower wage level than older Bombay companies in Maharashtra. But the high relative wage figure for SF is not confirmed either by the trade union or by the management, who both maintain that SF does not pay above the average in West Bengal.

The most reliable type of wage statistics available shows the wage levels in the same grade of skill in specific companies. Such statistics for Ambernath, Dhubri and Poona are shown in Table 15. There are usually six grades of skill: unskilled, semi-skilled, skilled I, skilled II, highly skilled and very highly skilled. By showing the minimum wage in a certain grade, the age differentials are neutralized, which makes old companies like WIMCO appear to be paying relatively less.

The WIMCO factories in Ambernath and Dhubri pay the highest minimum wage in their respective areas for semi-skilled personnel. In fact, all the WIMCO factories pay relatively high wages for unskilled and semi-skilled workers, who make up the bulk of the labour force in the match factories. Other and more technology-intensive companies use more skilled personnel, and their average wages are therefore higher than in WIMCO. The typical position is thus that a WIMCO factory pays relatively high wages for unskilled labour but that its average wages are lower than in some 3-4 companies in the same geographical area (usually chemical companies, oil refineries, etc.).

In Poona, Philips is reputed to be the best-paying company (not included in Table 15). Philips resembles WIMCO in the sense that it is an old foreign company with high declared profits and a relatively labour-intensive production. In comparable age groups and grades of skill, the new Swedish firms are said to pay better than Philips. There are some 40 big companies in Poona, and the Swedish firms all pay in the highest bracket. The highest wage bracket is in effect made up almost exclusively of foreign-associated companies. This is not an uncommon feature: "Foreign firms in new manufacturing industries generally pay well above ruling wage rates."[1]

---

1) Kidron, M., Foreign Investments in India, London 1965, p. 248; cf. Sveriges Allmänna Exportförening, op. cit., p. 34.

Table 15. Minimum monthly earnings for a semi-skilled worker in
selected companies in 1967-68

Company	Area	Minimum monthly earnings for a semi-skilled worker 1967-68
WIMCO, Factory 1	Ambernath	253
Dharamsi Morarji Chemical Co.	Ambernath	198
Century Rayon	Ambernath	164
WIMCO, Factory 4	Dhubri	107
Mornai Tea Estate	Dhubri	85
Dhubri Cotton-ginning Factory	Dhubri	72
Vulcan-Laval	Poona	205
Atlas Copco	Poona	204
Sandvik	Poona	207
SKF	Poona	169
Buckau Wolf	Poona	203
Cooper Engineering	Poona	191
Bajaj Electricals	Poona	183
Mahindra Owen	Poona	182
Bajaj Auto	Poona	119
Kirloskar Pneumatics	Poona	116

Sources. Company statistics. The Poona figures are calculated on daily
rates for 26 days per month. The figures include "dearness
allowance" (see p. 127). "Minimum" refers to the wage for new
employees, without seniority increments.

Wages in India are fixed according to the industry-cum-region principle,
which means that companies in the same industry in the same region should
pay about the same wages. The principle allows for quite a large spread,
illustrated by the fact that Atlas Copco pays nearly double the wage of one
of its main competitors, Kirloskar Pneumatics, which is also located in
Poona. Of the Swedish companies, SKF has the lowest wage and Sandvik
the highest. The low figure for SKF is, however, somewhat misleading,
as the maximum wage on piece-rates in SKF is quite comparable with the
wages paid by the other Swedish firms. In 1968 the maximum wage ob-
tainable for a very old and very highly skilled worker in Sandvik was Rs.
625 per month, which equals the average annual per capita income in the
Poona region.

The stated policy of the Swedish companies is to pay in the highest brackets. Several Swedish managements take the view that it is better to pay handsome wages than to "fiddle around" with small changes in social benefits etc. But, on the other hand, none of the Swedish companies wants to leave other companies behind and pay very much higher wages. "We do not wish to go against the interests of other employers in the region"; "we are responsible to the country, we cannot disrupt the economy by raising the wages".

In connection with the employment effects, it was stated that the Swedish companies did not really have any direct employment effects - they recruit people already employed and employment is therefore created only indirectly, as a chain reaction throughout the industrial structure.[1] The wage effects run parallel to the employment effects.[2]

It seems likely that the Indian companies that have been replaced by the Swedish firms would have paid the going wage, which (one hopes) reflects the social opportunity cost of their labour. Employees in the jobs created by the resources released by the Swedish investments would probably also have been paid the going wage. But the Swedish companies generally pay more than the going wage for essentially the same type of labour as is employed in comparable Indian firms.

It is not possible to obtain an exact measure of the average wage difference between Swedish firms and other firms, and the best I can do is therefore to try to get an approximate percentage. Referring to Table 15, it seems likely that, if the average wage of a worker in the Swedish companies was Rs. 200 in 1968, his average wage in former occupations would have been around Rs. 150. This would mean, by my reasoning, that the alternative product of labour in the Swedish companies, the social-opportunity cost, would be Rs. 150, and Rs. 50 per month per worker or 25 per cent of the total wages could be regarded as a social gain.

In this connection I would point out that lower wages in India are not the same thing as lower total labour costs. Wages in India are about one-tenth of European wages, but other labour costs are higher. Skilled labour is expensive, office staff is more numerous in Indian companies, and various kinds of bonus must be paid out. Moreover labour costs are just one item in the total production costs. Materials are expensive, imports are scarce and the Government bureaucracy is a tough obstacle. If direct wages in an Indian company are 10 per cent of European wage rates, labour costs

---

1) See p. 90.
2) Little, I.M.D. and Mirrlees, J.A., op. cit., p. 158.

are perhaps 50 per cent and production costs 150 per cent of the European costs.[1]

Wages and standard of living

The wage system in India is quite complicated. The employee does not just get a simple "wage". The main components in the total wage are the basic wage, the dearness allowance and the annual bonus.

The practice of paying dearness allowances was initiated during the First World War to compensate the employees for rapidly rising price levels. After the war the practice was discontinued, but it was revived during the Second World War, and this time it was not abolished afterwards. The idea behind the dearness allowance was that, when the cost of living rose, wages should automatically rise too. Hence, part of the wages is linked to a price index and varies from month to month and sometimes from week to week.

In the absence of any laws regulating the calculation of dearness allowance, different companies adopted different practices and a lot of confusion was created. When it became clear that the new national Government would not abolish the dearness allowance, the employees clung to it as a safety measure in a world of rising prices. The result has been that a large number of wage increases have been effected in the form of automatic increases in the dearness allowance, and the original "basic wage" has become a progressively smaller part of the total earnings. In the WIMCO factory in Calcutta, for example, the basic wage in 1969 was, on an average, 17 per cent of the total wages, while the dearness allowance constituted 52 per cent.

The dearness allowance does not vary with skill and experience, and its predominance has therefore militated against an increase in productivity. This is probably true also of the annual bonus. The bonus has the same history as the dearness allowance; it was introduced during the First World War by profitable companies, discontinued after the war, re-introduced in the Second World War and afterwards retained.

The bonus was at first a truly ex-gratia payment, paid once a year by very profitable companies to its employees. But the national Government endorsed the opinion of the employees that they had acquired a permanent right to bonuses, and a lot of confusion and disputes over bonuses ensued. The Bonus Commission of 1965 finally laid down a formula stating that a

---

1) Cf. Kidron, M., op. cit., p. 249, and Baranson, J., Manufacturing Problems in India. The Cummins Diesel Experience, New York 1967, p. 87.

minimum bonus of 4 per cent of wages should be paid even by companies that had sustained a loss. The maximum sum was fixed at 20 per cent of profits. In money terms, the annual bonus for a worker in the Swedish companies, spread out on a monthly basis, represented in 1968 Rs. 10-20 per month.

Standard of living. The dearness allowance was originally intended as an insurance against price increases, but full compensation for increased prices has not been permitted by labour courts. Without enough upward revisions of basic wages, the Indian factory workers would therefore have suffered a deterioration in the standard of living. At least in later times, it appears that total wages have not increased fast enough to maintain real earnings. After several ups and downs, the real wage for factory workers in 1967 was lower than in 1939, according to the available statistics. [1]

In the period 1961-67 real wages in India decreased by 13 per cent. The workers became poorer, although nominal wages increased. This is apparently true also of WIMCO, but the new Swedish companies in Poona differ from the all-India average insofar as they seem to have had an increase instead of a decrease in real wages in the sixties. This can be explained by the newness and buoyancy of the Poona industrial area and by the fact that the new Swedish firms were expanding rapidly during this period.

Real wages are not always identical with real income, but there is tangible proof that at least the employees in SKF are in one sense better off each year. The SKF company doctor has measured the weights of the employees at different times and found that the average weight of all classes of employees is continuously rising (Table 16). This is presumably a consequence of the rising real wages and/or a result of the subsidized meals and snacks provided by the company.

Table 16. Average weight of SKF employees 1965-69

Category	Average weight (kilograms)		
	1965-66	1968 (January)	1969 (January)
Hourly-paid workers	51.4	53.8	54.1
Monthly-paid workers	58.1	60.0	61.5
Foremen	56.5	58.8	60.8

Sources. Company statistics.

---

[1] India. Labour Bureau, Indian Labour Statistics 1969, op. cit., p. 78; Pant, S.C., op. cit., p. 212.

Even if real wages do increase, it is not certain that the standard of the worker or of his individual family members also increases. In fact, the presumption is that individual living standards are kept almost constant when real wages go up, because of the number of dependents added to the families that benefit from the increases: "... the increase in earnings is often neutralized by a corresponding increase in the dependency load on the earners".[1]

Such a "neutralization" seems to take place also in the case of workers in the Swedish companies. Scattered data give the impression that the sizes of the families of workers in the Swedish firms exceed the average by some 1-2 persons. This "living-standards equilibrium" for the employees may operate as a disincentive to higher productivity. It has happened in the Swedish companies that workers have been averse to the introduction of piece-rates because the increased earnings would just be spread out among their families. Also, the prospects of promotion under such circumstances are not likely to be very alluring to the workers.

Wages and productivity

In the section on recruitment I assumed that "modern" recruitment methods were more conducive to higher productivity and rapid economic development than the old, personal and discriminatory type of recruitment. The same type of assumption is made here concerning the principles for wage-fixing. The more wage differentials reflect genuine differences in skill and experience the better.

As in the case of recruitment, there is little discrimination in the Swedish companies between religious and geographical communities in wage-fixing. In the few secretarial and lowly occupations in which women are employed, they seem to get the same wages as their male colleagues. As concerns age, the common practice in Indian industry is to give annual wage increments for seniority up to a certain point (the "efficiency bar"). To cross this bar, a minimum of skill must be shown. The Swedish firms follow the common increment practice, except for a few of the new companies that, notwithstanding protests from the employees and their trade unions, give less than normal weight to seniority in wage-fixing.

The only category that really is discriminated against, as concerns wages in the Swedish companies, is the casuals. As we have seen, casual labour is also discriminated against in recruitment and in other respects, [2] and

---

1) Vaid, K.N. , op. cit. , p. 49; cf. Lambert, R.D. , op. cit. , pp. 40 and 56.
2) See p. 113 ff.

on top of this there is the discrimination in wage-fixing. The Swedish firms follow the common inequitable practice, although not all to the same extent. The WIMCO factories seem to pay their casuals less, sometimes only half as much as the new Swedish companies. A casual worker in the new Swedish firms can earn up to two-thirds of the wage of a permanent unskilled worker.

The preferential treatment or "over-prizing" of formal educational qualifications found in countries like Sweden is rampant in India. Even when they have only a modicum of education the clerks constitute themselves a "petty literati class" in the company hierarchy.[1] They have higher wages and fewer working hours than the supervisors, although a supervisor in India on an average probably contributes more to the company's profits than a clerk. The Swedish companies are here doing some useful work by pressing down the relative wages of clerks. About half the number of Swedish firms have, in their own view, reached a state of adequate wage differences between clerks and supervisors, which in most cases means that supervisors are on an average paid more than clerks. One manager even states that his target is a lower wage for clerks than for workers.

Piece-rates. There is no general correlation between the extent of the application of the piece-rate system and economic development.[2] The system of payment in Indian industries also shows no uniformity. Piece-rates are common in the textile industry, plantations and mining. The general trend is that the piece-rate system is being extended, but there are obstacles in the form of a deep-rooted suspicion between labour and management and a lack of exact methods of job evaluation.[3]

WIMCO introduced piece-rates from the beginning, and at present some 70 per cent of the workers in the WIMCO factories are paid at piece-rates. The general opinion of the management cadre in WIMCO is that the piece-rate system forces the workers to do a certain minimum amount of work but that the present system has several drawbacks. It is sometimes applied where the machines and not the machine-minders set the pace of production. The rates are sometimes set not by job evaluation but by negotiation. Another factor working against higher productivity through piece-rates is the circumstance that the piece-rate part of the wages is becoming a progressively smaller part of the total wages, which are now dominated by the dearness allowance and the bonus.

---

1) See p. 116.
2) Kerr, C., et al., Industrialism and Industrial Man, London 1962, p. 255.
3) Pant, S.C., op. cit., p. 170.

A special feature in WIMCO is the "production bonus" payable in most of the factories. It started as an incentive for supervisors when a certain production target was over-fulfilled. Through labour-court awards the production bonus has been extended also to workers and clerks, even though the latter category has no direct influence on production. At the same time the original production target to be reached has seldom been revised upwards, with the result that the production bonus in some of the factories is now more than double the basic wage.

Of the new Swedish companies, SKF introduced a piece-rate system from the beginning. In 1969 about 60 per cent of the employees were covered. The rates were in the beginning set high enough to enable the company just to retain its workers. The maximum production on each machine was evaluated and the remuneration for the maximum production possible was set equal to the average wage in the best-paying companies in Poona. Through the piece-rate system the company has obtained high productivity, and the job evaluation made necessary by the system has saved the company from employing too much labour. Piece-rates have been a prerequisite for high profitability in SKF. "Without piece-rates we might as well pack our things and go home again". The workers are not equally fond of the piece-rate system and its abolition was one of the demands in recent negotiations.

In Vulcan-Laval and SF the production is stated to be too heterogeneous to make piece-rates profitable. Atlas Copco and Sandvik have started to introduce piece-rates on the SKF lines, with good results in the form of increased production. One problem is that a workable system of piece-rates must be based on substantial incentives, which is not the case when a large part of the wage is made up of a constant dearness allowance. Sandvik has managed to bring the dearness allowance down from about 70 per cent of the total wages to 20 per cent.

Pant says that "... what the workers really want is increasing real income and not stable incomes".[1] In that case they ought to be in favour of a change-over from the dearness allowance to a more remunerative piece-rate system. But the trade unions have all the time been against piece-rates. The original trade union formed in 1937 in a WIMCO factory had as its first demand the abolition of the piece-rate system ("it makes a beast of man").

Especially in the new engineering industry, the trade unions have been wary of the introduction of piece-rates. It is felt that, as the industry is new, the workers are ignorant of what should be the correct job evaluation and the management could therefore take undue advantage of the workers.

---

1) Pant, S.C., op. cit., p. 197.

The main obstacle to the introduction of piece-rates in the new Swedish companies has, however, not been the trade unions but Government officials. Although the Five-year Plans are moderately in favour of piece-rat types of payment, the practice of labour courts and labour commissioners has been more restrictive.[1]

I have already pointed out that labour costs in India are not particularly low.[2] The realization of this fact by the managements is a major motive for the introduction of piece-rates. One hard-working, well-paid employee is more productive than two slow but cheap workers. One of the main problems in the Swedish companies is said to be the low labour productivity. With piece-rates, workers are more productive and the company becomes more profitable.

In so far as the fruits of the increased productivity are shared by the employees, they too get some benefit from their extra effort. The suspicious attitude of the workers to productivity-raising measures originates to a large extent in the fear that the benefits of increased productivity will larg ly be appropriated by their employers. Even if the workers were to get so economic benefit from the introduction of piece-rates, they may be right in rejecting them. The social costs of a constantly increasing tempo of wor would perhaps be greater than the economic gain.[3]

The growth of wages and labour productivity in the Swedish companies is shown in Table 17. I repeat that the productivity measure used is extremely crude and is only very roughly corroborated by physical productivity figures.[4] Nevertheless, the wages for workers in the Swedish firms see to keep pace well with the growth of productivity. This has also been the common trend in India since Independence.[5]

The fact that wages increase at the same pace with productivity does not mean that the workers get as large a share as the capitalists of the gains from increased productivity; it only means that their relative shares grow at the same pace. The proportion of wages to total costs is commonly low - although not extremely low - in Indian companies, as compared with

---

1) Cf. Pant, S.C., op. cit., pp. 226 and 356 ff.
2) See p. 126.
3) In some industries in the developed countries, notably in a big mine and a shipyard in Sweden, all the very refined piece-rate systems have been replaced by monthly wages, because of the stress and health risks that are considered to be inherent in the piece-rate systems.
4) See p. 95.
5) Pant, S.C., op. cit., p. 212.

Table 17. Development of wages and productivity in the Swedish companies in 1965-68

	Average growth (per cent) of per capita wages for workers 1965-68		Average growth (per cent) of sales per worker 1965-68	
WIMCO				
Factory 1 (1964-67)	8.1			
Factory 2 (1964-67)	13.5			
Factory 3	-	8.4		8.4
Factory 4 (1964-67)	5.8			
Factory 5	6.3			
Vulcan-Laval	12.5		-5.3	
Atlas Copco (1964-67)	25.0		13.0	
Sandvik	15.5	18.2	9.8	8.8
SKF	27.9		35.2	
SF	10.0		-8.9	

Sources. Company statistics. For productivity figures, see Table 8, p. 96.

European companies. The Indian capitalist can therefore be a little less sensitive to increases in labour costs than his European counterpart. This is one reason given for the friendly attitude to labour and trade unions that is found in the Swedish companies. Better wages and incentive wage systems both raise productivity, and the largest absolute share of increased productivity goes to the owners of the Swedish firms.

Welfare

Social benefits

What has been said about the positive and negative effects of increased wages is in the main true also of non-monetary benefits and other welfare outlays, although the social benefits are quantitatively much less important than wages. Qualitatively, it is probable that an increase in social security and welfare operates more directly than a wage rise to bring about increased productivity. Both from the social and the business point of view, an increase in social benefits should therefore be preferred, on the margin.

Social benefits in the shape of medical aid or subsidized food are a kind of "forced consumption" that prevents the employees from squandering their remuneration on non-necessities. At the same time, the workers' contributions to the provident fund and other social-security funds are "forced savings", which may have the additional effect of inculcating the habit of personal saving.

Most of the social benefits in India are statutory and are therefore enjoyed by employees in all kinds of companies. The statutory benefits are largely a product of post-Independence legislation.

Before Independence, the Government was not very active in this field. The first Factory Act was passed in 1881, as a result of the combined efforts of philanthrophists and selfish textile manufacturers in England. The British textile manufacturers wanted improved conditions for Indian workers, because that would mean higher costs and lower competitiveness for Indian textile manufacturers. The Factory Act prohibited the employment of children below 7 years of age, fixed the maximum hours of work (for children!) at 9 hours a day and provided for the appointment of factory inspectors.[1]

The Factory Act was amended several times and completely rewritten in 1948. The last amendments in the colonial period, in 1945-46, introduced provisions for holidays with pay and reduced the maximum hours of work for male workers to 48 hours a week. As concerned social security, the Workmen's Compensation Act of 1923 provided for a lump-sum payment in the case of the death or disablement of a worker. But it was the employer and not the State who was responsible for reporting accidents and paying compensation, and there was much evasion of the Act. The worker who protested risked losing his job.

The same conditions prevailed in connection with the maternity-benefit acts that were passed by a few provincial governments from 1929 onwards.[2] If a woman worker was dismissed at the first sign of pregnancy, the employer could save the maternity benefit. Another neglected field was housing. The Industrial Commission of 1918 issued a warning that, if the housing problem was not tackled at once, the difficulties would be insurmountable.

---

1) Pant, S.C., op. cit., p. 410.
2) Pant, S.C., op. cit., pp. 266 ff.

But the warning went unheeded. In 1929 the Royal Commission on Labour found the conditions very bad and made recommendations, but to no avail.[1] In 1947, slums abounded in most large towns in India.

General welfare legislation (canteens, rest shelters, etc.) is also a predominantly post-Independence phenomenon. In 1938 an observer stated that "even today the position is that more than 60 per cent of Indian industrial workers are still not covered by any schemes of welfare work whatever".[2] Some welfare was introduced in ammunition factories during the Second World War "to keep up morale and boost war production", and after the popular governments were formed, there was also welfare legislation in some of the provinces. Without legislation nothing much happened in the welfare field, because the employers were not by themselves very philanthrophic."...on the whole, it may be stated that employers who take a most indifferent and nonchalant attitude towards welfare work ... constitute the majority".[3] And the general laissez-faire attitude of the colonial government prevented it from introducing any far-reaching measures. The social-security and factory-welfare legislation in India is therefore to a very large extent the work of the national Government.

During the first 20 years of WIMCO´s existence there was therefore little legislation in force in the field of welfare and security, and the workers had to depend on the benevolence of the employer. The extent of social benefits in WIMCO in 1927 was stated by the manager at the time:

We have our workmen´s quarters at Ambernath, Kanaung [in Burma] and to a certain extent Dhubri. In Calcutta the labour live in their own accommodation in the vicinity of the factory. At Ambernath we have built our own shop to keep living expenses down and at Kanaung there is a shop under our supervision. At Ambernath we have built a school for the children of the work-people, which is well attended and the teacher is paid by our firm and has also free quarters for himself and his family. We have also contributed towards the expenses for purchasing boods, etc. Some of our workmen prefer to live in Kalyan [township near Ambernath] and they had in the beginning to walk three to four miles distance mornings and evenings. Since over a year ago, however, the Great Indian Peninsula Railway at our request kindly arranged the local train service in such a way as to suit the working hours of our factory. We have our own doctors and compounders with

1) Pant, S.C., op. cit., pp. 302-3.
2) Ram, V.S., The State in Relation to Labour in India, no date, p. 169, quoted in Pant, S.C., op. cit., p. 322.
3) India. Labour Investigation Committee, no date, pp. 345-46. Quoted in Pant, S.C., op. cit., p. 323.

well-appointed dispensaries at Ambernath and Kanaung, whilst at Dhub and Calcutta we have a contract with an outside doctor, who attends regularly.[1]

The above quotation probably enumerates all the major measures undertaken. To a modern Western reader this is not much, but at the time the company probably considered itself a progressive employer. And so it was at least if compared with other match companies of the same size.[2] Especially at Ambernath many quarters were erected for the workers, and at one time 75 per cent of the Ambernath workers were housed. In 1927, accumulated housing expenses in WIMCO amounted to 10 per cent of the total fixed capital expenditure, split up fifty-fifty between staff bungalows and workmen's quarters.[3]

Data on welfare in WIMCO after 1927 are scarce. At the Madras factory the employees were given 96 hours' leave with pay in the early forties at the instigation of the popularly elected Congress Government in the State. Before that there was at this factory no leave, no security, no allowances and no welfare! During the war a dearness allowance was introduced at the Madras factory, and a voluntary provident-fund (pension) scheme was started in 1944.

Conditions in the other WIMCO factories were more or less the same as at Madras. The general picture is thus that, until the Second World War, the WIMCO employees worked 54 hours a week with a piece-rate wage as their only remuneration. In Dhubri, the only welfare given before 1940 was financed from a small fund formed out of the petty fines levied on late-coming workers. Annual leave and a canteen did not start until 1948 in Dhubri. In Bareilly a canteen was not built until 1959.

Present benefits in the Swedish companies

The attitude of the management in the Swedish companies to welfare and social benefits was ambivalent at the time of this study. Some managers were strongly against "haggling with petty welfare" and preferred wage rises to increases in benefits. Others were to some extent interested in welfare measures or were passive.

The precise attitude of the managements is probably unimportant, as the Swedish companies anyway seem to follow closely the laws and local prac-

---

1) India. Tariff Board, Match Industry, Vol. III, op. cit., p. 22.
2) India. Tariff Board, Match Industry, Vol. I-II, op. cit., passim.
3) India. Tariff Board, Report...Match Industry, op. cit., p. 33.

tices in welfare matters. In Table 18, the large variations between the new
Swedish firms are therefore probably spurious and may be due to classification mistakes. In 1964, the all-India average ratio of social benefits to
wages was 9.2 per cent, corresponding to an annual expenditure of Rs.
200 per employee. The average ratio in WIMCO is 12.3 and in the new
Swedish companies somewhat higher, according to the detailed data for a
few companies. The annual expenditure is rising in absolute figures but
the relations do not seem to change. If the average company in India paid
Rs. 300 per employee in social benefits in 1968, WIMCO paid Rs. 500 and
the new Swedish firms perhaps Rs. 600.

Table 18. Money value of social benefits in the Swedish companies as
percentage of wages and per employee

	Money value of benefits as percentage of total wages and benefits (annual average 1965-68)	Money value of benefits per employee 1965
WIMCO	12.3	392
Factory 1	12.3^a	437
Factory 2	12.0^a	329
Factory 3	-	-
Factory 4	10.6^a	292
Factory 5	10.0	361
Vulcan-Laval	6.7	283
Atlas Copco	9.5	735
Sandvik	(1.3)	(75)
SKF	12.8	302
SF	23.8	1,058
All industries, all India (1964)	9.2	200
Cotton textiles, Maharashtra (1964)	10.7	306
Cotton textiles, Tamilnadu [Madras] (1964)	10.7	257
Cotton textiles, Uttar Pradesh (1964)	8.4	184

Sources: India. National Commission on Labour, Statistics of Selected
Manufacturing Industries, Delhi 1968; company statistics. a =
average 1964-67. The Vulcan-Laval figures are for the factory
only and only for the period 1965-67.

The relative distribution of expenditure between different kinds of social benefits is shown in Table 19 for a WIMCO factory and for a new Swedish company in Poona. Expenditure on the provident fund, the gratuity and the Employees´ State Insurance (ESI) weighs heavy, particularly in the WIMCO factory. These statutory obligations constitute 62 per cent of WIMCO´s benefits but only 32 per cent for the new Swedish firm, as compared with an all-India average of 55 per cent.[1] The absence of payments of gratuities for the new Swedish firm is, of course, due to the fact that the company is only a few years old. We may note in Table 19 that very little is spent on housing and that the new Swedish company pays for transport and spends much more on uniforms than the WIMCO factory.

Table 19. Expenditure on social benefits in a WIMCO factory and in a Swedish company in Poona (percentage distribution)

	WIMCO factory 1964 (per cent)	Swedish company in Poona 1968 (per cent)
Provident fund	26	11
Gratuity	25	0
Canteen	21	19
Employees´ state insurance	11	21
Health	9	9
Free tea	3	6
Uniforms	3	19
Recreation	2	5
Housing	0	0
Transport	–	9
Credit society	–	1
	100	100

Sources: Company statistics. Expenses for annual, casual, holiday and sick leaves are not included.

Social security. The present official provident-fund scheme was introduced in 1952 for six industries and has gradually been extended to most other industries too. The company and the employee have each to contribute 8 per cent of the wages. At the time of retirement - in the Swedish companies usually at 58 years of age - the employee is entitled to his own contribution

[1] Employers´ Federation of India, Handbook of Labour Statistics 1968, Bombay 1968, pp. 74-75.

plus the company´s contribution, subject to deductions if the employee has been in the company less than 10 years. The Swedish companies follow the Provident Fund Act, and the only deviation is that a few of the new Swedish firms contribute 8 1/3 per cent of the wages insted of 8 per cent.

There is no scheme in India for unemployment benefit, but the Industrial Disputes Act of 1948 provides for some compensation in case of lay-offs and retrenchment.[1] In the case of a lay-off the employer has to pay 50 per cent of the basic wage and dearness allowance payable for 45 days in year, and in the case of retrenchment without notice a month´s wages plus gratuity at the rate of 15 days´ pay for every year of service is payable. The Swedish companies have, in addition, gratuity schemes of their own, providing for some payment also on voluntary resignation or retirement. The usual rate is half a month´s basic wage per year of service, subject to a maximum of 15-20 years (it should be remembered here that the basic wage is quite a small part of the total wages).

Besides the Provident Fund Act, the major piece of social-security legislation in India is the Employees´ State Insurance Act of 1948 (the ESI Act). It provides for cases of sickness, injury and confinement. Although the ESI Act was passed in 1948, it was not implemented until 1952, and then only in a few industrial centres. It is slowly being extended to other places. The ESI scheme was not introduced in Poona until 1965. Where applicable, the Swedish companies follow the ESI Act.

Under the ESI scheme an employee receives in case of sickness roughly half his normal pay for a maximum of 56 days. Sickness must be certified by specially appointed doctors. Medical care in kind is also provided. In case of employment injury, the employee or his dependants get a sickness or invalidity pension. The ESI Act also includes a maternity benefit to the extent of full wages for a period of 12 weeks. The ESI scheme is financed by the employers contributing 3 per cent of the total wage-bill and the employees contributing on a scale graded according to the rate of pay. Only employees earning less than Rs. 500 per month are covered by the scheme.

The working of the ESI Act has been criticized from all quarters. The employees complain of delays in getting their money and of faulty or non-delivered medicine. The Government complains about malpractices by doctors

---

1) Pant, S.C., op. cit., p. 291.

and chemists, and the employers contend that the workers use the ESI to get illegal compensation when they are absent for personal reasons.[1]

Welfare

The Factory Act of 1948 makes provision for welfare measures inside and outside the factories. Employers must provide drinking water, latrines, washing facilities, facilities for storing clothes, rest-shelters, and canteens (canteens only in the case of factories employing more than 250 workers). The Factory Act also prescribes rules on working hours and annual leave with pay.

Leave. Annual leave with wages was introduced in the Factory Act amendment of 1945 and was further extended in the new Factory Act of 1948. A worker earns leave at the rate of one day for 20 days worked after he has been in the company for more than 240 days, which means somewhat less than three weeks' leave per year. The Swedish companies follow the Act. The staff in the Swedish firms get more leave, usually four weeks, in accordance with the usual preferential treatment of white-collar workers. According to the same line of thinking, the clerks in the WIMCO factories work 42.5 hours a week, as compared with 48 hours for supervisors. Clerks in the new Swedish companies have even shorter working hours.

Prior to the introduction of the ESI scheme, the Swedish companies had various schemes of sick leave. Following the general practice, most of the Swedish firms abandoned their own sick-leave schemes when the ESI Act came into force, except for schemes for employees earning more than

---

1) The doctors issuing sickness certificates have come under heavy fire: "There are not many skilful and conscientious practitioners, and there are some who abuse their profession. We have already mentioned how in some cases workers are deprived of the facilities. Some of them, in collusion with the chemists and patients, cheat the [ESI] Corporation of its limited resources. Thus it has been found that doctors prescribe medicine in the name of [an] insured person for his relatives and friends, prescribe drugs not mentioned in the authorised list to please the worker, pay agents to bring patients, give bogus certificates so that the insured person may get leave to attend marriages, funerals, etc." (Pant, S.C., op. cit., p. 281). The system of issuing bogus certificates at least seems to be widespread. I checked with workers and staff in several companies around India and all of them were able at once to state the customary price (Rs. 1-5) in the area for getting a false ESI certificate.

Rs. 500 per month, who are not covered by the ESI. Two new Swedish companies and two WIMCO factories, however, retained their old sick-leave schemes, comprising 7-14 days with full pay also for the workers (the ESI pays only half the normal wage in sickness).

Nearly all companies in India allow their employees to take casual leave with pay. In accordance with common practice, the Swedish companies permit 7 days of casual leave per year. In addition, several holidays with or without pay are given in the Swedish firms, according to local custom in the respective areas. The workers normally get around 5 paid holidays per year, while the staff gets 10 or more.

Housing. "Before independence there was no housing policy of the central government...".[1] and the slums in industrial areas grew. In 1949, the Government announced a policy of incentives to the employers for the construction of industrial housing. The incentives were increased several times, but the employers still did not show any interest, and some 80 per cent of the construction of industrial housing has therefore been undertaken by the State Governments.[2]

The Indian private building industry is mainly interested in luxury housing, which is much more profitable than tenements for industrial workers. It seems probable that, unless housing is made a statutory obligation, the employers will not make any serious efforts to get proper quarters for their workers. The bad housing conditions of the industrial workers are reflected in the fact that they rank housing second in importance only to wages.[3]

The WIMCO factory at Ambernath has an early record of housing its employees, and some 50 per cent of the workers still rent quarters built by the company. The other WIMCO factories house only 5-10 per cent of their employees. Two of the new Swedish companies in Poona provide housing for some 5 per cent of their employees in the form of contributions to a Government scheme (the Government makes all arrangements and pays three-quarters of the cost), and the other Swedish companies do not have any housing schemes at all. In view of the fact that nearly all the big companies in Poona provide some housing for their workers, the performance of the new Swedish firms is not too impressive.[4]

---

1) Pant, S.C., op. cit., p. 307.
2) Ibid., p. 316.
3) Vaid, K.N., op. cit., p. 111.
4) Poona Metropolitan Regional Planning Board, op. cit., p. 209.

The employees in the WIMCO factories either live in the company's quarter or in a nearby township or village, and the provision of special transport for them is therefore not deemed necessary. The new Swedish companies in Poona, on the other hand, are located quite a long way from Poona City. They are served by public-transport facilities, but this service is not considered satisfactory by the employees, and nearly all the Swedish firms in Poona therefore have special transport arrangements at subsidized rates. Only 3 per cent of the companies in Poona provide such transport.[1]

Health and nutrition. As the ESI scheme does not cover employees earning more than Rs. 500 per month, the Swedish companies, as already mentione allow special sick leave for this category. Outside the statutory obligations ordinary medicines and vaccines from a dispensary are also provided. All the Swedish firms have a part-time doctor attending for a few hours every day. In several factories WIMCO formerly had a full-time doctor, but he h now been replaced by a part-time doctor, who thus spends about one hour on every 1000 workers. The trade unions in these factories have demanded that a doctor shall be available during all working hours.

Since 1965, company expenses for family-planning are deductible for tax purposes. Three new Swedish companies have introduced family-planning programs, which have had a moderate following. Four out of five new Swe- dish firms provide free uniforms - quite a costly measure - for their workers, which is not a common practice. In WIMCO, uniforms are provi- ded only in departments where the risk of spoiling clothes is imminent.

Factories employing more than 250 workers are required to have a cantee run on a no-profit-no-loss basis. All the Swedish companies of this size have canteens, which are run on a loss basis: prices, once fixed, cannot be raised and some companies have subsidized their canteens from the be ginning. The average subsidy on canteen food is around 60 per cent. In the Swedish companies in Poona and in one WIMCO factory, free tea is servec twice a day - a welfare measure over and above the common practice. Bu only one Swedish company has a co-operative shop, although such shops are quite common in Indian factories.[2] All the Swedish firms subsidize some marginal welfare activities, like sports clubs, credit societies and family days.

The Swedish companies thus observe the statutory obligations on welfare, and they also follow the general welfare practices in the respective areas

1) Poona Metropolitan Regional Planning Board, op. cit., p. 207.
2) Employers' Federation of India, Labour Statistics 1968, Bombay 196 p. 85.

The trade unions within a certain area all know the benefits available in other companies and press their demands accordingly, with the result that benefits in different companies tend to equalize after a time. The WIMCO factories do not, on the whole, go beyond the common practice in the respective areas, while the new Swedish companies often have more welfare than the average.

The new Swedish company presented in Table 19 (which shows the percentage distribution of welfare expenditure) spends roughly 35 per cent of the total cost of social benefits on welfare measures that exceed the normal practice, which is equivalent to somewhat less than 2 per cent of the total wages. The major measures within this "extra" group are free uniforms, transport subsidies and free-tea service.[1] As might be expected, the labour representatives are content with the relative level of welfare in the Swedish companies. The main complaints are about housing and about things which are marginal from the cost point of view but not therefore less important, like the quality of sports clubs and canteen contractors.

Labour and Management

As is the case with a high level of social benefits, good relations between labour and management are likely to benefit both parties. Labour in India is, it seems, likely to get higher wages and benefits if disputes are settled by tough, independent negotiations than if the disputes are solved by the Government's industrial tribunals. If there are no strikes, labour does not lose wages and the company does not lose profits. Good relations are also conducive to higher productivity.

The first piece of legislation on industrial relations in India was the Employers and Workmen Act of 1860. It was aimed at the speedy settlement of disputes and contained the obnoxious feature (to labour) that it made breach of contract a criminal offence. The earliest recorded strike took place in 1877 in Nagpur and from this date the labour movement in India dates its origin.[2] The first trade union was formed in 1890.

The colonial government at first ridiculed the trade-union movement and then became suspicious. Government spying on trade-union activities was

---

1) The welfare practices of the new Swedish companies in India correspond closely to the practices of Swedish subsidiaries in Latin America (Sveriges Allmänna Exportförening, op. cit., pp. 38 and 41).
2) Pant, S.C., op. cit., p. 69.

common. "At best the attitude of the government was that of neutrality".[1] In 1920, the Madras High Court sided with the employer in a dispute and declared trade-union activities illegal. British and Indian labour interests reacted sharply, and in 1926 the Indian Trade Unions Act was passed. It gave immunity to registered trade unions and protection to trade-union officials.[2]

The employers responded by forming the first employers´ union in 1933. Reforms in the labour field were proposed by the Royal Commission on Labour in its report of 1931, and the popular governments created in the provinces after the constitutional reforms in 1935 were also sympathetic to labour. But nothing much happened. During the Second World War the Government intervened in the labour market and prohibited strikes and lockouts "in the national interest".

The official attitude underwent a distinct change with Independence. The trade-union movement had developed more or less as a wing of the national independence movement, and the sympathies of the national Government were therefore with labour. In the major piece of industrial legislation passed at Independence, the Industrial Disputes Act (1947), labour was guaranteed the right to organize, and provisions were made for the compulsory recognition of trade unions, non-discrimination against trade-union officials etc.

The compulsory settlement of industrial disputes introduced during the war was included in the Act, and a regular Government machinery, comprising industrial tribunals, was set up. I have mentioned elsewhere the legislation that was also passed by the national Government on job security, social security, and welfare. No wonder that the Indian capitalists were shaken:

> ...Indian business, schooled in the crudest forms of exploitation; protected hitherto by the lightning rod of foreign rule; unused to the give and take of power; and generally ignorant, as much of India as of the wider world, was terrified, the more so as other measures affecting business seemed hostile and restrictive. For the moment it looked to them as if labour had the ear of the Government.[3]

But after the major policy changes enacted in 1947, the Government´s willingness to listen to the labour side has apparently not increased. The Industrial Policy Resolution of 1956 includes the following admonition: "The maintenance of industrial peace is one of the prime requisites of in-

---

1) Ibid., p. 74.
2) Ibid., p. 72.
3) Kidron, M., Foreign Investments in India, London 1965, p. 77.

dustrial progress. In a socialist democracy [= India] labour is a partner in the common task of development and should participate in it with enthusiasm".[1]

In the interests of economic development, the Government has been averse to large wage increases. The daring policy at Independence, including labour participation in management etc., has been perfunctorily repeated in the plans, but no measures have been undertaken to implement it. In the draft document on the Fourth Plan, industrial relations are only mentioned on one of the last few pages.[2]

Trade unions and negotiations

For obvious reasons, trade unionism did not flourish before Independence. In 1947 the total number of trade unions in India doubled, from 1,000 to 2,000. In 1966 there were 14,000 registered unions.[3]

The trade unions are usually not very strong. "Weakness is the dominant trait of the trade-union movement in the modern sector of manufacturing industry".[4] The main reason for this weakness is the relative inexperience of trade unions and collective bargaining on the part of both labour and employers. The trade unions in other countries built their strength up by fighting for the recognition of unions, job security and welfare measures. In India many of these issues have been settled by legislation, which narrows the scope of trade-union activity.

Another source of weakness has been the political affiliations of the trade unions. From the very beginning, trade unions in India were started and dominated not by workers but by politicians, "unsuccessful lawyers and careerist and opportunist outsiders".[5] Outside leaders have used the trade unions for their own political aims, and the trade-union movement has been a projection of Indian politics. "The fact that trade unions in

1) India. Industrial Policy Resolution 1956, reprinted in India. Estimates Committee 1967-68, Delhi 1967, p. 298.
2) "In the field of industrial relations, priority will be accorded to the growth of a healthy trade-union movement, the promotion of collective bargaining and the raising of productivity through labour-management cooperation" (India. Planning Commission, Fourth Five-year Plan, op. cit., p. 341).
3) India. Labour Bureau, Indian Labour Statistics 1969, p. 122. Cf. Pant, S.C., op. cit., p. 449.
4) Myrdal, G., op. cit., p. 1111.
5) Pant, S.C., op. cit., p. 103.

India derive strength from their political affiliations is the biggest obstacle in the way of the development of independent unionism", says Pant.[1]

The first trade unions in WIMCO were formed in 1935-37, a time of national manifestations and industrial unrest. In the Calcutta and Bareilly factories there were no unions until after the Second World War. Most of the original unions in WIMCO have been superseded by other unions - the weakness of the trade unions is also shown in their relatively short lives.

The position in the late sixties was that all the Swedish companies had trade unions for their workers - some WIMCO factories even had several. The staff in the new Swedish firms is normally not organized and often identifies itself with the management, while the larger number of low-paid clerks in WIMCO has proved a viable basis for staff unions. The staff unions are normally not affiliated to political organizations, while in the late sixties only three of the workers' unions were not affiliated - all of them operating in new Swedish companies,where the smaller number of workers and the relatively good conditions make it easier for the management to attach the workers more closely to the company. The trade unions in the Swedish firms were mostly affiliated to different Communist parties. Two unions were affiliated to INTUC, the Congress trade-union organization, but, according to the management, they too had from time to time been dominated by "Communists".

Half the number of unions in the Swedish companies have one or more outside leaders - lawyers or professional politicians - while the other half has only actually employed workers as office-holders. The existence of outside leaders does not mean that the unions are controlled from outside. The outsiders are normally contacted only at negotiation time, and the majority of trade unions in the Swedish firms have a large measure of independence.

In most cases the trade unions are not allowed to carry on their activities or to collect subscriptions on the premises of the company. This is common practice in India,and in fact several trade-union leaders in the Swedish firms thought that, for example, the collection of trade-union fees through the company's wage department would impair the independence of the union. The average union membership in the Swedish companies seems to be aroun

---

1) Ibid., p. 105. To advocate the development of strong labour unions is perhaps a second-best choice. The Indian workers may in the long run further their interests better by working instead through their political affiliations and thereby making the State work for them. But in the present situation, strong independent unions are probably necessary to safeguard the interests of labour.

75 per cent, and the union leaders maintain that their unions are much more democratic in their workings than the average union.

Negotiations. The attitude of the managements in the Swedish companies to trade unions is positive, particularly in the new Swedish firms. According to the trade-union representatives, this attitude is a constant surprise - in many Indian companies the one who tries to start a union is the first to be removed (if possible). But the (often foreign) managers in the Swedish firms are of the - probably correct - opinion that a strong trade union is good also for the company. One strong union keeps the rival unions out, and an agreement with that union can be relied upon as a basis for future planning.

One of the central issues raised by the trade unions in India and a recurring cause of disputes is the question of recognition.[1] The Indian Government has provided for compulsory recognition but only under certain conditions, which still makes recognition a more or less voluntary issue for the employers. The common practice is not to give recognition.[2]

The WIMCO factories do not have an impressive record as concerns recognition. They do recognize unions but only on tough conditions. In one factory no recognition was given for ten years (1955-65). The new Swedish companies seem more liberal and recognition of unions is accomplished more smoothly, although not automatically.

The practice of collective bargaining is less common in India than in Europe - at least the practice of reaching agreements through collective bargaining. Half the number of disputes are normally resolved by Government intervention.[3] The adjudication machinery provided by the Government at Independence assures the parties of a final settlement and thereby takes away much of the incentive for the employers and the trade unions to settle the conflict themselves. The adjudications are mostly made by industrial tribunals.

In the Swedish companies negotiations usually start by the workers handing in a list of demands. At times the demands are unrealistic, in the sense that the cost of meeting them would be several times the gross profit of

---

1) "Recognition" means the acceptance by the employer of the right of the trade union to represent the workers at negotiations.
2) Pant, S.C., op. cit., p. 102.
3) Employers' Federation of India, Handbook of Labour Statistics 1968, Bombay 1968, p. 104.

the company in question. All cases of that type are referred to industrial tribunals. But in ordinary cases, where demands are more realistic, there is only one Swedish firm that follows the traditional line of referring all disputes to tribunals - on the ground that "it is always better to have a third party".

At the other extreme there is another new Swedish company in which the management sometimes takes the initiative in starting negotiations and in which it has happened that the demands from the workers have been forestalled by offers from the management. But most of the Swedish firms lie somewhere between the extremes, and have a more positive attitude to negotiations than the average Indian company.[1]

Apart from the major negotiations, the management in several Swedish firm has a habit of settling most grievances before they are voiced in prestige-ridden documents like lists of demands. At the insistence of the management practically all negotiations are conducted between the management and trade-union office-holders in the company only. This sometimes involves a lot of running about for the "inside" office-holders between the "outside" trade-union leaders and the negotiation table. Some important topics, like the firing and hiring of employees, are excluded by the management from the negotiations. Most agreements are for three years or more.

Industrial disputes

The first period of intense industrial unrest in India was in 1928-29. In 1937-38 the number of strikes increased again in connection with the formation of popular governments in the provinces. The Second World War period was calm, but after the war there was an alarming rise in the number of industrial disputes.[2]

In 1947 the Industrial Disputes Act was passed, which provided, among other things, an adjudication machinery to solve industrial disputes. In the same year an Industrial Truce Resolution was accepted by management and labour, and peace was restored. Since 1947, the labour market has been relatively calm, except for a period starting in 1966-67, when the recession in Indian industry and political events in West Bengal produced a wave of strikes.

---

1) This agrees with the finding of Myers that foreign companies have a higher frequency of collective-bargaining agreements than the average in India. Cf. Myers, C.A., Labor Problems in the Industrialization of India, Cambridge 1958, p. 125.
2) Pant, S.C., op. cit., pp. 112 ff.

Before Independence the predominant cause of industrial disputes was wage issues. Since 1947, disagreement about wages has still accounted for 40 per cent of the disputes, but other causes, like retrenchment and personnel questions, have assumed increasing importance. The average duration of strikes has been reduced since 1947.[1]

Before Independence, most strikes were unsuccessful. But since 1947, about two-thirds of all strikes have been successful. This is usually attributed to the workings of the Government adjudication machinery.[2] The attitude of the Government has, on the whole, been pro-labour, and the industrial tribunals have interpreted the law in that spirit. In 1967, about 70 per cent of the awards from industrial tribunals were in favour of the workers.[3]

All the WIMCO factories, except one, had severe strikes in the late thirties. At this time there was industrial unrest all over the country and big factories, like those of WIMCO, were, of course, not spared. Trade unions were formed at this time too, and the main activity of unions before Independence was to organize strikes. During the war the conditions in WIMCO were peaceful, but since then there have been strikes in the WIMCO factories every five years or so, except for the Ambernath and Calcutta factories, which have an impressive record of industrial peace, broken only by a big strike in the Calcutta factory in 1954.

The numbers of strikes and man-days lost per thousand workers in the Swedish companies in 1962-68 are shown in Table 20. As WIMCO has had a fairly large number of strikes, which have often been of long duration, the average number of man-days lost is high. The reasons for strikes in WIMCO have usually been of an economic nature, for example, dissatisfaction with wages or bonuses.

According to Table 20, the new Swedish companies have also had more strikes than the average. This is because SKF has had several short strikes - the total number of man-days lost is much lower for the new Swedish firms than the all-India average. The statistics in Table 20 do not include what are called "political strikes", a type of very short general strike that has occurred especially in West Bengal. Barring such strikes, there have not been any work stoppages at all in Vulcan-Laval, Sandvik and SF.

---

1) India. Labour Bureau. Indian Labour Statistics 1969; Pant, S.C., op. cit. pp. 451 ff.
2) Ibid., p. 122.
3) India. Labour Bureau, op. cit., p. 212.

Table 20. Strikes in Swedish companies in 1962-68

	Average annual number of strikes per factory 1962-68	Average annual number of man-days lost per 1,000 workers employed 1962-68
WIMCO		
Factory 1	0.29	0.2
Factory 2	1.00	15.9
Factory 3	0.57 } 0.49	1.1 } 14.8
Factory 4	0.29	4.1
Factory 5	0.29	52.7
Vulcan-Laval	0	0
Atlas Copco	0.14	1.9
Sandvik	0 } 0.18	0 } 0.6
SKF	0.75	1.3
SF	0	0
All India, manu-facturing sector	0.03	1.6

Sources. India. Labour Bureau. Indian Labour Statistics 1968 and 1969;
company statistics. Only industrial disputes involving work stoppages are included. The figures for all India are averages for the
years 1960 or 1961, 1964, 1965, 1966, and 1967. The figures
for Vulcan-Laval and SKF are for the period 1965-68 only. Man-
days lost for SKF have been calculated on the assumption that
all the workers were involved in the respective strikes.

The recurring short strikes in SKF indicated unsatisfactory relations between labour and management. In 1969, the management started to pay
more attention than befor to labour questions, and a three-year agreement
was concluded with the workers. No strikes were recorded in SKF in
1969-70.

The only prolonged strike in the new Swedish companies occurred in Atlas
Copco in 1966 and lasted for 17 days. It was launched by outside leaders
on a bonus issue and was, it seems, justified. The strike ended in mutual
satisfaction. The management got rid of the outside leaders in the trade
union and did not concede anything to the workers during the strike. After
going back to work, the workers got the extra money they had struck for.

Labour and management

Labour-management relations in general are often said to be better in foreign than in Indian companies. According to Myers, there is a consensus between labour leaders and Government officials in India that foreign firms are in the forefront in their willingness to deal with unions and in their whole approach to labour-management relations.[1] One reason given for this is that the activities of foreign firms are followed closely by the Government and that trade unions often single out foreign firms for special attention.

In the opinion of Myers, the positive labour-management relations in foreign firms are mainly due to better organization.[2] In foreign firms, the managers themselves are often interested in good relations, and more money is usually spent on the personnel department than in Indian companies, which makes it possible for foreign companies to have a more flexible labour policy. Foreign managements, unlike Indian managements, are also not burdened with old attitudes and traditional views on labour.

This picture of foreign firms as more progressive than Indian firms seems to be true in the case of the Swedish companies. It is more true of the new Swedish firms than of WIMCO, where old habits and some suspicion between labour and management still linger. The following statements by workers in the Swedish companies illustrate in what respects the Swedish firms are considered better than Indian companies:

> The management in the Swedish companies is less snobbish than in Indian companies, it is more informal, the trade union can identify with the company, the managers mix with the workers both in the daily work and at celebrations, relations are more democratic, problems are settled by mutual discussions and in mutual understanding, the managers are sympathetic, there is an open-door policy, the union leaders can see any officer and they will help, relations are very friendly, the management has a more positive attitude than in Indian companies.

One union leader states clearly his low opinion of the labour policy of other companies: "The other companies decide their labour policy in the Chambers of Commerce". But there are, of course, problems also in the Swedish firms. Several union representatives complain that they are not taken into the picture early enough in suspension cases, and the handling of questions of promotion is always a source of discontent. But many problems

---

1) Myers, C.A., op. cit., p. 100.
2) Ibid., p. 102.

seem to originate more in clashes of personalities than in disagreements on concrete issues.

The majority of managements in the Swedish companies consider themselves more progressive in labour matters than their Indian counterparts. It is often pointed out that it would be much easier to have a labour policy of the type allegedly found in Birla and some other big Indian companies: "Birla never has any disputes or awards. Long before that the trade-union leader is either bribed or killed." At the same time the managements in the Swedish firms realize that good relations are perhaps more favourable, relatively speaking, to management than to labour. Productivity goes up, and the management can be more tough in firing people and keeping discipline when the trade union has a positive attitude to the management.

The managements in several Swedish companies also maintain that other companies are being influenced by the progressive labour policies in the Swedish firms - which will mean that these policies may to some extent become an external economy. They hold that Swedish companies set an example and that sooner or later other companies will have to come and find out why the Swedish firms have such harmonous relations between labour and management, with concomitant high productivity. The personnel officers in several Swedish companies maintain that they are often consulted even on quite small matters, by personnel officers and managers in other companies.

Works committees. In the 1948 Industrial Policy Resolution, in the Industrial Disputes Act of 1947 and in the Five-year Plans, there have been numerous provisions for workers' participation in management in the form of works committees, production committees and joint management councils. But the employers have not been interested, the trade unions have bee to weak and there has been too much suspicion between labour and management to allow for any such cooperation.

> The feeling of mutual distrust is too strong to be overcome by legislative measures...Any person with some understanding of Indian labour problems would have known that in the existing social framework and conditions, workers' participation in management could not be successful.[1]

Although the works committees are statutory, exemptions are often made. All the Swedish factories but one, a WIMCO factory, are exempted. In this WIMCO factory, labour-management relations are generally good and the

---

1) Pant, S.C., op. cit., pp. 129 and 153.

works committee is just a manifestation of these harmonious relations. The workers do not really participate in management. The works committee meets once a month and the management then presents its plans, which are accepted by the workers.

The works committees are to consist of an equal number of representatives of labour and the employers. In most industries in India, and also in the Swedish firms, labour is too suspicious to be willing to sit on such a joint committee, where it is felt that the decisions may be too much influenced by the management. The attitude of the management is not always commendable: "Our policy is to let the workers participate in the questions which they can absorb in their brains."

Summary. Before Independence WIMCO paid average wage rates, but at present both WIMCO and the new Swedish companies pay considerably more than the average wage, and the wage difference may be regarded as a social gain. Total wages are composed of basic wage, dearness allowance and annual bonus. Real wages and living standards have increased for employees in the new Swedish companies.

The wage policies in the Swedish firms are in comparison relatively non-discriminatory. Piece-rate incentive systems are used or are being introduced in most of the Swedish companies, which seems to raise productivity. The workers are usually not in favour of piece-rates.

Social security and welfare measures were introduced on a large scale in India after Independence. The Swedish companies fully observe the statutory obligations and conform to local welfare practices. The new Swedish firms also provide uniforms, transport subsidies and free tea over and above the normal local practice. This extra contribution amounts in money terms to about 2 per cent of the total wage bill in the new Swedish companies.

There are workers' unions in all the Swedish companies. Most unions are affiliated to political parties, usually some Communist party. Over the years WIMCO has had many strikes, but the new Swedish companies have a good record of industrial peace. Like other foreign firms in India, the Swedish companies seem to have relatively harmonious labour-management relations, which is largely due to the positive attitude on the part of the management in the Swedish firms.

Chapter 6.

EDUCATION, CULTURE AND POLITICS

This chapter will mainly be devoted to the effects of foreign investment which have been called here "external economies in a wider sense". The external effects of the labour policies discussed in the previous chapters should rightly be classified in this category too, but the impact in connection with education and culture is more typical of the "external economies in a wider sense". The effects I have in mind here are illustrated in the following quotation from Myrdal:

> Industrialization is expected to instill a new spirit of rationalism, enterprise, discipline, punctuality, mobility, and efficiency. People will be stirred to become mechanically minded and master unfamiliar skills, not merely within new industrial enterprises but elsewhere in the economy as well. More competitive and more perfect markets will be called forth and superior commercial and financial institutions developed. All in all, the organization of work and people's attitudes toward it will be altered in ways that raise the efficiency of work performance throughout the economy. Bottlenecks will be more easily eliminated and the potential for diffusion of spread effects of the logistic type will be extended. All these happy results are expected to follow as a direct consequence of industrial expansion.[1]

There is, as we have seen, a consensus of opinion that these possible, positive effects of industrialization and foreign investment are much more important than other types of positive effects.[2] The conclusion of Chapter 1 was that it is mainly the long-term effects of an indirect nature that may produce viable growth. The rationale for encouraging foreign investment in appropriate cases is usually its intangible effects - its contribution to the educational and social transformation necessary for development. The "external economies in a wider sense", together with the corresponding diseconomies, are therefore of major interest.

It is implicit in the reasoning on the "external economies in a wider sense"

---

1) Myrdal, G., Asian Drama, p. 1196.
2) See p. 6.

that new investments, being mainly of an "economic" nature, cause or embody changes in other fields.[1] This view is contained in the Marxian thesis that changes in the "superstructure" are caused by changes in the basic "modes of production". It is corroborated, for example, by Epstein in his study on two villages in South India: "Thus we have established a positive correlation between economic, political, ritual and organisational change, with economic change being the determining variable".[2]

But the findings of R.D. Lambert show that the changes embodied in industry are not always imperative and may leave many institutions and attitudes untouched.[3] Myrdal considers the assumption that industrial investments induce changes favourable to development in other fields to be "glaringly untrue".[4] According to him, industrialization is not a cause of such changes - without specific and vigorous policies in other fields the spread effects and external economies from industrial investments will be small or non-existent.[5]

In India's case there are not enough reliable data to form any general conclusions on the strength of the indirect effects of foreign investments. Here I shall discuss some indirect effects of the Swedish investments under three headings: education, culture and politics. In the section on education I shall consider the training of workers and staff and the transmission of technological and organizational know-how. Under the heading of "Culture" I shall discuss changes in attitudes and cultural values, while in the section on politics I shall deal with political effects and Government control.

Education

The education given in industrial establishments in India must be regarded against the background of the general level of education in the country. Only 20 per cent of the population enter secondary school, and only 6 per cent leave it. Standards of learning and teaching are miserable, as compared with western norms. Fifty per cent of the students trying for the matri-

1) Streeten, P.P., The use and abuse of models in development planning, reprinted in Meier, G.M., Leading Issues in Economic Development, Stanford 1970, p. 74.
2) Epstein, T.S., Economic Development and Social Change in South India, Manchester 1962, p. 334.
3) Lambert, R.D., op. cit., pp. 17 and 24.
4) Myrdal, G., op. cit., p. 1907.
5) Ibid., p. 1199.

culation examination fail, in spite of the fact that all education is geared
to examinations:

> Teaching in South Asian schools at all levels tends to discourage in-
> dependent thinking and the growth of that inquisitive and experimental
> bent of mind that is so essential for development. It is directed toward
> enabling students to pass examinations and obtain degrees and, possibly,
> admittance to the next level of schools. A degree is the object pursued,
> rather than the knowledge and skills to which the degree should testify.[1]

India has an outmoded, "literary" system of education that has not changed
much since colonial times. In spite of the fact that there are very many
"educated unemployed", who create special problems, there is therefore
a general shortage of people with an education and training suitable for industry. Skilled workers and good engineers are in very short supply, although "engineers" and half-educated workers abound. The minimum knowledge required for different posts in modern industries is even higher now
than in the early western industrialization, but the Indian educational system will in all probability change but slowly. The efforts of Indian companies to train their staffs may therefore be of great significance for development.

Workers' training

An obvious example of "external economies in a wider sense" is the training of workers. If a company trains an employee so that his productivity
and market value are raised, the company has "added a value" to the worker. But this value added cannot normally be fully appropriated by the company. To retain the trained employee, the company may have to raise his
wages, in which case the worker himself benefits from the unpriced training. If the worker leaves the firm to take up a position elsewhere, an external economy is realized to the benefit of the new employer (and the
worker).[2] A company can compensate itself for the training given by paying low wages during the training period, as is usually the case when apprentices are taken on.[3]

The employers in India have traditionally not been very interested in the
education and training of workers. "Typically, little provision has been

---

1) Myrdal, G., op. cit., pp. 1645-46; cf. p. 1747.
2) When the subject of the training is the tending of special machines
   not used in other companies, there is, of course, no scope for external economies of this type.
3) Little, I.M.D., and Mirrlees, J.A., op. cit., p. 211.

made for training, anu ᴗhe bulk of the labour force has remained with few
skills."[1] The responsibility for workers´ training has therefore been taken
over by the Government.[2] The first "national craftsmen training scheme"
was organised in 1940. In 1968 some 110,000 workers were undergoing
training in the Government´s Industrial Training Institutes, and the capacity
of these Institutes is a present considered satisfactory.[3]

The quality of the training at the Industrial Training Institutes has improved,
but still many of the workers trained in there are not fit to start work in industry. An apprentice scheme was therefore put into operation in 1961.
Every industry has to receive and train one apprentice per 6-7 skilled workers. The apprentices spend 1 1/2 years in industrial training and 1 1/2
years at Government institutes. Companies with more than 500 workers
are expected to undertake also the theoretical training of their apprentices.
In 1968, nearly 37,000 apprentices were undergoing training in 3,000 industrial establishments, and the programme is being expanded.[4]

WIMCO did not have any regular training scheme for its workers before the
introduction of the apprentice scheme in 1961. There has, of course, been
"on-the-job training" all the time in the company, and in the early years
this training involved an "industrial socialisation" of the new recruits. A
high rate of labour turnover in the early years probably resulted in substantial spread effects:

> Out of a total labour force of 1,517, only 80 remained from 1924, 410
> from 1925 and 665 from 1926, leaving a balance engaged in 1927. That
> is for Ambarnath. In Calcutta, of a total of 780, 61 remained from
> 1924, 196 from 1925, 333 from 1926 and 128 from 1927, and those
> are people whom we have trained at considerable expense and trouble
> and that is where we come in at a disadvantage. We train the people
> and then gradually they leave us.[5]

Later, with growing industralization, the initial socialization has been
passed on to other, smaller establishments and in some cases to the Government.[6] At present both WIMCO and the new Swedish companies recruit mostly experienced workers, which means that the on-the-job training in the Swedish firms does not add as much to the workers´ abilities as

---

1) Myrdal, G., op. cit., p. 1197.
2) India. National Commission on Labour, Report, New Delhi 1969, p. 85.
3) India, Labour Bureau, Indian Labour Statistics 1969, p. 51; India.
   Planning Commission, Fourth Five-year Plan, op. cit., p. 340.
4) India. Planning Commission, Fourth Five-year Plan, op. cit., p. 340.
5) India. Tariff Board, Match Industry, Vol. III, p. 140.
6) Mason, R.H., op. cit., p. 15.

did the early WIMCO training. Today such additions may come mainly from more organized educational activities in the Swedish firms.

The legal provision that factories with more than 500 workers should have a factory school means in reality only that such factories are supposed to have separate facilities for the theoretical and practical training of their apprentices. Exemptions are numerous - it seems that the only facilities required by the authorities are a blackboard somewhere and a promise that certain machines will be reserved for apprentice training.

Consequently, most industries and also the majority of the Swedish factories do not have any factory schools but only the required number of apprentices, who are given some training. Sometimes apprentices for certain crafts are not available, and the production processes in certain companies are deemed to be unsuitable for training. Exemptions as to the number of apprentices are therefore common. The WIMCO factories usual have only some 10-15 apprentices and the new Swedish companies have 2-! Apprentices get a monthly wage of about Rs. 50, and they are therefore nc great financial burden to their principals. One WIMCO factory in 1968 spe only Rs. 8,000 on its entire apprentice scheme.

The WIMCO factory at Ambernath is therefore exceptional in having a ver; ambitious scheme of training for the apprentices. Of the new Swedish com panies, Sandvik and SKF have actually started factory schools. The Sand-vik school started in 1966, when 10 boys were taken on for training. But it was closed again in 1968 because of the recession and the greater avail; bility of good people from the Industrial Training Institutes. Only SKF sti] has a full-fledged factory school. A course lasting three years is given, and the trainees are supposed to work for at least three more years in SK after the examination. In 1969, 17 trainees had passed the final examinati in the SKF school.

Atlas Copco and SF are somewhat smaller than the other Swedish compa-nies and are therefore not required by law to have a factory school. They give small courses in welding, reading drawings, how to avoid accidents, etc. WIMCO has lately started on-the-job courses run by the wood depart ment for contractors and workers on the felling side. The Calcutta factor pays four teachers in a primary school for the children of workers. Apar from what has been mentioned here, no other education is provided on the company's initiative for the workers in the Swedish companies. Workers are practically never sent on outside courses in India or to Sweden - for rational economic reasons. It should be remembered here that we do not place any moral blame on any company for having, for example, little in the way of training. The Swedish companies give as much training as they consider profitable, which is quite rational.

In 1958 the Indian Government started a scheme of "workers' education". The idea is that the common workers shall be taught some basic facts about industrial work and trade-union activities. In the developed countries the trade unions have usually been responsible for such education, but unions in India are weak and therefore the Government has taken over the responsibility. One or two trade-union officals per company are given a course of three months' duration, and after that they are expected to act as teachers of their fellow-workers.

The "workers' education" scheme has not been an unconditional success: "The union leaders have generally been indifferent towards the scheme and workers generally regard it as a paid holiday in a new form."[1] Only a few of the Swedish companies have sent workers to teacher-training and then started courses. One WIMCO factory has discontinued its scheme, as the classes were considered by the management to be masked propaganda for the trade union. The only WIMCO factory that has a running scheme has generally good labour-management relations, and the "workers' education" classes are used by the personnel officer to propagate the views of the management on different topics.

Thus, not very much organized training is given to the workers in the Swedish companies. Coupled with the fact that the turnover of labour in the Swedish companies is generally low, this means that the possibilities of spread effects to other companies are small. This is especially true of SKF and WIMCO, where the machines are so specialized that the experience gained by the workers is not applicable outside the company.

Staff-training

Since Independence, India has turned out more than 100,000 engineers.[2] Their training has often been of dubious quality. To rectify this, the companies employing new engineers can either give them additional training in the company or send them on outside courses. In most cases, inside training is to be preferred, as the outside courses are usually of the same relatively low standard as the general engineering training. What is said here about engineers is true also of other staff categories.

The general picture for WIMCO is that very little in the way of staff-training has been provided. In 1967, at the instance of the parent company, STAB, a one-month course in match technology was given to newly engaged engineers. A few accountants, engineers and supervisors have in recent

---

1) Pant, S.C., op. cit., p. 341.
2) Commerce, Annual Number 1968, Bombay 1968, p. 14.

years been sent on outside courses, and in a few special cases people have also been sent to Sweden. But in the main WIMCO has provided as little training for its staff as for its workers.

The new Swedish companies have a relatively good record of sending people for training in Sweden. On an average, more than one person per company per year has been sent, which is more than the average for foreign subsidiaries in India.[1] Actually, more people have been sent to Sweden than to courses in India. The managers of some of the Swedish companies consider Indian courses to be of a very limited value: "Courses are of no use either to the company or to the employees." But most of the new Swedish companies have a positive but passive attitude to staff courses - the company takes no initiatives, but registration and examination fees for courses actually taken are usually reimbursed. Within the new Swedish firms no training worth mentioning has been provided for the staff categories.

Foreign personnel. The question of foreign personnel and their replacement by local nationals is of current interest in many underdeveloped countries.[2] The basic policy statement concerning foreign investment made by the independent Indian Government in 1949 considers the employment and training of Indians for all posts as a question of "vital importance".[3]

But before Independence the (colonial) Government did not consider Indianization to be an important issue. The policy-making External Capital Committee of 1925 concluded that no rules should be set for Indian participation, except when the Government gave direct subsidies to a company. In such cases "a reasonable proportion of the directorate should be Indian."[4] This very weak condition was applied to WIMCO in 1927 by the Tariff Board, which proposed the Indianization of WIMCO's directorate.[5]

As no rules were set by the pre-independence Government, the foreign companies in India, including WIMCO, were not particularly interested in replacing their foreign personnel. "The foreign enterprises in such protected industries as paper and matches... were very slow in turning out

---

1) Reserve Bank of India, Foreign Collaboration in Indian Industry, Bombay 1968, p. 31.
2) Geiger, T., The General Electric Company in Brazil, New York 1961, p. 83.
3) India. Ministry of Finance. Pocket Book of Economic Information 1969 New Delhi 1970, p. 283.
4) India. External Capital Committee, Report, Calcutta 1925.
5) See p. 65.

160

locally trained people, specially in the higher categories of the technical and managerial jobs."[1] WIMCO had 25 foreigners in 1927 and this average number was maintained well into the 1950's. Sometimes second-rate foreigners were employed just to keep control in foreign hands.

Since Independence, the Indianization of foreign firms has generally shown considerable progress, except for the top managerial posts and some technical capacities.[2] From the point of view of the foreign companies, Indianization pays: local people are cheaper and are normally as efficient as foreigners, and they have valuable local knowledge. A major reason for the progressive Indianization of all but the very top managerial posts seems to be the fact that control need no longer be exerted by individuals - modern budgeting and accounting tools give the parent companies full control over their subsidiaries without the employment of foreigners.

By reason of the scale and international character of its operations, the typical new investing company has found it necessary to build a system of control into the structure of the organization. If it appears tolerant of the national origins of high-level staff in its foreign subsidiaries, if as in India its encouragement of "-ization" often precedes and exceeds the requirements of law, this is due more to it being able to displace decisive authority upwards than to any other factor.[3]

During the last ten years, Indianization in WIMCO has progressed rapidly. In 1955, WIMCO had 38 expatriates employed. In late 1969 three out of five factories were completely run by Indians and there were at that time altogether only six foreigners in the company. It is stated that the new accounting and budgeting system will in 10 years' time make almost all foreigners superfluous. The parent company will probably only keep one foreigner in the top echelon, and the new techniques and methods that may be required will be transmitted by temporary experts.

The number of non-temporary foreigners in the new Swedish companies in 1969 is shown in Table 21. On an average, the foreign subsidiaries in India have less than three foreigners, as against more than three in the new Swedish companies. The somewhat higher number in the Swedish firms may be explained by the fact that they are comparatively young.[4] 'he techno-

---

1) Islam, N., Foreign Capital and Development: Japan, India and Canada, Tokyo 1960, p. 182.
2) Economic Times, Bombay, 28 March 1969.
3) Kidron, M., Foreign Investments in India, London 1965, p. 39. Cf. Myrdal, G., op. cit., p. 663.
4) Reserve Bank of India, Foreign Collaboration in Indian Industry, Bombay 1968, p. 31.

logy-intensive character of SKF, Sandvik and SF shows in the relatively high minimum number of foreigners considered to be required.

Table 21. Number of foreigners in Swedish companies in 1969 and stated minimum number of foreigners needed.

	Number of foreigners 1969		Minimum foreigners needed	
WIMCO	6		1	
Vulcan-Laval	1		0	
Atlas Copco	2		1	
Sandvik	5	3	4	2
SKF	5		3	
SF	4		4	

Sources. Company statistics.

All the Swedish companies would like to have more permanent foreigners than the stated minimum, but they are compelled by the Indianization policy of the Government to reduce the numbers. The parent companies consider foreigners to be indispensable in quality control and sometimes in factory administration, while company administration, including the managing director's function, apparently can be Indianized without any problems. There is even no aversion to leaving the top management of the companies in Indian hands, because it is felt that presumptive managing directors can be indoctrinated to be "citizens" of the company rather than of India.

Technology and know-how

The main benefits to be reaped from foreign investment are said to be the "external economies in a wider sense". Perhaps the most obvious external economies are the spread of technological knowledge and know-how.[1]
To quote K.K. Subrahmanian: "The gains emerging from the transfer of

---

[1] In using the terms "technology" or "technical know-how", I have in mind the type of services that normally flow from a foreign technical collaborator to a recipient company in India: patents, specifications, designs, drawings, plant layout, etc.

technology account for the most important contribution of foreign investment to the host country."[1] The Indian Government has stressed the technological aspect of foreign investment, and investments with foreign majorities have been allowed in cases in which the new technology has been very much desired.

If the spread of technology is to be an external economy, it must be adopted and brought into use in other companies or bodies. This can be done piece-meal through the selling and purchasing activities of the foreign company, through contacts between the research department in the company and indigenous institutions and through imitation by other companies.

To be considered as a primary benefit, the new technology should be new, in the sense that it should not have existed in the country before in actual production. In this sense, the Swedish companies have not brought very much new technology. WIMCO started relatively late with conventional production methods. The new Swedish companies were also preceded by their competitors and therefore brought with them only a duplication of technologies that already existed in the country. Sandvik started at the same time as its main competitor and may, in this sense only, be said to have introduced new technology.[2]

But in the years following the original investment, the Swedish companies have introduced new varieties of their main product and also new products. WIMCO has started the production of chemicals, SKF continuously extends its range of bearings, and Atlas Copco introduces accessories to its main products. Sandvik tries to sell TEMAX inserts, and Vulcan-Laval and SF introduce new products within a broad range. In most cases the competitors carry on the same type of diversifying activities as the Swedish companies. It is difficult to judge who was actually first with a new variation of a product, but the power and will of the Swedish firms to introduce new products probably acts as a stimulant to technological development in Indian industry.[3]

The know-how spread in India by the Swedish companies originates from the Swedish parent companies. The know-how given by the parent companies is paid for by the Indian subsidiaries by way of royalties and research fees, but because of the strict rules of the Indian Government, the Swedish subsidiaries in India pay much less than their sister companies in other countries - and all subsidiaries normally pay less than the market rate for the technology supplied by the parent companies. In spite of the low payments,

---

1) Subrahmanian, K.K., A Study of Foreign Private Investment in India since 1950, Bombay 1967, Diss (unpublished), p. 17. Cf. p. 15.
2) Cf. p. 259.
3) Cf. p. 253.

the parent firms have a very generous attitude to their Indian subsidiaries. Most of the know-how supplied is of an ad-hoc and unpatented nature. Generally, the Swedish subsidiaries in India can get as much know-how as they want - it is there for the asking. This naturally gives them an edge over the Indian competitors, who are mostly dependent on successive renewals of expensive collaboration agreements.

But there is one limitation to the generosity of the Swedish parent companies the actual research and development of new products is not transferred to the subsidiaries. This is quite normal, because economies of scale and concentration very frequently arise in connection with research and development. The foreign parent companies and also the foreign collaborators of purely Indian companies are therefore generally very reluctant to part with their research activities:

> While there are some firms which find it necessary to adapt their products or methods to local needs, and so undertake a modicum of development research, this is usually done on a modest scale, if at all, an for strictly limited ends. Fundamental research and ma·or developments in the private sector are, with perhaps the sole exception of Tata, a foreign responsibility.[1]

The Indian Government tries to reduce the country's technological dependence by giving all sorts of tax concessions to companies that conduct research of their own. But still most research in India is on a laboratory level, and 90 per cent of the total research expenditure is incurred by the Government.[2] The existence of foreign collaborations in technology-intensive industries hampers the development of indigenous research and may have very serious long-term effects.[3] The only Swedish company in India that does some rudimentary research of its own is Vulcan-Laval, which is forced by competition to undertake some independent product-development work.

Spread of technology. The technology embodied in the production of the Swedish companies can be spread either through imitation by other companies or through selling and purchasing activities. The imitation process

1) Kidron, M., op. cit., p. 287.
2) Namjoshi, M.V., Monopolies in India, Bombay 1966, p. 95.
3) Södersten, B., op. cit., p. 465. Cf. Choudhari, A., Oligopoly and industrial research in India, in Monopolies and Their Regulations in India, Bombay 1966.

probably does not operate as regards the Swedish companies, with their large-scale and technically complicated production.[1] The Swedish firms are also not willing to disclose any manufacturing secrets; in SKF, for example, 80-85 per cent of the machines are patented and are not sold outside the SKF group. This leaves selling and purchasing as possible channels for the spread of manufacturing technology.

The production of the Swedish companies replaced former Swedish exports, and the direct effect of local production was therefore naturally not a fresh spread of technology through sales but an intensification of former efforts by sales agents. Technology is spread simply by way of the fact that the customers learn how to use the Swedish products. The Swedish firms try through service and by other means to maintain close relations with their customers, who are told which machines are suitable for Sandvik detachable bits, how bleaching is done with WIMCO's sodium chlorate and what maintenance is necessary on Atlas Copco's compressors. Atlas Copco even arranges formal "customers' courses" to make its products known.

The Swedish companies also sometimes give technical advice on matters not directly connected with their own products. Atlas Copco has made a study of a complete tunnel project, and SKF helps with measurement problems concerning the building in of bearings in larger units. Vulcan-Laval and particularly SF offer consultancy services on a large scale, because a sizeable part of their sales consists of specially made equipment. In this consultancy process know-how is communicated, for example, from a SF sales engineer to the engineers of the customer.

The educational effects through purchases are, of course, dependent on the amount and variety of goods purchased. Companies with strong "backward-linkage effects" usually have more educational effects through purchases than companies of a more basic type.[2] Atlas Copco has much "backward linkage" - many small components are bought from a large number of suppliers. When imports are replaced by indigenous supplies, it may be that Atlas Copco will give detailed technical instructions to the supplier and even sometimes provide the jigs and tools needed for production.

But generally not much genuine technology is transferred to the suppliers of the Swedish companies. Instead the difficult and sometimes time-consuming task is stated to be to teach the suppliers to maintain the quality and keep to delivery schedules.[3] When a new supplier is taken on, a representative of the Swedish company in question often has to pay frequent vi-

---

1) Cf. Meier, G.M., The International...,p. 158.
2) See pp. 84 ff.
3) Cf. Rosen, G., Industrial Change in India, Bombay 1966, p. 156.

sits to him to reject bad-quality work on the spot, to give advice and to check delivery dates. In one case it took three months just to get a reliable supply of a simple thing like wooden boxes. Even when supplies flow regularly, the Swedish companies have to maintain a rigid inspection system, even for such goods as oil from reputable companies like Esso (India). But all these strict measures are stated to have had the desired effects: suppliers have developed a quality consciousness and some of them are even said to be proud to be suppliers to the Swedish firms.

WIMCO is a special case. The main product bought is wood in different forms and some training of felling contractors and their workers has been started, in order to bring down costs. For the raw materials bought as splints (wooden sticks) a special scheme has been introduced. Splint manufacturers are given technical and managerial advice in the form of package deals, in which the manufacturer is tied closely to WIMCO. In this way WIMCO gets better splints and the splint manufacturer in question can expand his production.

Organisation and personnel

The managerial know-how brought by foreign private investment is stated to be as important as the technical know-how transferred.[1] The idea is that the underdeveloped countries do not have any entrepreneurs willing to take risks and able to handle modern industrial organizations. Even if these countries have entrepreneurs, they are said to be mostly of the raw profiteering type, and the smooth, modern type of manager-administrator with the coordinating abilities and instruments needed to run a large-scale modern enterprise can consequently only be brought by foreign investment. The image of modern western management includes high business standards and "progressive" personnel policies.

India evidently has good entrepreneurs of all kinds.[2] But a sizeable proportion of the managerial class seems to have retained the trader's mentality:

> This proportion speculates as other people bet, for excitement; it lends money at extortionate rates of interest; it prefers the short view to the long; its tradition is trading rather than industrial; it cheats its

---

1) "The missing bit and that most crucial to the success of an enterprise is managerial and administrative know-how". Mason, R.H., An Analysis of Benefits from U.S. Direct Foreign Investments in Less-developed Areas, Diss., Stanford Univ., no date, p. 32.
2) Rosen, G., op. cit., p. 163.

customers, evades its taxes, exploits its workers and defrauds its shareholders. Worst of all, it is not even enterprising.[1]

The present distribution of Indian managers between the old, personal-trading type, on the one hand, and the modern, integrative type, on the other, is not known. It has been contended that foreign managers are no better than the Indian average.[2] But the general tenor of the evidence is that foreign investments have more modern and more efficient management than the average Indian company.[3]

The new Swedish companies have from the beginning used the latest management tools and methods. There is a continuous stream of managerial know-how flowing from the Swedish parent companies to their subsidiaries in India. Managers in the new Swedish firms go on courses in Sweden, and new methods of budgeting, accounting and marketing are introduced in India as soon as they have been tested by the parent companies. The performance of the new Swedish companies is usually judged by the same standards as are used for their sister companies in the respective concerns, and to meet this competition the new Swedish companies have to have the latest management tools.

In contrast to this, WIMCO has all the time followed age-old Indo-British methods of accounting and management. Not until in the late sixties was this tradition broken, and then quite abruptly. The parent company (STAB) is introducing in all the companies in the concern a new budgeting system, a new divisional system and new concepts of profit measurement. The new methods are slowly being disseminated through the WIMCO organization and will in due course probably have substantial effects on the workings of the company.

In the field of business standards and business ethics, all the Swedish companies seem to differ from the average in India. They represent the "modern" way of doing business: less personal, with less elaborate negotiations and with more reliance on written agreements and contracts.[4] The Swedish companies also, at least at the higher staff levels, have avoided joining in the ever-increasing practice of corruption.[5] The goodwill earned

---

1) Zinkin, M., Development for Free Asia, quoted in Myrdal, G., Asian Drama, p. 822.
2) Subrahmanian, K.K., op. cit., p. 295.
3) Kidron, M., op. cit., p. 230; Baranson, J., op. cit., pp. 103 and 112; Choudhari, A., op. cit., p. 9.
4) For an elaboration of this point, see Geiger, T., The General Electric Company in Brazil, New York 1961, p. 81.
5) Cf. Myrdal, G., op. cit., pp. 944 ff.

by abstention from corrupt practices is considered to be worth more than the possible gains from bribery.

In the field of personnel policies, the traditional picture of the average Indian management is a highly centralized, authoritarian and, at best, paternalistic structure.[1] WIMCO has in this field followed British-Indian personnel traditions and not deviated much from the prevalent civil-service atmosphere. Without having any hard statistics to support my judgment, it seems that the new Swedish companies, together with most new foreign investments, tend to have more "progressive" personnel policies than the Indian average. There is said to be in the new Swedish companies an emphasis on personal motivation, delegation of power, job satisfaction, punctuality, open-door management and democratic working. But one shoul perhaps not over-rate the differences. There are many Indian companies that are as progressive as foreign companies, and it has to be remembere that the personnel policies in foreign firms are invariably carried out by Indian nationals.

Still, it seems likely that the management and personnel policies of the new Swedish companies are more "modern" than the Indian average. It will be recalled that this was the case also with, for example, the recruitment, welfare and labour policies of the new Swedish firms. Granted this superiority, what are the consequences for development? How are the goo management practices in the Swedish companies spread to other agents an put to use for development?

Very little management know-how is consciously spread to other companie management know-how is, after all, a major ingredient of the competitive advantage of the Swedish companies. Complex accounting systems and othe modern management tools are in any case not easily transferable. Some in fluence is excercised by managing directors and personnel officers in the Swedish firms in their normal intercourse with colleagues, but the transfer of managerial know-how in this way cannot be significant. The social intercourse of management personnel in the Swedish companies is restricted to a small and very select westernized group, and the foreign personnel are usually even more secluded.

This leaves us with spread effects through employees leaving the Swedish companies and taking up jobs elsewhere. The staff turnover is very low in the Swedish companies, but a few persons leave every year. If they are not specialists, they cannot bring with them all the complex management

---

1) Myers, C.A., Labor Problems in the Industrialization of India, Cambridge 1958, pp. 175-6.

tools used, but they may have imbibed the business ethics and the general approach to management and personnel questions prevalent in the Swedish firms.[1] The Swedish companies are adamant about keeping foreigners in some technical jobs, but the top-management cadre is normally open to Indians and therefore there is usually some scope for on-the-job training in management (separate training for officials is generally not provided in the Swedish companies).

Culture

Under this heading I shall treat the more elusive effects of foreign investments. Foreign companies can provide direct education and transmit technical and managerial know-how. But industrialization per se also brings new patterns of thinking and reacting. Institutions, habits and fundamental attitudes may be affected.

The possible changes in institutions and attitudes are perhaps not only incidental effects of industrialization. According to many writers, such changes are imperative,and they may also be necessary for long-term economic growth.[2] Those who live in industrialized countries perhaps tend to underrate the importance of attitudes and institutions, living, as they do, in a society in which attitudes are already conducive to growth. Gunnar Myrdal´s central thesis in his book on Asia is that institutions and attitudes in southern Asia are the primary obstacles to development.[3]

The Indian leaders are convinced that attitudes and institutions must be changed,and the Five-year Plans reiterate the need for remoulding and refashioning existing institutions.[4] But the Indian Government has not

---

1) The better the management spirit, the lower is usually the turnover and thereby also, paradoxically enough, the positive spread effects.
2) Myrdal, G., op. cit., pp. 454 and 690; Gadgil, D.R., The Industrial Evolution of India in Recent Times, London 1933, p. 192.
3) "The prevailing attitudes and patterns of individual performance in life and at work are from the development point of view deficient in various respects: low levels of work discipline, punctuality, and orderliness; superstitious beliefs and irrational outlook; lack of alertness, adaptability, ambition, and general readiness for change and experiment; contempt for manual work; submissiveness to authority and exploitation; low aptitude for cooperation; low standards of personal hygiene; and so on." (Myrdal, G., op. cit., p. 1862).
4) India. Planning Commission. Fourth Five-year Plan, op. cit., p. 2.

done very much to accomplish any social changes. Instead, nearly all hopes have been attached to industry. Industries are alike over the world, and the new industries in India are expected to bring also changes in institutions and attitudes. The difficulties and the inertia are played down: "Nothing changes as fast as customs".[1] The argument is well put by Lambert:

> ... it is assumed that the introduction of the factory system has certain institutional imperatives that flow from this form of work organisation, imperatives which are instrumental in moving a society from one end of the polarity to another, from a static, acquired-status-ridden tradition-bound, primary-group-oriented, particularistic, fatalistic society into one that is rapidly changing, achieved-status-dominated, progressive, secondary-group-oriented, universalistic and aspiring. In fact, the factory is presumed to embody the latter set of characteristics and thus, by its example, to upset the stable, traditional structure.[2]

But the conclusion of Lambert´s own study is that industry is not a major catalyst in bringing about a modernization of institutions and attitudes. Myrdal points out that changes in institutions are dependent on the cultural, social and economic levels already attained.[3] Industries, especially foreign ones, easily become social enclaves with little impact on the institutions and attitudes in their environment. In the following pages I shall discuss a few indirect effects of a "cultural" nature in relation to caste, religion, commitment, and superficial and fundamental cultural changes.

Caste and religion

The caste system may perhaps be regarded as part of the Hindu religion, but I prefer to treat the two as distinct subjects. Religion, in India mainly Hinduism, is often said to be a major obstacle to change. But it seems probable that the Hindu religion at the present time is not in itself very important - it is mainly a philosophical expression of deep-rooted social values and customs. "Religion has, then, become the emotional container of this whole way of life and work and by its sanction has rendered it rigid and resistant to change."[4]

---

1) Kerr, et al., Industrialism and Industrial Man, London 1962, p. 8.
2) Lambert, R.D., Workers, Factories and Social Change in India, Princeton 1963, pp. 16-17.
3) Myrdal, G., op. cit., p. 1196.
4) Myrdal, G., op. cit., p. 112.

According to the National Commission on Labour of 1969, industrial workers in India are, as a consequence of industrialization, gradually becoming more secularized.[1] The relatively insignificant role and status value of religion is shown by the fact that both rural and urban dwellers rank . the vocation of priest as absolutely the lowest in a scale of occupational rankings.[2] The Swedish companies have had some communal strife in factories with two dominant religious groups, but, on the whole, religion has not been of practical importance.

In comparison with religion, caste is socially much more important. Caste serves as a delineator of different economic and social classes. According to competent observers, this curse of Indian society is increasing in importance, especielly in the political field.[3] Caste typifies ascribed status, as opposed to achieved status, and the caste system perpetuates age-old economic and social differences. It is often assumed that economic change in the form of industrialization will loosen the grip of ascribed caste status in favour of achieved status within and outside the factory.

This also seems to happen. Industrial work gives low-caste people opportunities of economic and social emancipation from dependence on the high-caste Hindus. The low-caste worker can become part of a new class system based only on economic differences.[4] Many high-caste Hindus have by economic necessity overcome their prejudice against manual work - Brahmins are found nowadays in all factories, tending machines and doing other "lowly" jobs.[5]

Instead of caste, occupation is developing into a primary status criterion. A majority of urban dwellers in a Poona sample referred to themselves by saying, for example, "I am a fitter", while rural people tended to introduce themselves with "I am a Brahmin...".[6] Industrialists are considered to have high status in both rural and urban areas. The personal quality given highest rank is education, while caste was ranked as number 5 and 7 in the respective samples.[7] The workers apparently no longer fear

1) India. National Commission on Labour, Report, Delhi 1969, p. 33.
2) Bopegamage, A. and Veeraraghavan, P.V., Status Images in Changing India, Delhi 1967.
3) Cf. Myrdal, G., op. cit.. p. 763.
4) Myers, C.A., op. cit., p. 39; Niehoff, A., Factory Workers in India, Milwaukee 1959, p. 104.
5) National Commission on Labour, op. cit., p. 34; Niehoff, A., op. cit., p. 103.
6) Bopegamage, A. and Veeraraghavan, P.V., op. cit., p. 41.
7) Ibid., p. 64.

that caste is taken into account when industries recruit new people - which corroborates my findings that in the Swedish companies caste is not of importance in recruitment.[1]

But the caste system is still in force, although it is somewhat crippled in urban areas. Dining is still largely an inter-caste affair, and 44 per cent of the urban dwellers in Poona do not wish to marry outside their own caste.[2] Caste prejudice is very noticeable at the extreme ends of the scale, for example, in the discrimination against the "untouchables": "... we find that the social stigma of untouchability continues to stick", says the National Commission of Labour.[3] Also in factories the extreme caste differences are observable.

In the factories studied by Lambert, the majority of both the highest and the lowest castes were employed as production workers. But the Brahmins were only found in the more advanced jobs, and up to one-half of the Brahmins were either supervisors or clerks. In contrast, there were no clerks from the lowest caste, and all the lowest jobs were performed by people from the "backward classes".[4] There was a marked covariance between caste and educational level, but Lambert is of the opinion that separate influences of caste are quite probable.

The Swedish companies generally do not take caste into account. Recruitment and promotion appear to be based on merit only. The foreigners in the Swedish firms, not being brought up in the caste system, are mostly ignorant of the caste status of individual employees. The Indian managerial personnel in the Swedish companies are naturally more conscious of caste, and in rare cases they appear to have a discriminatory attitude towards the lower castes.

But the most caste-conscious category has been the workers themselves. In one WIMCO factory, high-caste workers used to refrain from accepting a job when they were told that they would sometimes have to sweep the floor themselves (a job traditionally reserved for untouchables). There was formerly also trouble when low-caste people drank from the common tea-pot. The promotion of a low-caste sweeper to be a machine operator in a WIMCO factory provoked a strike, and the managing director of a new Swedish company had to flush the new water-closet himself for three weeks before the workers came round to doing it.

1) See p. 106.
2) Bopegamage, A. and Veeraraghavan, P.V., op. cit., p. 78.
3) India. National Commission of Labour, op. cit., p. 429.
4) Lambert, R.D., op. cit., p. 154.

The overt manifestations of caste seem to be on the wane in the Swedish companies, but it still makes quite a difference whether a worker is a Brahmin or low-caste. The pattern shown in Table 22 is the same as in the Lambert study: nearly half the staff category of the Swedish companies in Poona is made up of Brahmins, but there is not one single low-caste staff member. The WIMCO factories employ quite a number of unskilled workers, which gives the low-caste workers a somewhat higher representation than in the new Swedish companies. [1]

Table 22. Distribution of employees from the highest and the lowest castes in Swedish companies in 1969

	Highest caste as percentage of workers	Highest caste as percentage of staff	Lowest caste as percentage of workers	Lowest caste as percentage of staff
WIMCO				
Factory 1	2	11	23	0
Factory 2	1	20	33	5
Factory 3	33 ⟩ 8	33 ⟩ 19	2 ⟩ 16	0 ⟩ 1
Factory 4	2	2	8	2
Factory 5	1	33	15	0
Vulcan-Laval	5	50	5	0
Atlas-Copco	18	30	5	0
Sandvik	20 ⟩ 15	55 ⟩ 45	7 ⟩ 8	0 ⟩ 0
SKF	20	60	8	0
SF	10	30	15	0
Poona factories	12	64	12	0
Kota factories	24	28	46	23

Sources. Company statistics; Lambert, R.D., op. cit., p. 153, for Poona figure; Vaid, K.N., op. cit., p. 38, for Kota figure. The "highest caste" is identical with the Brahmin caste. The category of "lowest caste" is mainly made up of "untouchables".(= "Harijans"), but it also includes some tribals and other "backward classes". The percentage figures for the Swedish companies are in no way exact.

[1] It may be noted that in a very new industrial centre, Kota, nearly half the work force is low-caste, which gives this category representation also on the staff level.

173

The Brahmins on the shop floor in the Swedish companies are mostly supervisors, and most of the untouchables employed are still sweepers. A few untouchables have advanced to semi-skilled jobs, and in very rare cases one can find untouchables working as machine operators. This is an improvement compared with the situation 10 years ago, but progress is slow. But if I may venture to make a qualitative judgment, it appears that the Swedish companies are contributing to the weakening of the caste system as much and perhaps even more than comparable Indian companies

Commitment and absenteeism

A basic change brought about by industrialization is the creation of an industrial labour force. The workers do not only change their locus of emplc ment. from land to factory. They normally also settle near the factory in urban areas, take up new social relationships and gradually adjust to urban-industrial life. The work force becomes "stabilized" and "committed"

The National Commission on Labour states as its opinion that the Indian labour force is gradually becoming more and more committed.[1] The reasons for this are said to be the added facilities for workers in factories and the social security offered by the State, which reduce dependence on the village in contingencies. Some employers offer incentives for regular attendance and high productivity. Also, urban families traditionally averse to taking up factory jobs are now seeking employment. People fror such families are not severed from their social background when they begin to work. An increasing proportion of new jobs are taken up by descendants of the first migrants, who do not have any memories of village life.

Lambert, in his study of workers in Poona, criticizes the notion of "workers' commitment".[2] According to him, the attitude of the employer is s important that one should not talk of workers' commitment without also taking "employer commitment" into account. For example, the employer attitude to casual labour and absenteeism is very important. Lambert ma tains further that the fact that workers stay in urban areas and stick to th factory jobs does not imply that they have accepted the "industrial values" The workers may still have "a village-based set of inter-personal relatio norms", and in many cases they may just regard their factory job as an e tension of the paternalistic "Jajmani" system prevalent in the villages.

---

1) India. National Commission on Labour, op. cit., p. 31.
2) Lambert, R.D., op. cit., pp. 90 ff.

Regarding the Swedish companies, I stated earlier that, by and large, their work forces seem to be settled and adjusted to factory work.[1] Few farmers are recruited - most workers come from the factory area - which contributes to stability. The Swedish companies also have relatively few workers employed in causal or temporary capacities, which probably results in a higher degree of commitment.

Absenteeism. One indicator of labour stability is the rate of absenteeism. A low rate of absenteeism may be a sign of high stability and strong commitment. It may also, like a low turnover of labour, indicate good relations between management and labour.[2] In India, the rates of absenteeism are generally higher than in industrialized countries.

Absenteeism in Indian industry is largely seasonal. It is highest in the dry season, March-June, and lowest in December-January. In the dry season the harvest is brought in and then all hands are required. In this season also all celebrations take place: weddings, funerals and religious festivals. A more recent cause of absenteeism is the introduction of the ESI sickness-pay scheme in all major industrial centres (see p. 140). The employees more often stay at home, due to real or feigned sickness. Workers in a bad physical condition can now afford to stay at home, and the cheapness of false ESI certificates constitutes a strong temptation for others. According to a study made by a WIMCO factory, absenteeism increased by 4 percentage points after the introduction of the ESI scheme.

Absenteeism rates in the Swedish companies are shown in Table 23. The highest figure is reached by WIMCO´s Madras factory, with nearly 18 per cent. The maximum in this factory is 35 per cent, which is a very high figure. Of the new Swedish companies, Vulcan-Laval has a relatively high ratio, and the management of the company also considers absenteeism to be the main labour problem. The new Swedish companies have relatively low rates of absenteeism, while the WIMCO factories come closer to the Indian average.

One would really expect the Swedish companies to have higher rates of absenteeism than the average, as they are relatively generous with sick leave and casual leave, which are included in the absenteeism figures. But at least the new Swedish companies have lower rates, and this may then be taken as a sign that the labour force in the new Swedish companies is more committed than the average. But one has to be careful with such conclusions

---

1) See p. 105.
2) See pp. 91 ff.

Table 23. Absenteeism in Swedish companies in the period 1965-68

	Average annual rate of abstenteeism 1965-68	
WIMCO		
Factory 1	13.3	
Factory 2	17.6	
Factory 3	11.5	14.2
Factory 4	15.2	
Factory 5	13.5	
Vulcan-Laval	13.5	
Atlas Copco	11.4	
Sandvik	10.0	10.9
SKF	8.6	
SF	11.1	
Engineering industry, Bombay	16.6	
Enginering industry, West Bengal	14.7	

Sources. India. Labour Bureau, Indian Labour Statistics 1969, Simla 1969, p. 173; company statistics. Absenteeism is measured as the ratio of man-shifts lost due to absence to the corresponding total of man-shifts scheduled to be worked. All leave is included. The figure for Sandvik is an average for 1967-69. The figure for SKF was arrived at by adding to the average unpaid leave the average paid leave for SF in 1965-68.

- the labour force in the WIMCO factories is presumably also becoming more committed, but WIMCO's absenteeism rates are rising continuously.

Several Swedish companies have attendance incentive schemes, with a maximum annual bonus of as much as one month's pay, but these schemes hav apparently been less effective than strict attendance policies, threats and warnings. This means that economic incentives cannot increase attendance, and that the employees attend more regularly only when they are forced to do so. This may be an indication that family and tradition still exert a stron pull - the workers are perhaps committed to factory work but not to industrial values and incentives.

The industrial order

Under this heading I shall discuss some of the superficial changes in "culture" that are said to flow from industrialization. In the next section, more fundamental value changes will be examined. This division into "superficial" and "fundamental" values and customs is, of course, arbitrary. The superficial values are of much the same kind as the modern job attitudes formed by progressive personnel policies.[1)]

The changes in values and customs that I designate "superficial" are those that would follow directly from the "industrial order" - an adjustment on the part of the employees to the industrial imperatives and a general westernizing of institutions and attitudes, resulting from the fact that Indian industrialization is very much influenced by western industry. More specifically, I have in mind the fact that the employees have to accept rules on hours of work, methods of payment, movements in and out of work, the continuity of the work process, the responsible care of machines, regular attendance and work load.

When employees have been conditioned by industry, they will probably also place a high value on promotion, on being modern, on the English language, on success in business contra Government service, on western clothes and on harmonious labour-management relations. They will accept the objectives of their company and show a positive interest in its productive performance.[2)]

The harshness of the impact of the industrial culture is disputed, and we have seen that a certain scepticism regarding the extent of the impact may be warranted. But one can find students who are fully convinced that industry will impose its own cultural patterns on the pre-existing culture and that the employees are very adjustable to the internationally valid rules set by modern industry:

> As individuals we may not approve of all the implications of the mature industrial society. But an argument against industrialization in general is now futile, for the world has firmly set its face toward the industrial society, and there is no turning back... In the modern world, the new spreading culture is an industrial one, and the future into which the laboring masses are going is much more determinative of what

---

1) See p. 168.
2) Cf. Lambert, R.D., op. cit., p. 5; Myrdal, G., op. cit., p. 61; Giesecke, H., Betrachtungen zum Entwicklungsbeitrag überseeischer Privatinvestitionen, in Wirtschaftsdienst, 1963:1, p. 13.

happens than the past from which they are drawn. <u>They must and will</u>
<u>conform to the logic of industrialization.</u>[1]

The National Commission on Labour of 1969 is of the definite opinion that a
process of "industrial culturization" of the Indian working class has set in.[2]
This means that eating habits in large industrial centres have become more
cosmopolitan, partly as a consequence of the existence of subsidized industrial canteens. Styles of dress have also changed: the Indian worker nowadays prefers trousers and pyjamas to his traditional dress. Footwear has
become a necessity.

It is very difficult to form an opinion as to what changes, if any, in these
and other, more subtle matters have been brought about by the Swedish
companies. Foreign industries in general are part of a much larger complex of foreign influences, working through the press, cinema films and
personal contacts.

But it seems that the Swedish companies have to some extent increased
the discipline and the productive habits of their work forces. Turnover and
absenteeism are relatively low. Labour-management relations are
kept peaceful by the positive attitude of the management to trade unions.
Intra-factory mobility is encouraged and the management´s attitude to internal promotion is positive. Progressive personnel policies instil rational attitudes and responsibility.

A marked change in dress has been noticed also in the Swedish companies.
Most of the Swedish firms force their employees to wear western-style
shirts and trousers at work, as these are more practical than the traditional <u>dhoti</u>. The western dress habits are said to be adopted by workers
also in their spare time. Besides dress, a general influence in a western
direction is felt in the Swedish companies, but Indian observers in the
companies consider that these small changes emanate more from the ubi-
quitous Indian films with westernized actors than from contact with the
Swedish companies.

Traditionally, the businessman has had a low status in Indian society.
With the economic success of Indian industrialists, the situation has
changed - in the opinion of the Monopolies Commission for the worse:
"Inevitably, the position and glamour of these very rich persons has also
seriously undermined social values in the country. Culture and education,
scientific pursuits and research are for many young men at a discount,

---

1) Kerr, C. et al., <u>Industrialism and Industrial Man</u>, London 1962, pp.
   19 and 174. My italics.
2) India. National Commission on Labour, New Delhi 1969, p. 32.

compared to a career that is likely to help to climb the dizzy tops of business success."[1] In India, everything "foreign" is in vogue, and posts in foreign companies are preferred to jobs in Indian companies. The presence of foreign business helps to give a business career in general a higher status, and people with jobs in foreign companies seem to have the highest status of them all.

By necessity, the foreign companies, including the Swedish firms, have to use English as their working language to a larger extent than in Indian companies. English is thus favoured at the expense of indigenous languages. This is a positive feature, in the sense that international and intra-Indian communication is facilitated. But at the same time healthy nationalism and mass mobilization are rendered more difficult. English is spoken by only 1 per cent of the population and can never become a truly national language.[2]

The staff positions in foreign companies are exclusively reserved for English-speaking persons, which perpetuates the privileges of the small English-speaking class. The Indian nationals in foreign companies usually constitute a "distinct and often conspicuous group in their own society", a superior upper class with high education, high salaries and high status.[3] Foreign firms may thus create new social barriers, of which there are already too many in Indian society.

Fundamental cultural values

"The industrial order" may thus bring superficial changes in customs and habits, but it is also possible that after some time the more fundamental values of the society and its members will be affected. The "fundamental values" are things like basic understanding and outlook, beliefs, ethics, individual goals, moral issues, basic social habits, psychological inclinations and cultural heritage. Are basic Asian values and Indian attitudes transformed into western attitudes? What is the result of this transformation? What role does foreign investment play in such a transformation?

Gunnar Myrdal has delivered a pervasive critique of the concept of "Asian values", which makes one sceptical as to the alleged basis for the cultural transformation.[4] I shall illustrate the issue with an example of a

---

1) India. Monopolies Inquiry Commission, Report, Delhi 1965, p. 136.
2) Myrdal, G., op. cit., p. 259.
3) Harbison, F. and Myers, C.A., op. cit., p. 381. Cf. Kidron, M., op. cit., p. 295, and Lambert, R.D., op. cit., p. 148.
4) Myrdal, G., op. cit., pp. 93 ff.

typical western value, materialism, defined as a desire to have money and to buy and consume non-necessities.[1] The western influence is said to be detrimental to India, because it gives a "materialistic twist to Indian thought and has introduced a worship of wealth".[2] Spiritual India is degenerating into a materalistic, solely consumption-oriented society. Myrdal retorts: "Against the claim that people in Asia are peculiarly spiritual and non-materialistic must be placed the common observation of a propensity for narrow materialism in all social strata."[3]

We have seen that wages are considered by Indian workers to be more important than other aspects of work.[4] It is gradually being agreed that most people farmers included, respond positively to economic incentives.[5] Fatalism melts away when money is in sight.[6] The National Commission on Labour is of the opinion that workers want to earn more money to be able to buy non-necessary consumer goods, while others contend that a conspicuous consumption society is not yet in the offing in India.[7]

The picture in the Swedish companies is indeterminate. Many Indians in the Swedish firms maintain that the employees are gradually becoming more materialistic, in the sense that they want to buy radios and bicycles and that they are now ready to work longer hours, even overtime, to get such goods. How much of this alleged increased materialism is attributab' to the influence of the Swedish companies is impossible to say.

Another cultural trait allegedly introduced by industrialization is individualism. Economic change breaks up the old social harmony and joint

---

1) "Non-necessities" must, of course, be considered in the Indian context, in which a radio, for example, would be considered a non-necessity.
2) Griffiths, C.I.E., The British Impact on India, London 1952, p. 485.
3) Myrdal, G., op. cit., p. 97.
4) See p. 119.
5) Myrdal, G., op. cit., p. 441; Ohlin, G., Den ekonomiska teorin inför u-ländernas problem, in Ekonomisk politik i förvandling, Stockholm 1970, p. 202; Gårdlund, T., Främmande investeringar i u-land Stockholm 1968, p. 73.
6) Lambert, R.D., op. cit., p. vii.
7) "By and large, however, there were few signs of a conspiuous consumption society in the making. City as well as country people would for instance rather invest a year's additional income in land, cattle, industry than spend it on jewellery, cars or radios" (Bopegamage, A. and Veeraraghavan, P.V., op. cit., p. 205. Cf. India. National Commission on Labour, op. cit., p. 35).

families are replaced by nuclear families and individual wage earners.[1]
The greater the opportunity for profit, the weaker seem the ties of extended kinship.[2] The National Commission on Labour of 1969 finds a trend
from joint to nuclear fimilies in urban areas, presumably because of the
protection offered to nuclear families by the social-security system.[3]
Lambert, on the other hand, finds no differences between industrial families and other Poona families.[4] In my material on the Swedish companies there is nothing that indicates a disintegration of the joint family
system.

A contempt for manual work may be regarded as a basic value in Indian
society:

> Throughout South Asia there is a traditional contempt for manual
> work, and the educated tend to regard education as the badge that
> relieves them of any obligation to soil their hands. In India, the
> Brahman prescriptions against plowing and various other types of
> manual work have, of course, helped to strengthen this prejudice...
> After a Western engineer obtains his degree and takes a steady job,
> he is prepared to use his hands and even get them soiled, if necessa-
> ry, but a South Asian engineer often prefers to stand beside his ma-
> chines when something goes wrong, and give orders to inferiors.[5]

One would certainly expect this value to be affected by industrialization —
the work situation forces engineers and others to undertake manual jobs.
This effect should perhaps more appropriately be considered as emanating from the "industrial order" treated in the foregoing paragraph. According to the National Commission on Labour, the old Brahman distaste for
manual work is gradually wearing off.[6] In the Swedish companies, an
increasing number of engineers are seen with soiled hands. This is appreciated by the workers and leads to more democratic working on the shop
floor. The somewhat improved status of manual work may in the long run
have effects on even more basic values like the "indifference towards the
empirical and the concrete" said to be found in India.[7]

---

1) Lewis, A., The Theory of Economic Growth, London 1955, p. 426;
   Lambert, R.D. op. cit., p. 147.
2) Linton, R., Cultural and personality factors affecting economic growth,
   quoted in Epstein, T.S., op. cit., p. 322.
3) India. National Commission on Labour, op. cit., p. 30.
4) Lambert, R.D., op. cit., pp. 39 ff.
5) Myrdal, G., op. cit., pp. 1646 and 1648.
6) India. National Commission on Labour, op. cit., p. 34.
7) Shils, E., The Intellectual between Tradition and Modernity: The
   Indian Situation, The Hague 1961, p. 27.

The industrialization of India is modelled on the western industrialization process. Many Indians fear that the acceptance of western industrial methods will imply also a wholesale acceptance of all the western patterns and values. Fundamental indigenous values and attitudes may be changed for the worse. But it seems likely that many western values are only accidentally associated with western economic growth.

India has to some extent to conform to the "logic of industrialization", but the industrial system is grafted on a stratum of indigenous culture. It is to some extent possible to assimilate western business behaviour without accepting all the cultural traits associated with it. "Abegglen´s study of the Japanese factory also shows that a pre-industrial social system may continue in the midst of a radically changed technological system and the two may jointly produce one of the most developed economies of the world."[1]

The Swedish companies have generally tried to follow the old colonial policy of "not disturbing the natives". The specific "Indian" customs and values perceived have been left alone as much as possible, and the foreign personnel in the Swedish firms has tried to take part in the traditional culture, instead of pushing their own. There have been very few clashes between foreign and Indian employees, which may be a sign that cultural influences are minimized. It seems therefore that the Swedish companies do not have any noticeable effects in the realm of fundamental customs and values, outside the industrial order.

Politics

It may be argued that the possible political effects of foreign investment should not be taken into account in this type of study. We should perhaps restrict ourselves to the "economic", "social" and possibly the "cultural" effects. It may be true that the political effects are of a somewhat special character. But as I am trying an integrative approach here, I cannot see any reason to exclude any one category of effects. The relevant political objectives of the Indian Government are being vigorously publicized,are well diffused throughout Indian society, and are often deeply felt.

---

1) Sheth, N.R., The Social Framework of an Indian Factory, Bombay 1968, p. 179. Also Epstein believes in partial assimilation - money does not dissolve everything: "The answer seems to be that it dissolves what stands in its way, but nothing more" (Epstein, T.S., op. cit., p. x).

The political effects of foreign investment are mostly of a negative character. Theoretically at least, they can be weighed against the economic benefits. H.G.Johnson suggests that political "benefits", the absence of negative political effects, should be treated as a collective consumption good, for which a sacrifice of possible economic benefits could be made.[1]

The weighing of economic and political effects would be easy in a strictly socialist country, where, for political reasons, foreign private investment would not be allowed, even if it brought ample economic benefits. In "pseudo-socialist" countries like India, the weighing is more difficult, but the Indian Government should in principle allow foreign private investment when the net economic and other benefits are larger than the negative political effects. The trouble in India is that the Government does not always have enough reliable information on the different aspects of prospective foreign investments to take correct decisions.

One type of political effect of foreign investment may be said to influence negatively the "economic independence" of a recipient country. "No country wants to see its basic industries controlled by foreigners - even by efficient and friendly foreigners."[2] Some countries allow certain types of foreign investment but want to reserve ownership and control of basic industries, for example, for their own nationals, often with the argument that foreign control of important industries restricts the scope and effect of national economic policies. The monopolization of entire sectors by foreigners may also be feared.[3]

Apart from the fact that foreign investment may not be wanted in certain sectors, it may be considered to have negative effects as such because the presence of foreign investment may affect important objectives like national independence and prestige.[4] This is best illustrated again by

---

1) Johnson, H.G., The efficiency and welfare implications of the international corporation, in Kindleberger, C.P. (ed.), The International Corporation, Cambridge 1970, p. 49.
2) Model, L., The politics of private foreign investment, in Foreign Affairs, July 1967, pp. 644-45.
3) "Among the social costs should also be included the social strain and dissatisfaction arising from the continued stay of foreign ownership and monopoly control in certain sectors of the economy" (Subrahmanian, K.K., op. cit., p. 144). Cf. Little, I.M.D. and Mirrlees, J.A., op. cit., p. 46; Lewis, A.W., Report on industrialization and the Gold Coast, reprinted in Meier, G.M., Leading Issues in Economic Development, Stanford 1970, p. 310.
4) Little, I.M.D. and Mirrlees, J.A., op. cit., pp. 47-48; Rosen, G., op. cit., p. 10.

the extreme case of strictly socialist economies, where political dogma would be enough to keep a foreign investment out. But capitalist countries may also have too much foreign investment: "A workable capitalist system is one which is made up of local capitalists, not foreign capitalists and local workers". [1] This type of negative political effects may be based on xenophobic attitudes, but they are none the less a reality in a number of underdeveloped countries and to some extent also in developed countries like Canada and France.[2] The two types of political effects described so far are not very distinct categories, and they are not always separated:

> In terms of the broader economic and social objectives in India, it is fairly obvious that the larger the share of foreign firms in the total capital invested in the business sector in India, the greater is the cost to the economy. Foreign control over business activity in India and concentration of power in the hands of foreigners have an adverse impact on India's economic independence. [3]

It is also possible that foreign investment may have political effects in the form of more or less direct influences on actual policy-making in favour of individual foreign companies or the foreign sector as a whole. Such influence can be made effective through financial donations, through bribery or simply through personal contacts. The interests of foreign enterprise may be backed up by the home governments or aid agencies, sometimes quite openly: "The United States Government is prepared to intercede on behalf of American firms and make strong representations to host governments in cases of economically unjustified expropriations or harassment." [4]

Foreign investment can also influence other policies than those concerned only with the foreign sector. Foreign enterprises often co-operate with and strengthen the position of large-scale local business interests, and in countries like India, where a weakening of the large-scale business sector is a declared national objective, this may be said to constitute a negative political effect. Also positive political effects are, of course, conceivable, and it should be emphasized that it is sometimes difficult to differentiate the political effects from other types of effects.

---

1) Pazos, F., The role of international movements of private capital in promoting development, quoted in Alejandro, C.F.D., op. cit., p. 330.
2) Södersten, B., op. cit., pp. 442-43.
3) Kurian, K.M., op. cit., p. 248.
4) Rusk, D., Trade, investment and United States foreign policy, in Department of State Bulletin, November 5, 1962, quoted in Bernstein, M.D., Foreign Investment in Latin America, New York 1968, p. 183.

Big business

In India, foreign investments are found in several strategic industrial sectors. But basic industries, like the steel plants, are under national control, and India has a relatively well-diversified industrial structure, in which there is little scope for such total domination by large multinational companies of individual industrial sectors as is found in some smaller underdeveloped countries. But the foreign sector in India is in the aggregate relatively large. More than one-third of the industrial output is controlled by foreigners, which is considered to be a large proportion by the Indian Government and by all political parties in India.[1)] Every addition to the foreign sector has therefore, from the Indian point of view, a marginally relatively high "political cost".

Foreign investments in India, with or without the support of the respective home governments, apparently have some influence on the policies toward foreign enterprise, and their activities may also have some effect on the Government's policies towards the large-scale business sector. I shall start here with a discussion of the political ramifications of the large-scale private-business sector in India.

The impression conveyed by the Five-year Plans is that India is a planned economy striving towards a "socialistic pattern of society", with a large public sector and a complementary private sector. In reality, it is "one of the world's least controlled or 'planned' economies", and it is overwhelmingly a free private-enterprise economy.[2)] The private sector has encroached on the industrial fields reserved for state-owned companies, and a few big industrial houses control a large part of the economy.

Reading Indian newspapers, one would perhaps think that Parliamentary politicians lead a life of their own, without contact with other groups in society. But all tours, detours and defections have to be financed, and finance is concentrated in the hands of big business. "In the background are powerful big-business interests, who provide the necessary funds for political activity."[3)] Official business donations to political parties have recently been abolished, but these constituted only a minor part of the total contributions.[4)]

---

1) Cf. p. 51.
2) See p. 42. Cf. Kidron, M. op. cit., p. 314; Myrdal, G. , op. cit., p. 902.
3) Myrdal, G., op. cit., p. 768.
4) The official business donations to the Congress Party during a span of four years were only a quarter of what is spent by the Party in a general election. "It follows that funds have to be obtained by individual candidates and that donations in a systematic or unsystematic manner have to be accepted from interested parties." (Namjoshi, M.V., op. cit., p. 85).

Most of the election money from the business world goes directly to individual candidates or, informally, to local political organizations. On the national party level, the Congress Party has received most of the official contributions. No statistics on local donations exist, partly because there is officially quite a low limit on the maximum election expenditure by individual candidates. Following the pattern of contributions, the political influence of businessmen is proportionately larger at the local level than at the national level, where political leaders sometimes show a considerable degree of independence.

As in the western countries, Parliament in India is not the only or perhaps not even the main centre of political authority. The business world exercises its most pervasive political influence not through party donations but in more indirect and subtle ways:

The problem of relationship between the private industrialists and the political parties certainly exists, but in my opinion, this is not the sole or even the main reason for the influence which big business has on the affairs of the State. Concentrated economic power involves control of large resources, and also of large areas of production and of the economy as a whole. Those who have this control are in a position to influence the economic policy in a large measure, irrespective entirely of their relationship with political parties, whether in opposition or in power, or even their relationship with individuals in authority... The economic decisions of Govt. do not exist in isolation. They are taken in a certain context, in response to the decisions and attitudes of the persons engaged in economic activities, and must, therefore, necessarily be influenced by the latter. There is still another factor which gives rise to this influence, and that is the ability of big business to influence public opinion through their predominance in the press. In a democratic society Government must necessary be responsive to public opinion. To the extent, therefore, that articulate public opinion can be influenced by big business, they can also influence the decisions of Government. [1]

The economic power of big business has continuously increased and thereby also the possibilities of indirect influence. Contrary to the original in-

---

1) India. Monopolies Inquiry Commission, Report (Note of dissent by R. C. Dutt), Delhi 1965, pp. 193-94.

tention, the planned economy has been a "potent factor for further concentration". [1] The large, established manufacturers are greatly favoured in the race for industrial licences, import licences, government credit and tax concessions. [2] Until recently, big business also controlled most of the large banks which were used as channels for economic and political influence. The nationalization of the banks does not seem to have materially changed the situation. [3]

The connections between big business and the press were examined by the Monopolies Inquiry Commission to assess the truth of the allegation that "the press has an unhealthy influence on society, inasmuch as it obstructs the free formation of public opinion and moulds people's minds in a manner unduly favourable to the selfish interests of businessmen".)

Most important newspapers are owned by business families like the Birlas, the Jains and the Goenkas. [5] A few of these newspapers, notably the Times of India, have shown some degree of editorial independence, but the general picture is that the press is under the control of big business.

We have read many of the issues of the daily and weekly press which is within the control of these businessmen and we are inclined to think that in spite of the so-called "editorial independence", these newspapers or financial journals do tend to prejudice the reader in favour of businessmen in general, and big business in particular. [6]

Most big companies have "industrial embassies" in New Delhi with a sizeable staff employed full-time in circulating papers and persuading Government servants to favour their company. [7] Corruption is, of course,

---

1) Ibid., p. 6. Cf. p. 45 and Myrdal, G., op. cit., p. 930.
2) India. Industrial Licensing Policy Inquiry Committee, Report, Delhi 1969, pp. 56, 74, 180.
3) The restrictions on the largest business houses introduced in 1970 may have effects on their future growth but even this is far from certain.
4) India. Monopolies Inquiry Commission, op. cit., p. 186.
5) Ibid., pp. 186-87; Cf. Namjoshi, M.V., op. cit.,.p. 85.
6) India. Monopolies Inquiry Commission, op. cit., p. 187.
7) "It is well known that many of the Larger Industrial Houses maintain liaison officers in Delhi, where licensing decisions are taken. These persons try to maintain contact at business and social levels with senior persons in Government and seek to influence the exercise of discretionary powers in their favour" (India. Industrial Licensing Policy Inquiry Committee, Report, Delhi 1969, p. 63.).

rampant.[1]   But also more subtle influences are at work. India is ruled by a "select group of upper-class citizens who use their political power to secure their privileged position".[2]   This new raj mostly has the same background and common interests as the representatives of big business. The type of amalgamation between business and Government prevalent in countries like the United States is to some extent found also in India.[3]

Big business in India thus has decisive economic and political power. It finances party politics, dominates business organizations, controls the press and has intimate relations with the ruling class. Still, we should not forget that there are some public men and Government officials who are truly independent. They try to implement the Directive Principles in the Constitution that say that there should be no concentration of wealth and economic power. They also try to implement the official policy of intro- ducing a "socialistic pattern of society". The intention behind the Mono- polies Commission, the new industrial licensing policy and the nationaliza- tion of banks is to break the economic and political power of big business for the benefit of the medium- and small-scale industrial sector, and al- so to strengthen the public sector at the expense of the private sector.

Foreign capital. A natural outcome of the economic forces prevailing in India is that big business has easier access to foreign collaboration than others. The licensing system and the distribution of collaboration appro- vals tend to favour financially strong and already reputable companies.[4] The big Indian business houses can often mobilize the foreign sector for their own benefit. The alleged interests of foreign investors and collabo- rators have been used to ensure tax concessions for large Indian compa- nies and to give big Indian industries a "toe-hold of extra-territoriality from which to confound the planners in every aspect of their work".[5]

---

1) Diwedy, S., and Bhargava, G.S., Political Corruption in India, passim; Segal, R., op. cit., p. 279; Myrdal, G., op. cit., Chapter 20.
2) Myrdal, G., op. cit., p. 766.
3) "We have thus arrived at the curious position that most officials who exercise large discretionary powers in relation to regulation of busi- ness might yet look on businessmen as potential employers or patrons of their sons and relatives and even of themselves" (Gadgil, D.R., Convocation Address at Nagpur University, 20 January 1962, quoted in Kidron, M., op. cit., p. 233).
4) India. Monopolies Inquiry Commission, op. cit., p. 7; Myrdal, G., op. cit., p. 930.
5) Kidron, M., op. cit., p. 315.

Foreign interests have also been used to propagate the cause of the private sector as a whole:

Since foreign investors prefer to collaborate with private industry... the government is influenced by the desirability of foreign investments to favor the private sector more than it otherwise would. The same influence is exerted by the biggest providers of foreign grants and credits - the United States and the World Bank, which has been very much of a United States agency, though it operates with considerable independence. Both regularly advise greater reliance on the private sector". [1]

Foreign capital has political influence in its own right, apart from its connections with big business. The Indian Government cannot control foreign companies in the same way as Indian companies. "While there are no direct political strings to private capital there are political limits to what you can do to it". [2]   Individual firms can be controlled by the Government, but private foreign capital as a whole enjoys a wide immunity. [3]

Quite often the interests of foreign companies in India are backed up by the respective governments and foreign aid agencies. In view of India´s heavy dependence on foreign assistance, the aid authorities have a considerable "leverage". With the present donor constellation, a generous attitude towards assistance to India is dependent upon a reasonably good "foreign investment climate", which gives the Indian Government little freedom in the formulation of its foreign investment policies. The "back-stopping" services from home governments and aid agencies are sometimes offered openly and bluntly, but mostly the support for foreign investment and the direct influence on policy of the foreign companies themselves are managed more adroitly.

Enough has been said in this chapter to sustain a view that foreign capital wields considerable influence with the Government... Documentation is naturally difficult. It is impossible, if anything approaching comprehensiveness is aimed at. Such interrelated developments as the growth of government, the absorption of many former ICS men - not all expatriates - into foreign firms, the centering of head offices or strong 'industrial embassies' in the capital, and the development of a Delhi 'cocktail-party round' embracing business, government, and foreign aid missions, are scarcely amenable to formal description.

---

1) Myrdal, G., op. cit., p. 824.
2) Desai, A.V., Potentialities of collaboration and their utilisation, in Hazari, R.K. (ed.), Foreign Collaboration, op. cit., p. 123.
3) Kidron, M., op. cit., p. 315.

And yet the channels embedded in them are almost certainly more im portant than many others which are more easily demonstrated. [1]

The Government and the companies

Government control. The large-scale private corporate sector in India, in cooperation with the foreign private capital, thus seems to have considerable political influence. But this is true only in the aggregate. Individual firms have to be very careful with the Government and are for all practical purposes at its mercy. "The fact is that no major and, indeed, few minor business decisions can be taken except with the prior permission of the administrative authorities or at the risk of subsequent government disapproval." [2]

The Constitution and different acts empower the Government to regulate production, prices and profits and it can also take over management and control of any company. Through legislation, the Government has **given** itself "powers of life and death" over industry. [3]) In practice, however, these powers are seldom used and up to 1966 only 12 industrial units had been taken over. There seems to be a consensus of opinion that these early take-overs were not "ideological" but were necessary to prevent mismanagement and shutdown. [4]

No companies with foreign equity participation have been taken over, but this does not mean that the Government leaves such companies alone. The are restricted by exactly the same controls as other companies in the private sector. When foreign companies have become too dominant in an industry, the Government has in some cases entered that industry itself or encouraged Indian companies to do so. "Finally, the constraints placed on foreign capital emerge quite clearly. Wherever it appears to exercise unchallenged control in an important industry, whether as a single firm (matches...), or as a group of firms acting in concert (oil...), the Government has attempted to curtail that power." [5]

The Swedish companies feel themselves to be in the hands of the Government. Every month they have to supply reports on production, personnel, progress in development of indigenous components and other facets of the

1) Ibid., p. 232.
2) Myrdal, G., op. cit., p. 921.
3) Kothari, M.L., Industrial Combinations, Allahabad 1967, p. 181.
4) Cf. p. 41; Kust, M.J., Foreign Enterprise in India, Supplement, Bombay, 1967, p. 34.
5) Kidron, M., op. cit., p. 223.

activities. All the time, different Government agencies require some information on labour questions, import licences or tax payments. This "coping with officialdom" takes a lot of time and personnel.

Hence, the Swedish companies are closely watched and no major decision is taken without Government sanction. Several Swedish companies produce essential goods or products for defence purposes, and they are therefore particularly closely watched, in the sense that ostentatiouns monopoly tendencies are prevented: "One can be sole producer of filing cabinets, but not of ball bearings, matches, dairy machinery or tungsten carbide." Several Swedish firms therefore try to diversify into industrial sectors which are less controlled. Vulcan-Laval, for example, is trying to leave the dairy-machinery sector and instead wants to sell minor components to breweries and other big industries, where Government "interference" is unlikely.

Political effects of the Swedish companies. The Swedish companies produce mostly priority industrial goods, but they do not dominate any basic industrial sectors. They do, of course, add to the aggregate of the total foreign sector, and as a marginal addition they have a relatively large negative political effect, because of the already very large size of the total foreign sector. [1]

The Swedish companies do not have any "Parliamentary" political influence, either directly or by giving donations to political parties. Several Swedish managers have a clause in their employment contracts saying that they are not to involve themselves or their company in politics. Requests for contributions to political parties are regularly turned down. All foreign companies in India seem to refrain from this type of political activity.

On the local government level, the Swedish companies seem to have some influence of an informal character. This is particularly true of the WIMCO factories, where over a long period personal contacts between Government officials and WIMCO officials have been built up. They meet socially, and the goodwill built up in this way is used when the company is in trouble. One WIMCO factory has created such good relations that a Marxist minister in the State has several times intervened personally·to resolve labour conflicts at the factory.

Foreign companies in India can voice their political views in business organizations and through them exercise political influence. This is relatively easy, because the Chambers of Commerce in India have traditionally

---

1) Cf. p. 183.

more power than the corresponding organizations in the west. All the Swedish companies are members of Chambers of Commerce and other business organizations, but they seem to be rather timid at the meetings and to a large extent they leave both the talking and the policy-making to Indian industrialists. The political influence of the Swedish companies through business organizations therefore only consists of passive support for the large-scale private industrial sector.

In several developed countries the banks have played an important role as coordinators of business activities and political influences. In India, before nationalization, most banks were owned and controlled by various big business houses and were subservient to them. They were therefore more instruments of policy than policy-makers.

The foreign banks, which are still not nationalized, are of some importance as co-ordinators of foreign business interests as a whole. British companies use British banks "come what may", and all foreign firms have at least one foreign bank affiliation. The Swedish companies are in this respect more "Indianized" than the average: WIMCO has traditionally Indian bank connections, and SKF's main bank is the Bank of India, formerly owned by Tata, an important shareholder in SKF.

On the national level, a few big Indian business houses have had considerable direct influence. Birla, who supported financially the Congress-led nationalist movement, had for some time much influence with the Congress Government, but in view of his aggressive and corrupting behaviour and the recent radicalization of the ruling Congress Party, his star is now waning. Other business houses exercise varying degrees of influence.

But foreign companies do not as individual firms have any perceptible direct influence on the national level. This is so because, even if a foreign company is big (WIMCO is number 31 on a list of the biggest companies in India) it is still much smaller than the medium-sized Indian business houses that control a number of individual companies. The head of a business house is also the owner, while foreign companies, including the Swedish firms, are mostly run by professional foreign managers. The managers of foreign firms spend a relatively short time in India, and they usually do not have any political contacts, while the head of a business house is an Indian national with a network of relatives and contacts through which he can work politically.

All the Swedish companies have special representatives in Delhi, which is considered very necessary.

There is so much to be done on so many levels, from obtaining licen-

ses and favourable interpretations of regulations and procedures in
New Delhi, to expediting goods through congested ports and getting
hold of a couple of railway wagons, that easy access to Governmental
authority is itself an important "factor of production". All foreign
firms require this factor. [1]

The Swedish companies often have several people, usually employees of
the sales office in Delhi, who are specially assigned to encourage the
movement of papers in Government offices, while a contact man of higher
status keeps in constant touch with higher Government officials, either
directly or through the medium of the "Delhi cocktail round".

The idea behind the special Delhi representations is, of course, that the
company in question shall get fair or preferential treatment. The high-
level contact men are employed to anticipate major policy changes and,
if possible, to change policies in a way favourable to the company. The
temptation to bribe is evident, especially when the conditions are such
that "officials require compensation, not to speed an application, but merely to desist from unduly delaying its progress". [2] According to Myrdal, the western companies can render a useful service to India by refrain-
ing from giving bribes:

> However, a Western company that tries to maintain higher standards
> finds itself up against the unfair competition of companies that resort
> to large-scale bribery. Here Western businessmen could contribute
> significantly to remedial action in the South Asian countries by adher-
> ing to the stricter practices they follow at home. This would consti-
> tute a very substantial "aid" to development. At the same time it
> would be to the advantage of Western business interests, for collecti-
> vely they have much to gain by stamping out unfair competition of
> this type. [3]

Many foreign companies do bribe; West German and Japanese firms are
said to be the worst. [4] The Swedish companies may have some petty
corruption in the rank and file, but it seems that they do not resort to bes-
towing illegal gratifications at the top level in Delhi. This means that the
Swedish companies have to go the "stony and cumbersome way" - the straight
approach and persistency have to replace the easy way out offered by corruption.

---

1) Kidron, M., op. cit., p. 26.
2) Segal, R., op. cit., p. 279.
3) Myrdal, G., op. cit., p. 958.
4) Ibid., p. 947.

Michael Kidron states of WIMCO that "together with Hindustan Lever, it became the paradigm 'imperialist investor' during the fifties", and there has been some talk of "Swedish match imperialism".[1]   Some of the new Swedish companies have been discussed in the Lok Sabha (the Parliament) in similar terms. In such cases, some theory of imperialism is invoked, according to which the Swedish investments are regarded as part of the total international capitalist system, in which Swedish companies in India work closely with diplomats and foreign aid people from Sweden and from other countries to further the cause of Swedish capital, as opposed to the true national interests of India.

It is natural that Swedish diplomats in India should try to further the interests of Swedish companies, and several honorary Swedish consuls around the country are, for obvious reasons, employees of Swedish companies. Swedish foreign aid was also in the 1960´s partly geared to Swedish business interests. To some extent there is therefore substance in the allegation of collusion between different Swedish interests, although the tie-up is not as close as is the case with U.S. or British interests.[2]   The Swedish interests are, in an unplanned way, also inter-linked with other foreign interests and with the Indian Government through the social contacts in Delhi already mentioned.

The political effects of the Swedish companies are not materially changed if alternative events are taken into account. It is assumed here that the investment of the Swedish firms to a large extent substitutes for Indian investment in the respective industries. Without the Swedish companies, the political effects related to the size and influence of the foreign sector would therefore not have materialized. Further, the Indian companies that the Swedish firms have replaced would probably have belonged to the large-scale business sector. and most of the resources "freed" by the Swedish investments are therefore also likely to be used to further the cause of big business. The support for the large-scale Indian business sector from the Swedish companies could therefore also be regarded as a net addition of a negative political influence.

Summary. The Indian Government is responsible for almost all organized training and education of workers in India. The Swedish companies follow the statutory obligations to have a certain number of apprentices. On the whole, workers and staff in the Swedish firms are given as little training as in average Indian firms. WIMCO has over the years been slow in substituting Indian for foreign personnel.

---

1) Kidron, M., op. cit., p. 215; Das Gupta, S.C., op. cit., p. 175.
2) Hazari, R.K., interview, 23 January 1969.

The Swedish firms get practically all the know-how they want from their parent companies, but all research activities are located outside India. The manufacturing technology of the Swedish companies was not new to India at the time of investment, but it is actively spread by the new Swedish firms through their sales activities. The Swedish companies seem to have more efficient and modern management methods and personnel policies than the average Indian firm, but the diffusion of management know-how to other parties is probably insignificant.

In itself, religion in India is probably not of much social importance, as compared with the caste system. The extreme caste categories are stratified also in the Swedish factories, but the Swedish firms, together with other industries, seem to be helping to weaken the caste system.

Although the Swedish companies have relatively low absenteeism rates, the employees do not seem to be fully committed to the industrial system. But the "industrial order" has probably brought at least superficial changes in customs and habits. More fundamental values seem unaffected. The general process of westernization, for good or ill, is more likely to be caused by extraneous influences like films than by the activities of Swedish and other foreign firms.

The political effects of foreign investment are usually of a negative character. The Swedish companies add to an already large stock of foreign capital in India, and, together with other foreign interests, they can influence official policies in favour of foreign investments. Foreign capital in India is also sometimes used by the Indian large-scale business sector as a political lever against the Government.

Chapter 7.

CAPITAL INFLOWS AND FOREIGN TRADE

In the last chapter, and to a large extent also in the previous chapters, I dealt with the indirect effects of the Swedish investments. Starting with physical external economies and diseconomies, I discussed the "external economies in a narrow sense", which are mainly identical with industrial linkages, and quite a number of "external economies in a wider sense" in relation to employment, welfare, labour-management relations, skill formation and culture.

I shall now turn to the more traditional "economic" effects. An obvious benefit of foreign industrial investment is increased production. The forei§ investor provides savings and thus makes additional investment possible. But we should remember here that the indirect impact, the "external economies in a wider sense", of foreign investments are in all probability mo re important for long-term growth than the effects of pure savings and pro duction. The obsession with savings, investment and capital-output models found in some quarters may even have negative consequences, in the sense that it may "deflect attention from crucial relationships". [1]

With these reservations in mind, the savings and production effects of the Swedish companies will be treated in the next two chapters. Special attention will be given to the balance-of-payments effects. The main economic cost of foreign investment is the foreign-exchange drain through dividend remittances. The original inflow of foreign exchange is sooner or later outweighed by outflows of dividends and other payments. I shall start this chapter with a discussion of the inflows and after that I will deal with the foreign-trade aspects of the Swedish companies. Exports and imports are, of course, of great interest from the point of view of the balance of payments.

Foreign Capital Inflows

An inflow of foreign capital can be treated in two ways, as an addition to

---

1. Myrdal, G., op. cit., p. 2007.

savings or as an increase in the supply of foreign exchange:

> ... an inflow of private capital contributes to the recipient country´s
> development program in two general ways - by helping to reduce the
> shortage of domestic savings and by increasing the supply of foreign
> exchange. To this extent, the receipt of private foreign investment
> permits a more rapid expansion in real income, eases the shortage
> of foreign exchange, and removes the necessity of resorting to a drive
> toward self-sufficiency and the deliberate stimulation of import sub-
> stitution industries out of deference to foreign exchange considerations.[1]

In traditional growth theory. the inadequacy of savings is recognized as
the primary obstacle to economic growth.[2] The need for foreign capital
has consequently been estimated on the basis of calculations of a "savings
gap" that needs to be filled, and different assessments of the "absorptive
capacity" of various underdeveloped economies have been made. But at
present it is realized that in many countries there are other factors than
physical capital that are of primary importance for development - the
bottlenecks are often found in other fields. Institutions and attitudes are
sometimes of the greatest interest, and in many countries the supply of
foreign exchange is the limiting factor.[3]

India is a typical case of foreign-exchange shortage - the "foreign-exchange
constraint bites before the savings constraint".[4] The notion of a foreign-

---

1) Meier, G.M., The International Economics of Development, New
York 1968, p. 138.
2) Cf. the famous statement of A. Lewis: "The central problem in the
theory of economic growth is to understand the process by which
a community is converted from being a 5 per cent to a 12 per cent
saver - with all the changes in attitudes, in institutions and in techniques which accompany this conversion" (Lewis, A.W., The Theory
of Economic Growth, London 1955, pp. 225-26).
3) Incidentally, the stress on savings and capital inflows is not even
warranted by the available historical evidence: "If it is claimed that
the present underdeveloped countries need a substantial increase in
capital to bring about an economic take-off, making a large inflow
of capital from other countries necessary, their situation in this
respect would thus differ, and not coincide, with the actual conditions
in the present rich countries during their take-off" (Gårdlund, T.,
Främmande investeringar i u-land, Stockholm 1968, p. 20).
4) Little, I.M.D., and Clifford, M.J., International Aid, London 1965,
p. 144.

exchange gap as distinct from a savings gap assumes the existence of structural rigidities and limited substitution possibilities, and it can be criticized on a number of counts.[1] But there is full agreement that foreign exchange is a "primary bottleneck" to development in India, and the foreign-exchange aspect of external capital is therefore of main interest. "Its importance in bridging over the savings-investment gap in developing countries is only marginal, as compared to its role in easing the foreign-exchange constraint of growth..."[2]

Savings

Before dealing with the foreign-exchange aspects of foreign investment, I shall here briefly discuss foreign capital as savings. The primary inflow of capital, of external savings, is, of course, in itself an addition to the national product of the country. This effect is of a non-recurrent nature and insignificant as compared with the future flow of production and savings emanating from the foreign investment. But I am interested here in the primary inflow of savings; subsequent increments in savings will be treated in the chapter on profits.

The theoretical approach in India to the development problems of the country has followed the international trend. The first Five-year Plan stresses the savings approach: "...on capital formation, in the main, depends the rate of development of the economy".[3] But in the subsequent Plans the role of savings has been played down. In the Third Plan the associate concept of an overall capital/output ratio was dropped, and the Fourth Plan stresses social objectives, economic discipline, equitable distribution and efficiency.[4] Hence, savings are no longer considered to be the main bottleneck to development.

The contribution of the Swedish companies of savings in the form of fresh share capital is shown in Table 24. WIMCO (Swedish Match) invested Rs. 7 million in 1923, half of which was repatriated in 1938 when the company was forced by the Government to sell 50 per cent of its share capital to Indian investors. In 1925, Swedish Match provided 70 per cent of the share

---

1) Meier, G.M., The International ..., pp. 91 ff.
2) Subrahmanian, K.K., op. cit., p. 90; cf. Myrdal, G., op. cit., p. 919; Chenery, H.B., Foreign assistance and economic development, in Adler, J.H. (ed.), Capital Movements and Economic Development, New York 1967, pp. 270 and 275.
3) India. Planning Commission, First Five-year Plan, op. cit., p. 2.
4) Cf. Myrdal, G., op. cit., p. 1963.

capital for the Dhubri factory, which is formally constituted as a separate company, AMCO. AMCO is in this study treated as part of WIMCO.

Table 24. Inflow of foreign share capital to Swedish companies in the period 1923-68 (Rs. million).

	1923	1925	1930	1938	1960	1961	1962	1963	1964	1965	1966	1967	1968	Total
WIMCO	7.0	0.4		(-3.5)										7.4
Vulcan-Laval			0.2			0.7	0.2		1.5		1.6	2.4	0.4	7.0
Atlas Copco				0.2		0.5	0.6	0.2		0.1			0.2	1.8
Sandvik							2.4	1.2		0.9	1.5			6.0
SKF							1.5	11.3	5.3	2.3	0.8	2.5	1.7	25.4
SF						0.5	0.4	0.4						1.3
	7.0	0.4	0.2	(-3.5)	0.2	1.7	5.1	13.1	6.8	3.3	3.9	4.9	2.3	48.9

Sources. Stock Exchange Directory. Bombay: company statistics. The figures show actual inflows (for example, loans taken by Vulcan-Laval later converted into equity are shown as the amount of converted equity for the year the loan was taken). Bonus issues of shares are not included.

Vulcan-Laval was formed in 1965 as a result of a merger between an old trading company, Vulcan Trading. and an Alfa-Laval subsidiary in Poona, which explains the erratic inflows of capital for this company. The other new Swedish firms show a regular inflow during their respective starting periods, culminating, on an average, in 1963. The picture is dominated by SKF, which has invested a share capital of Rs. 25 million in its capital-intensive production outfit. The sales bias of SF and Atlas Copco shows in their relatively small initial capital investments.

Since 1968, inflows of fresh share capital have been and will probably continue to be insignificant. After the first lean years the new Swedish companies all show nice profits, and they will probably follow the WIMCO pattern of financing further expansions mainly out of created reserves. In 1969, the original inflow for WIMCO of Rs. 7.4 million constituted only 11 per cent of the accumulated net worth.

The Swedish companies have generally not financed their investments by external loans. Sandvik has obtained two long-term loans of together Rs. 1.6 million from its parent company. During the difficult reconstruction period Vulcan-Laval received substantial loans from Sweden, but at the instance of the Indian Government these were promptly converted into equity or paid back in cash. The other Swedish companies have not taken any foreign loans other than for minor imports of capital goods.

The Swedish companies have thus not resorted to financing through foreign loans, but this does not mean that the total capital employed has been mainly risk-bearing equity capital. WIMCO has a long tradition of internal financing, and SKF has supplied large quantities of equity capital, mostly in the form of machinery, but otherwise the Swedish companies have financed the larger part of their investments on the Indian capital market. The Indian laws are very liberal as concerns debt-financing, and companies are allowed to have as high a debt-equity ratio as 2:1.[1]

Only long-term debts bearing a fixed interest rate are included in the calculation of the ratio. Vulcan-Laval, Atlas Copco, Sandvik and SF all have at some time or other had a higher debt-equity ratio than the permitted maximum, especially in the early sixties,when control was not as strict as it has become since. Atlas Copco has all the time utilized the debt-financing facilities to the maximum. When one takes into account the fact that these Swedish companies, on top of their substantial long-term debt-financing on the Indian capital market, have also used extensively the short-term bank-loan facilities placed at their disposal, one really wonders if the investments should be called "Swedish" at all.[2]

The savings actually contributed by the Swedish companies are an addition to the supply of investible savings and they are used productively in industrial production. But at the same time it is probable that the Swedish companies substitute for Indian investment in the respective industries. The net addition of savings is therefore realized in the form of indigenous resources released by the Swedish investments.[3]

---

1) Swedish subsidiaries in other countries show an increasing tendency to finance their activities on the local capital markets (Lund, H., Svenska företags investeringar i utlandet, Stockholm 1967, pp. 78 and 80.

2) The high gearing ratios in the Swedish companies are not exceptional: "It is this ease in gaining loans (coupled with a reluctance to commit too much of their own resources) that explains the exceptionally high gearing ratios (between owned and owed capital) featured by foreign firms. They are high not merely in relation to their parent firm but even in the Indian context" (Kidron, M.,op. cit.,p. 231).

3) See pp. 260 ff.

Foreign ownership

All the Swedish companies are majority-owned.[1] The basic policy document concerning foreign ownership of industries is still the Prime Minister's statement of 1949, in which it is said that "... as a rule the major interest, ownership and effective control of an undertaking should be in Indian hands".[2] The "51 per cent rule" was relaxed after a time, first in practice and then also officially, but in the last few years policies have again become more restrictive. Foreign majority participation has usually been allowed in industrial sectors where specialized technology has been required, when the foreign-exchange cost of a project has been higher than 50 per cent of the proposed equity, and also when the company in question has agreed to export a substantial part of its production.

Foreign majority has thus been allowed in certain cases, but full foreign ownership has very seldom been permitted. In the 1960's the Indian Government aimed at a maximum foreign ownership of 60 per cent of the shares, and old collaborations would at the time of expansion also be brought down to this percentage. In 1956-64, out of a total of 270 new foreign financial collaborations, 211 had a foreign minority and 59 a majority. Of the majority companies, only 7 had full foreign ownership.[3]

Before Independence, most of the foreign companies in India were fully owned. Swedish companies in other countries usually have 100 per cent ownership, and it is safe to assume,that in the absence of an active Indian policy to the contrary, the Swedish companies in India would have been fully owned too.[4] WIMCO started out with 100 per cent foreign ownership, and Indian investors were admitted in 1938 only at the explicit request of the Indian Government.

---

1) That is, all the Swedish companies treated here, majority ownership being the criterion for selection. The other Swedish collaborations in India have little or no Swedish financial stake, except for a company in Madras, in which a substantial minority investment has been made by Facit for the production of office calculators.
2) A more detailed account of the policy towards foreign capital will be found in Chapter 2.
3) Reserve Bank of India, Foreign Collaboration in Indian Industry, Bombay 1968, pp. 14 and 41.
4) Lund, H.,op. cit., pp. 76 and 104; Sveriges Allmänna Exportförening, Svenska produktionsinvesteringar i Latinamerika, Stockholm 1970, p. 33.

The foreign ownership in the Swedish companies in 1969 is shown in Table 25. WIMCO has kept a few shares in addition to the 50 per cent to retain the majority. Vulcan-Laval, in which the foreign ownership was brought down in 1969 from 99 to 75 per cent, was created as a result of a merger between Vulcan Trading, a 100 per cent trading subsidiary of WIMCO-Swedish Match, and Alfa-Laval(India), a 99 per cent subsidiary. Vulcan Trading had 100 per cent foreign ownership, because it started long before Independence. But why Alfa-Laval(India) was allowed as much as 99 per cent is hard to understand. All its main competitors were already in production at the time of the investment, the foreign-exchange component was small, and no exports were envisaged.

Table 25. Foreign ownership of Swedish companies in 1969

	Foreign ownership as percentage of total share capital
WIMCO	50 +
Vulcan-Laval	75
Atlas Copco	100
Sandvik	60
SKF	60
SF	60

Sources. Company statistics.

The same reasoning applies to Atlas Copco, which has kept its initial full ownership for a long time. The only reasons offered for the low or non-existent initial local participation in Atlas Copco and Alfa-Laval(India) are that the Swedish companies were tough negotiators and that the administrative interpretation of the official policy was at the time very liberal. Vulcan-Laval had to sell 25 per cent of its share capital to the Indian public, as a condition of further expansion. The Government has put the same type of pressure on Atlas Copco, but this company dodged the pressure throughout the 1960´s first by interpreting its licence rules very liberally and then by offering to export a large part of its production.

Sandvik, SKF and SF all have a 60 per cent foreign majority. Sandvik probably got it because it was offered it, while SKF insisted on it and also pointed to the fact that the required foreign machines would cost the equivalent of 60 per cent of the proposed share capital. SF was a small company with new technology. The 60 per cent has not been a magic figure (except perhaps to the Indian Government). The Swedish companies would have liked more and might have been content with less, but it is improbable that many of them would have relinquished the absolute majority.

When a majority foreign ownership is approved, the Indian Government usually insists that, at the very least, half the Indian participation shall be made available to the public.[1] The rationale behind this is the desire that ownership and wealth shall be in as many hands as possible - foreign companies should not exclusively benefit Indian capitalists and thereby increase the concentration of wealth. This is also, on another level, the basic reason for the demand for local participation as such - profits accruing from a foreign project should, at least to some extent, be shared by the inhabitants of the host country.

The number of Indian shareholders in the Swedish companies in 1968 is shown in Table 26. WIMCO, Sandvik and SKF are quoted on the Stock Exchange in Bombay, on which Vulcan-Laval was also introduced in 1969, when it sold 25 per cent of its share capital to the Indian public. Before that, Vulcan-Laval had only about 45 Indian shareholders, all prominent Indian capitalists. Incidentally, Vulcan-Laval's first attempt to go to the market in 1967, in the middle of a severe recession, failed, because it could not get any underwriters. In contrast to this, Sandvik's first share issue in 1962 was oversubscribed 40 times. The Swedish companies are in general very confident about their possibilities of getting local equity finance, if required.

Table 26. Number of Indian shareholders in the Swedish companies in 1968

	Number of Indian share-holders in 1968
WIMCO	4,050
Vulcan-Laval	45
Atlas Copco	0
Sandvik	2,158
SKF	13,832
SF	40-45

Sources. Stock Exchange Directory, Bombay; company statistics.

---

1) Kust, M.J., op. cit., p. 145.

WIMCO, Sandvik, SKF and now also Vulcan-Laval are quoted on the Stock
Exchange and have many Indian shareholders, but this does not mean that
their Indian ownership is evenly spread. With the exception of WIMCO, the
Swedish companies have reserved as many shares as they are allowed to by
the Government - usually up to half the Indian-owned capital - for Indian
capitalists. In SKF, half the Indian share is owned by one company, Tata,
one of the best-known Indian big-business houses. SF does not want its
shares to be introduced on the Stock Exchange at all and restricts all transfers of shares. Three-quarters of the Indian capital in SF are in the hands
of two rich families that have long-standing connections with Sweden. Atlas
Copco has, of course, no Indian shareholders at all.

Foreign-exchange inflow

The inflow of share capital shown in Table 24 (p. 199) is not only an inflow of
savings but also of foreign exchange. [1] In India, foreign exchange undoubtedly commands a premium - one million rupees in foreign exchange
is more worth than one million rupees in local currency. Just how much
more is a tricky question to answer, and I will discuss that problem later,
in the section on foreign-exchange outflows.

The inflow of foreign share capital as an addition to the supply of foreign
exchange may have a positive effect in that it "permits a more rapid expansion in real income, eases the shortage of foreign exchange, and re-
moves the necessity of resorting to a drive towards self-sufficiency and
the deliberate stimulation of import-substitution industries out of deference
to foreign-exchange conditions". [2] As we have seen, the Swedish com-

---

1) I do not include re-invested earnings in the foreign-exchange inflow,
   but they are included, as part of the gross profits, in the total benefits of the Swedish investments. Re-investments, as such, are very
   seldom repatriated. Their foreign-exchange effects are of an indirect
   nature; re-invested earnings enlarge the basis on which future profits
   are earned and then remitted as dividends. What is characteristic of
   foreign companies is not that they re-invest part of their profits - the
   Indian companies do this too - but that they bring foreign exchange at
   the time of investment and that they give rise later on to foreign-exchange outflows in the form of dividends. Cf. Wells, D.A., Economic
   analysis of attitudes of host countries toward direct private investment, in Mikesell, R.F. (ed.), U.S. Private and Government Investment Abroad, Eugene 1962, pp. 561-2.

2) Cf. p. 197.

panies appear to have financed their operations as much as possible in India and kept their own contribution to a minimum. [1]

But even the minimum amounts supplied by foreign investors do not always have the positive effects enumerated above if they are not supplied in cash. The general practice is to supply a large part of the foreign share capital in kind, in the form of plant and machinery. According to Kidron, only 24 per cent of the fresh foreign-capital inflow into India in the period 1948-61 was a true cash inflow. [2]

Investment in kind may, of course, also be very valuable, but it is not at flexible as a cash receipt. When an investment is made in kind, there may be a temptation to mark up prices. [3] There may also be a temptation to import "too much", more than the Indian Government would have allowed if the investment had been made in cash. The foreign investors may have an understandable inclination to import what they have, which is a relatively capital-intensive technology, and their wish to do so may be reinforced by other factors:

> ...the fact that the foreign investor normally has a direct interest in supplying equipment and know-how; is almost universally in charge of the technical operation of a joint venture; is often chary of imparting skills or development information; is very often ignorant about Indian conditions; and might wish to keep out equipment that can be copied easily - mean that the natural tendency to over-import techniques receives powerful reinforcement. [4]

Because of the severe foreign-exchange shortage, the Indian Government does not normally allocate free foreign-exchange resources to private companies for the import of capital goods. "For more than five years now, the policy of Government has been to allow the private sector to import capital goods only against credits, investments or similar facilities." [5] Cash imports being rare, it is difficult to judge whether "over-imports" have taken place. Most of the indigenous firms import their capital goods from their foreign collaborators, instead of buying them on the free mar-

---

1) In this they are in the same boat as other foreign firms: "Conforming to the almost universal reluctance to place risk capital in India, foreign operations are starved of convertible currencies..." (Kidron, M., o. cit., p. 309).
2) Kidron, M., op. cit., p. 310.
3) See p. 218.
4) Kidron, M., op. cit., p. 302; cf. Subrahmanian. K. K., op. cit. p. 95.
5) India. Planning Commission, Industrial Planning and Licensing Policy, Final Report, Delhi 1967, p. 23.

ket, which makes comparisons with foreign investments somewhat uninformative. But, on the whole, it seems that foreign investments do not have a larger import content in their investments than Indian firms.[1]

It is often suggested that underdeveloped countries should use second-hand equipment instead of the latest capital-intensive machines available. Second-hand equipment is cheaper and would permit smaller plants with more labour-intensive techniques. But in India it has happened that western collaborators have sold defective machines at high prices. The Government is therefore suspicious of second-hand equipment and demands to see photographs, quality certificates and other guarantees before second-hand imports are allowed.

Swedish companies. The cash proportion of the foreign share-capital inflow in the Swedish companies is shown in Table 27. The average cash proportion of 19 per cent is lower than the average for foreign companies (24 per cent). The only company that seems to have put in more than a notional amount of cash is WIMCO. Vulcan-Laval was flooded with machinery in the export interests of Alfa-Laval but has also bought many machines in India. Atlas Copco is fully foreign-owned and therefore in the beginning had to supply also some working capital from abroad, which explains the cash inflow. SF uses quite simple machines, which were mainly bought in India or in eastern Europe, and its entire share capital therefore had to be supplied in cash.

SKF is responsible for the major part of the total share-capital inflow of the Swedish companies, and all of SKF´s foreign capital was supplied in kind. To a limited extent, this was a case of excess imports. To safeguard against more difficult import policies in the future, SKF imported machinery in the beginning that were not put into production until 1969. Sandvik has also made some little use of this device, and in both cases it is stated to have been a profitable measure. But, on the whole, the capital-goods imports of the Swedish companies have not been excessive.

The guarded attitude of the Indian Government towards imports of second-hand equipment is reflected in a passage in the collaboration agreement between a Swedish subsidiary in India and its parent company: "The machinery and equipment to be supplied by [the parent company] shall be modern machinery and equipment of the same type as [the parent company] use in their own factories in Sweden and shall mostly be of [the parent company´ own design and construction." The new Swedish companies have mostly so new machines. SKF contemplated sending used equipment but did not, which

1) Ibid., pp. 46 and 47.

206

was afterwards looked upon as a wise decision, because in that way employment and the consequent risks of labour trouble have been minimized.[1]

Table 27. Cash proportion of foreign share-capital inflow in Swedish companies up to 1968

	Cash inflow (Rs. million)	Cash inflow as percentage of total share-capital inflow up to 1968
WIMCO	6.0	81
Vulcan-Laval	Not available	Not available
Atlas Copco	0.8	44
Sandvik	0	0
SKF	0	0
SF	1.3	100
	8.1	(19)

Sources. India. Tariff Board, Report ... Match industry, p. 33; company statistics. The figure for WIMCO is calculated as the total original flow, less the book value of plant and machinery in 1927. Inflows for Vulcan-Laval are not included in the calculation of the total proportion of cash inflow.

Nearly all the machines that WIMCO brought into India in the 1920's were second-hand. In some cases they had already served 35 years in Sweden before they came out. Many of these machines have since been rebuilt beyond recognition to facilitate larger production. But the basic process of manufacturing matches is essentially the same, and the machines are still there, which means that a substantial part of WIMCO's basic machinery is very old. WIMCO has also in late years imported second-hand reconditioned machines. As WIMCO is a majority-owned subsidiary, it can safely be assumed that the quality of the second-hand machines has been satisfactory. The prices may have been in some way artificial, but there is no information on this issue.

---

1) Cf. pp. 99 ff.

Exports

During the last decade, the export opportunities of the underdeveloped countries have been much discussed. With the realization that the main bottleneck to development is often the balance of payments, exports and import-substitution measures have grown in importance. But exports have generally remained sluggish and many countries have difficulties in meeting their foreign-exchange obligations. Some countries have tried to secure at least the foreign exchange needed for the servicing of private foreign investment, by requiring that new foreign companies shall provide for the transfer of their own dividend income. By such measures, foreign investment has been directed mainly to the traditional export sectors, where this condition can most easily be fulfilled. Such a policy is from a dynamic point of view unsatisfactory:

> The servicing of foreign investment in the long run is not a question of merely earmarking foreign capital for use in the production of existing export products but of overall monetary, fiscal and exchange policies. In a dynamic context of changing demand and technology at home and abroad, comparative cost situations change, new export lines develop, old ones are replaced, and invisible export earnings assume an increasing role. [1]

India has partly resorted to guiding foreign investments to the export sector. Foreign collaboration is generally not permitted in low-priority sectors, unless a major share of the production is allocated to exports. Likewise, foreigners are not allowed to take part in trading activities unless the investment is meant exclusively for exports. Foreign investments are permitted without any export obligation only in the case of the priority sectors.

Exports are usually the most difficult economic factor for a government to influence. Yet increasing exports are probably indispensable for self-substained growth; import substitution is apparently not enough to avoid long-term balance-of-payments difficulties. [2] The Indian Government has certainly tried hard to encourage exports. Exporters are offered tax concessions, refund of duties on materials used, cash assistance for the ex-

---

1) Islam, N., *Foreign Capital and Development: Japan, India and Canada*, Tokyo 1960, p. 243. Cf. Kindleberger, C.P., *American Business Abroad*, New Haven 1969, p. 170.
2) Chenery, H.B., *Foreign...*, p. 275.

port of non-traditional products, guaranteed replenishment of the import component of exports made, export credits and refinancing, and railway freight-rate concessions.

The Indian export policy is of the carrot-and-stick variety. A company exporting more than 10 per cent of its production in any one year is granted preferred sources of import supply, facilities for expansion and all the incentives enumerated above. On the other hand, the Government has selected some industries that have to export at least 5 per cent of their production, otherwise they will get less imports, country-tied import licences and no expansion facilities. The stick is often wielded in more informal ways:

> The Indian Government is as capable as any other of putting pressure on firms to export, and many firms have seen wisdom in doing so at a discount or at some other inconvenience to themselves, in order to obviate yet greater inconvenience from the Government, or to benefit from more generous treatment. [1]

As yet, the Government's encouragment of exports has not yielded any impressive results. Exports have risen but slowly, and in spite of the special incentives, the export of non-traditional goods did not show any major increase until the late 1960's. [2]

The foreign sector has traditionally been prominent in exports, and one-quarter of the total exports are still produced by foreign companies. But the main export products of the foreign sector are tea and jute manufactures, which show a declining trend. The total export share of foreign subsidiaries and branches is therefore declining. [3] The foreign companies played an important role in the early development of exports of tea and jute manufactures, but it has been questioned whether these exports should at present be regarded as a contribution uniquely associated with foreign capital and foreign technology. [4]

The Indian Government is primarily interested in developing non-traditional exports. Some headway in foreign markets has been made by light-engineering goods, like machine-tools, fans and sewing machines. But these products are mostly financed by Indian capital, and new foreign investments

---

1) Kidron, M., op. cit., p. 280.
2) India, Planning Commission, Fourth Five-year Plan, op. cit., p. 93; Commerce, Annual Number 1968, Bombay 1968, p. 281.
3) Subrahmanian, K.K., op. cit., p. 431.
4) Ibid., p. 431. Cf. Kumarasundaram, S., Foreign collaborations and Indian balance of payments, in Hazari, R.K.(ed.), op. cit., p. 210.

have contributed little to the non-traditional exports. "The impact of foreign collaboration has not been of any marked significance in strengthening our competitive ability in regard to exports."[1]

The exports of foreign branches have, relatively speaking, been most disappointing. Foreign subsidiaries have increased somewhat the ratio of exports of manufactured goods to the total production, despite the fact that most foreign subsidiaries are found in the import-competing sectors.[2] The Indian Government has shown particular interest in the export performances of foreign companies, which often have a world-wide sales network at their disposal and sometimes produce better-quality goods than their competitors, which should, in the Government's view, qualify them for relatively larger exports.

The exports of the Swedish companies are shown in Table 28. Quantitatively, they are not very significant. Percentage-wise, the low export performance of the Swedish firms is commensurate with that of other foreign subsidiaries, while purely Indian companies appear to have, on an average, somewhat higher exports.[3] One reason for this may be that the Swedish companies have been channelled into import-competing sectors more than average Indian firms. The domestic resources released by the Swedish investments may and may not have been used for export production, but it would in any case probably be a question of insignificant quantities.

WIMCO does not have much to offer on the export market, only some paper and matches of medium or low quality, and Vulcan-Laval only sells some bulky stainless-steel tanks etc. on nearby markets. Atlas Copco has had increasing difficulties in getting licences for expansion, because of its full ownership, and has therefore linked up with governmental trade agreements with other countries. Exports, mainly to Greece, of more than Rs. 10 million in 1969-70 automatically gave Atlas Copco the desired expansion licence, besides the usual export incentives. Sandvik sells tungsten powder to its parent company. SKF's exports are channelled through the extensive sales network of the SKF group and are better characterized as "getting rid of surpluses" than as genuine export efforts.

---

1) Mehta, G.L., Development and Foreign Collaboration, Indian Investment Centre Publication, Delhi 1968, p. 16. Cf. Kidron, M., op. cit., p. 311.
2) Reserve Bank of India, Foreign Collaboration in Indian Industry, Bombay 1968, p. 24.
3) Ibid., pp. 24, 73 and 127.

Table 28. Exports from Swedish companies in 1968

	Exports in 1968 (Rs. million)	Exports as percentage of total sales in 1968	
VIMCO	0.5	0	
Vulcan-Laval	0.1	0	
Atlas Copco	0.5	2	
Sandvik	2.2	8	2
SKF	0.2	1	
SF	0.0	0	
	3.0		

Sources. Company statistics.

Export restrictions

The primary reason for investment by foreign companies in India and in many other underdeveloped countries has been tightened import restrictions. Foreign companies start local production to substitute for former exports. The new subsidiaries are usually not given any special export orientation; the normal thing is to continue to supply third countries from the parent company.

The parent companies in many cases also have other reasons for keeping exports for themselves. There is sometimes a quality prejudice against goods from underdeveloped countries, costs are often lower in the parent company, export contacts are usually centred in the parent firm, export markets are mostly found in developed countries, and there may be pressures from the home government in the direction of increased exports from the parent company.

To ensure that exports are reserved for the parent company, many concerns issue export restrictions in the form of the outright prohibition of exports from subsidiaries or permission to export only to certain countries. Presumably, such export clauses are more common in purely technical collaborations than in the case of majority-owned subsidiaries. This is anyway the case in India, where, out of a total of 224 subsidiaries, only three had export clauses with outright prohibition of exports. This does not mean that exports are allowed in the other 221 subsidiaries; it is just that there are normally few formal restrictions on majority-owned companies. "Thus, once again, as in the case of tie-in clauses, parent-subsidiary relations on restrictive features operated more at the level of tacit understanding rather than the written word."[1] The Indian Government has become more strict on export clauses during the past few years.

The Swedish companies are all majority-owned subsidiaries. The only company with explicit export restrictions is SKF, which may export only to nine specified countries. These nine countries are those in which Indian exports in general can be expected to be in good demand. They include Ceylon, Iran, Iraq and Singapore. Although the other Swedish companies do not have any formal export restrictions, no exports seem to take place without prior consultation with the respective parent companies, also with regard to prices.

The special emphasis on exports in the Indian Government's policy is well known to the Swedish parent companies, and they therefore tend to show their Indian subsidiaries special consideration in this matter. SF has explicitly been favoured in comparison with other SF companies, WIMCO sells its export paper mostly to other companies in the concern in Asia, and Sandvik's most important export customer is the main factory of the Sandvik group in Sweden. At the time this study was made, several Swedish companies were discussing with their headquarters arrangements of the IBM type, in which individual companies specialize in making a few components which are then exported to an assembly plant within the group.

Export prices. The main deterrent to exports from Indian companies is the high price level on the sheltered Indian market. In spite of low wage scales, the Indian prices are sometimes several times the world market price for identical products.[2] As shown in Table 29 the prices charged in 1968 by the Swedish companies on the Indian market were, on an average, about 50 per cent higher than the world market prices, and the general price level in India is possibly still higher.[3]

---

1) Reserve Bank of India, Foreign Collaboration..., p. 34.
   Bombay, 1968, p. 34.
2) The same conditions are found in Latin America. Cf. Sveriges allmänna exportförening, op. cit., pp. 36 and 46.
3) Myrdal, G., op. cit., p. 663; Baranson, J., Manufacturing Problems in India. The Cummins Diesel Experience, New York 1967, p. 82; Kumarasundaram, S., op. cit., p. 209.

Table 29. Prices on Indian market of products of Swedish companies in excess of world market price.

	Price on Indian market in excess of world market price (per cent)	
WIMCO	10	
Vulcan-Laval	150	
Atlas Copco	20	
Sandvik	15	46
SKF	50	
SF	30	

Sources. Company statistics. The average is unweighted and the figures are very rough estimates. They refer to the year 1968. The WIMCO figure refers to paper exports only.

The high prices prevailing in India can be explained in part by the fact that labour costs may be high, in spite of low wage scales.[1] Raw materials are also either produced at high cost in India or imported with heavy duties. But the most important cause of high costs and prices is probably the lack of ancillary facilities. Many goods and services, the supply of which is taken for granted in developed countries, do not exist in India. The Indian industrial market, being of the same economic size as the Danish market, is so small that many goods considered standard in developed countries have to be specially ordered or produced by the company itself (importation is in most cases not a possible solution).

... the efficient modern industrial production is achieved through a network of supply relationships in which firms depend on a large number of other firms for steady supplies of components made to strict and reliable specifications. The final product can only be produced efficiently if all the inputs are produced efficiently. If the substructure of efficient supplying firms are lacking, and the enterprise is instead obliged to go into the business of producing parts itself or depend on unreliable and inefficient local parts producers, the cost of production can rise to incredible heights. This fact is extremely relevant to the explanation of costs and inefficiency of the industrial sector in India.[2]

---

1) See p. 126.
2) Baranson, J., op. cit., p. ix. Cf. Myrdal, G ., op. cit., p. 651; Meier, G., The International..., op. cit., p. 196.

The high costs in India are one important reason why the Swedish concerns would prefer to export only from the parent companies. In the absence of incentives and pressures to export, the Swedish companies in India would in all probability have supplied only the local Indian market. The fact that some exports are still made from the Swedish companies means that the Government's policies make such exports profitable one way or the other.

WIMCO's paper exports are stated to be as profitable as home sales, while the match exports show a nominal loss. But the match exports automatically result in the allocation of import licences, for which components for match production can be bought from outside, components which would be more expensive in India or sometimes impossible to obtain. The loss on match exports is in fact a premium paid for foreign exchange, ranging from 5 to 100 per cent.

In the case of Atlas Copco, exports have become a condition for survival. With full ownership retained, expansion has not been allowed, except when substantial exports have been made. Without expansion, profitability would be drastically reduced. Seen in this light, exports have been very profitable for Atlas Copco. For Sandvik, exports are said to be as profitable as home sales when the cash incentives and the less exacting marketing work is taken into account. For SKF, exports are primarily a means of getting rid of unsaleable surplus stocks.

Hence, in one way or the other, the exports actually made have been profitable for the Swedish companies. Some of them will in the future have to export more, for the simple reason that the Indian market is not growing fast enough. Comparable Indian companies are in the same situation as the Swedish firms, except for one special feature. The Government has hinted at the possibility that the big foreign companies in an industry should perhaps take care of the necessary exports and leave the home market to the Indian companies, who for quality and marketing reasons might not always have the same opportunities to export as the foreign firms. The Swedish companies dread such a situation, because it would probably mean lower profits. But they show a marginally better export performance than their present competitors, and they may therefore be more exposed to Government pressures.

Imports

Import control was introduced in India during the Second World War and has been in force since then. Up to 1958, India still had some reserves of foreign currency, built up during the war, and imports were regulated mainly by duties. Since the foreign-exchange crisis in 1957-58, import restrictions have been the main vehicle for protection. All "non-essential" imports are banned, and "essential" imports are also gradually being banned as soon as indigenous production comes into being.

The policy of rigid import control in India is more of a necessity than a free choice. Without it, foreign-exchange reserves would soon be depleted. Devaluation is not a real alternative, because of the existing rigidities.[1] The fact that no imports are allowed when indigenous production is deemed sufficient makes the Indian market very sheltered. "There could be no more effective protection of new industries."[2] Protection ensures high prices and profits on the local market and acts at the same time as a disincentive to exports.

Exports being sluggish, India cannot increase the supply of foreign exchange, except by rigid import control and active import substitution. Import substitution works in two ways. Companies in India can buy an increasing share of their raw materials and components from local Indian instead of from foreign suppliers and thereby save on imports. Also, new investments can take place in fields in which imports are large, substituting local production for former imports.

The latter type of import substitution (new investment) has been very much encouraged by the licensing policy of the Indian Government. Industrial licences in a new field have been issued until the proposed local production has exceeded the imports, and then licensing has been stopped. Companies without a licence for local manufacture were thereafter excluded from the Indian market, because, when the original licensees came into production, imports of the product in question were completely banned, giving total protection to existing producers.

Foreign companies have generally been channelled into import-substituting industries.[3] The production of the Swedish companies also substitutes for former imports. This is as true of matches in the early days as of the new products: ball-bearings, compressors and hard-metal tools. In so far as foreign exchange is more scarce in India than is shown by the official exchange rate, this import substitution has had positive effects, by expanding the foreign-exchange bottleneck.

It is difficult to estimate the actual import savings resulting from this kind of import substitution. The direct effect is limited to the actual im-

1) Myrdal, G., op. cit., p. 2081; Little, I. M. D. and Clifford, M. J., International Aid, London 1965, p. 144.
2) Kust, M. J., op. cit., p. 209.
3) Reserve Bank of India, Foreign Collaboration..., p. 23.

ports in existence when production in India started, but it may be more relevant to regard the whole present production of the industry in question as substituting for imports. At the same time it does not seem right to classify, for example, the whole of WIMCO´s production as a gain in import substitution. In a historical perspective, practically all industries substitute for imports.

A calculation of import savings must allow for the fact that the price level is much higher in India than on the world market. Expenditure on imported raw materials incurred by the company in question should also be deducted from total savings, and in the case of foreign investments one may take into account the fact that the local factories can in different ways promote exports from their respective parent companies. The calculation is further complicated by the existence of product substitutes. This fact, coupled with the rigorous import policy of the Indian Government, makes it probable, for example, that imports of ball-bearings would not be as large as the total present production in India if there were no local production.

It is also very difficult to distinguish the effects of the Swedish companies on import substitution from the total effects of the Indian and Swedish companies in the respective fields. SKF produces small quantities of precision bearings that other Indian bearing manufacturers do not have in their range, but, with this sole exception, the Swedish companies and their competitors produce exactly the same products. If the Indian manufacturers had brought about import substitution to the same extent as now without help from the Swedish companies, it is doubtful if any specific import-substitution effects could be ascribed to the Swedish companies. As will be further elaborated in Chapter 9, it is quite probable that the Indian companies would, in the absence of the Swedish companies, have brought about the import substitution themselves. The direct import-substitution effects of the Swedish firm are therefore likely to be cancelled out. The resources released by the Swedish investments may have been invested in import-substituting industries, but to what extent is not known.

Import content. The other form of import substitution mentioned here is when companies already working in India reduce their import content, i.e. when indigenous supplies of components and raw materials are substituted for imports, so that the proportion of imports to the total output of the company is reduced. The Indian Government actively encourages such import substitution, by demanding from new companies that they shall commit themselves at the time of investment to a phased program of reduction of the import content. The import-licensing system in itself also provides strong stimuli towards a reduction of the import content.

The import-licensing system is very bureaucratic. Foreign exchange from different sources, most of it from tied foreign-aid credits, is sifted through the Ministry of Industry and other bodies to the individual companies. Each import-licence application is very carefully scrutinized, and many companies have special representatives attending at the ministries with the sole aim of moving the applications from desk to desk. The bureaucratic discretionary system has favoured big companies. [1] Each import licence is de facto a subsidy to the company in question, in the sense that it can be sold for double its face value or more. [2]

The imports and the relative import contents in 1968 of the Swedish companies are shown in Table 30. WIMCO, SKF and Sandvik predominate quantitatively, because they have to import raw materials (potassium chloride, phosphorus, steel tubes and tungsten ore) which are not at present produced in India. The components going into the products of Atlas Copco and Vulcan-Laval are easier to replace indigenously.

Table 30. Import contents of the Swedish companies in 1968

	Imports in 1968 (Rs. million)	Imports in 1968 as percentage of total sales	
WIMCO	9.3	4	
Vulcan-Laval	1.7	13	
Atlas Copco	0.6	3	
Sandvik	6.2	24	13
SKF	6.3	25	
SF	0.0	0	
	14.8		

Sources. Company statistics. The few cases of capital-goods imports that occur are not included. The quantity figures denote in most cases import-licence allocations for 1968 and not actual imports. The figures for SKF are calculated from data on raw-material consumption.

Before the Second World War, WIMCO imported practically everything from Sweden, including such things as nails and bolts. Since the war, imports have been reduced, and the import content of WIMCO in 1968 was as

1) See p. 187.
2) Myrdal, G., op. cit., pp. 924 and 2084.

low as 4 per cent. The average import content of the new Swedish companies, 13 per cent, is in line with the average figure for all foreign collaborations.[1] The general trend in India is that the import content of indu
strial production is being progressively reduced, and also the Swedish co
panies have during the last few years substantially reduced their depende
on imported spare parts and components.

Sandvik and SKF will probably for a long time to come be dependent on im
ported raw materials, and they cannot therefore reduce their import contents much further. The other Swedish companies are also near their low
possible import contents. The Indian competitors of the Swedish firms
show more or less the same import dependence as the Swedish companies
which is to be expected. The import content of a company in India - becau
of the pressure from the Government to substitute for imports - is mainly
determined by objective technical requirements. This implies that one
critical argument against foreign investment, that it is a masked way of
forcing imports into a country, is not applicable in the case of the Swedis
companies in India.

The Swedish companies all belong to the 59 "priority industries" that shot
in principle receive imports according to their needs. But every batch of
imports still has to be fought for, intensively. Like other companies, the
Swedish firms have agreements with the Government on a gradual phasing
out of imports, and reports have to be sent every month on the progress
made in import reduction.

But the agreements are not followed to the letter. Instead, actual import-
licence allocations are decided in protracted negotiations between civil se
vants and the Swedish firms. To get the desired licences, the Swedish
companies have in some cases found it necessary to threaten to take away
the international trade-mark on their products, and one company once ha
serious thoughts of closing the factory and sending the workers to demonstrate outside the licensing office in Delhi.

Import prices. One argument against foreign investment is thus not applicable to the Swedish companies, namely, that imports are excessive. Also the original capital-goods imports, the investments in kind, have, on
the whole, been limited to needs.[2] In connection with the argument on
excessive imports, it is also sometimes alleged that foreign companies
send home part of their profits secretly by boosting the prices of imports

1) Reserve Bank of India, Foreign Collaboration..., pp. 23, 51 and 73.
   23, 51 and 73.
2) See p. 206.

218

from their parent companies. Such practices are not unknown in India, where foreign collaborators in the pharmaceutical field seem particularly keen to use this device.[1]

The average import content for the Swedish companies of 13 per cent does not give much scope for marking-up practices under the present conditions of Government control. All imports do not come from Sweden; according to Table 31, half the already relatively small imports come from the world market, where the Swedish companies naturally have to pay the ruling price. A formal deterrent to profit transfers through over-priced imports is that the Swedish tax laws do not allow any such tampering with prices.[2]

Table 31. Imports from Sweden to Swedish companies in India

	Imports from Sweden to Swedish companies as percentage of total imports	
WIMCO	5	
Vulcan-Laval	70	
Atlas Copco	85	
Sandvik	60	50
SKF	80	
SF	0	

Sources. Company statistics. The percentages are averages for the late 1960's. The figures include purchases from other companies in the respective concerns, not necessarily located in Sweden. The average figure of 50 per cent is an unweighted average.

Furthermore, the raw materials and components exported to the Swedish companies in India from Sweden are in several cases sold by separate companies within the respective groups, which try to keep prices as high as possible to all customers, in order to be able to show good profits. Most of the Swedish companies in India state that they buy their components at list prices. The original machinery supplied in kind was apparently also valued at list prices. In some cases there are special lists for group com-

1) Kidron, M., op. cit., pp. 266 and 300. Cf. Subrahmaniam, K.K., op. cit., p. 95.
2) Eisler, H., En saklig betraktelse, Uddevalla 1969, p. 325.

panies with lower prices than for outsiders, which means that, in buying from the group, the Swedish companies are subsidized - realizing a profit transfer in the "wrong" direction.

In the collaboration agreement between a Swedish company in India and its parent company, it was specified, at the instance of the Indian Government, that "the prices for raw materials and semi-finished products to be supplied by [the parent company] to [the Indian subsidiary] hereunder shall be in line with the world market prices therefore from time to time in force". The implementation of the agreement is closely watched by the Government. The Indian subsidiary in question used to have a long-term contract with its parent company for imports of an important raw material from Canada at a fixed price. At one time this price was higher than the spot rate for supplies from South Korea, and the Government then forced the Swedish subsidiary to cancel the fixed-price agreement in favour of Korean supplies. When the spot rate soon afterwards rose again, the company ended up buying at a much higher price than the original Canadian rate.

As regards the Swedish companies, I have only found two cases of over-pricing of imports. Raw-material imports to one company were for a few years priced somewhat higher than the world market rate. One Swedish company is charged a higher rate for components than other manufacturing firms within the group to compensate the parent firm for technical services not otherwise paid for. The exact amount of the concealed profit transfers to the respective parent companies is not known, but in both cases it seems to be a question of only small sums that do not really appear to be worth the trouble.

Summary. The "savings gap" is apparently not the most serious bottleneck in India. The Swedish companies, with the exception of SKF, have not contributed any substantial amounts of fresh capital. Instead, the greater part of the capital employed in the Swedish firms has been raised on the Indian capital market.

Foreign companies normally wish to have full ownership, but the Indian Government wants Indian majorities. Vulcan-Laval was at an early stage allowed 99 per cent and Atlas Copco 100 per cent foreign ownership, apparently without plausible reasons. Part of the Indian share capital in the Swedish companies has normally been reserved for prominent Indian capitalists. The greater part of the Swedish share capital has been supplied in kind.

The Indian Government has tried in many ways to stimulate exports. Exports from the Swedish companies have been insignificant. This is mainly due to the fact that the price level in India is high, but it is also relevant that the Swedish firms are found in import-competing sectors and that the parent companies normally want to reserve the export markets for themselves.

Import substitution has been one of the key policies of the Indian Government. The production of the Swedish companies, together with the production of their competitors, substitutes for former imports. Through the pressures of the import-licensing system, the Swedish firms have been forced to reduce the import content of their production. There is therefore little scope for excess imports, and over-pricing of imports in the Swedish companies is also not of any importance.

Chapter 8

PROFITS AND OUTFLOWS

After the more general discussion of the foreign-exchange and savings
aspects in the last chapter, I shall here concentrate on the measurable
economic benefits and costs of the Swedish companies. The main measurable benefit of foreign investment is the gross profit, and the outflow
of dividends is the main cost. The quantified benefits and costs will be
compared at the end of the chapter.

Profits and Benefits

Profits

I shall use the private profits earned by the Swedish companies as a basis
for an assessment of the measurable economic benefits to India of the
presence of the Swedish companies. Private profits are essentially the
difference between the total output of a company and the total costs of
producing that output.[1] To arrive at the social benefits, private profits
have to be corrected for differences in the social and private valuation
and the classification of output and costs.

The main difference between private and social benefits is that dividend
remittances to the foreign investor are included in private profits but sho
be excluded from the social benefits. Another difference is the valuation
of labour costs - the social-opportunity cost for labour is sometimes low
than the private cost.[2] There are also other possible differences betwee
private and social benefits but, if these are taken into account, private

---

1) I am not concerned here with any refinements of the private profit
   measures as such. Cf. Little, I.M.D. and Mirrlees, J.A., Manual
   of Industrial Projects Analysis in Developing Countries, Vol. II,
   Social Cost-Benefit Analysis, OECD, Paris 1968, p. 19.
2) Cf. p. 126. Here and in the following paragraphs I shall disregard the
   fact that part of the total wages accrues to foreigners employed in the
   Swedish companies.

profits are a correct and convenient indicator of the net social benefits.

The valuation of total output, and thereby also of profits, may in itself be problematic. But output, including output of intermediate goods, can usually be valued at market prices. "Where the output of a project has a market value, this value plus any consumers' surplus can be taken as the measure of the gross benefit arising from the project."[1] assume here that market prices are appropriate for my purposes. The question of consumers' benefits will be treated later.

When it is said that private profits measure the social benefits, all taxes are included. The gross private profit from a foreign investment before taxes is equivalent to the gross social benefit. This gross benefit is then distributed to the Government in the form of taxes and to shareholders as dividends, and some part of it is usually re-invested in the company. The employment of a uniform term "profit" for all these different uses is really an over-simplification.[2] Leaving taxes aside for a moment, I shall here discuss the net profit after taxes of the Swedish companies.

Table 32 shows the profit situation for the Swedish companies. An average Indian company earns 9 per cent on net worth, while foreign companies in India usually earn around 12 per cent. The Swedish companies have earned even more and therefore follow the general trend that foreign companies are more profitable than domestic firms.[3] The reasons for the greater profitability of foreign companies in India are, according to Kidron, as follows: foreign capital is invested in high-yielding protected industries, it is often found in monopolistic positions, there is a xenophile prejudice in India, foreign firms are more efficiently run, and foreign companies are privileged in having access to cheap finance.[4]

Incidentally, there is - to quote A. Lewis - "a great tendency to exaggerate the profitability of foreign investment".[5] Available figures show that, on an average, the U.S. and British investments at home, in industrialized

---

1) Prest, A.R., and Turvey, R., Cost-benefit analysis: A survey, in Surveys of Economic Theory III, New York 1967, p. 161.
2) Ibid., p. 159.
3) Cf. also Reserve Bank of India, Foreign Collaboration...,pp. 16 and 70.
4) Kidron, M., op. cit., pp. 228-232.
5) Lewis, A., op. cit., p. 259.

Table 32. Profits of the Swedish companies

	Total net profits up to 1968 (Rs. million)	Net profit in 1968 (Rs. million)	Average ratio of net profit to net worth in all years up to 1968 (per cent)	Average ratio of net profit to net worth 1965 68 (per cent)
WIMCO	142.4	5.7	12	8
Vulcan-Laval	1.1	0.6	8 ⎫	2 ⎫
Atlas Copco	6.2	1.3	27 ⎪	23 ⎪
Sandvik	10.5	1.8	18 ⎬ 15	21 ⎬ 14
SKF	1.1	3.4	2 ⎪	5 ⎪
SF	4.0	0.5	21 ⎭	21 ⎭
	22.9	7.6		
Indian companies, average 1946-66			9	
Foreign-controlled companies in India 1957-65			12	

Sources. Reserve Bank of India, Financial Statistics of Joint-stock Companies in India 1951-63, Bombay 1966; Reserve Bank of India, Bulletin up to 1968; company statistics. Net profits = profits exclusive of depreciation, interest and taxes. For WIMCO there are no detailed profit figures available before 1929, but the company probably sustained a total loss of Rs. 1.6 million in the period 1923-28. The profits of Vulcan-Laval´s predecessor, Vulcan Trading, are available from 1953 only. The profits of Atlas Copco have been estimated from balance-sheet figures. Losses are not included in percentage calculations.

countries and in underdeveloped countries alike, have all had a profitability of 8-12 per cent.[1] There are, of course, cases of greater average profitability, for example, U.S. investments in Asia.[2]

1) Gårdlund, T., Främmande investeringar i u-land, Stockholm 1968, p. 60 (based on data from the U.S. Department of Commerce, the First City National Bank, the "Reddayway Report" and the U.K. Board of Trade).
2) Adler, J.H., op. cit., p.98.

WIMCO has, over the years, amassed an impressive amount of profits, and its profitability has, on the average, been on a par with that of other foreign companies in India. But the average figure conceals wide variations: profits were low until the 1940´s, when war conditions brought high yields, and since Independence the profit rate has slowly decreased. At present, WIMCO´s earnings are on a par with those of Indian companies. If internal company transactions are made at market prices, it may be noted that more than one-third of the profits comes form the new products - paper, chlorates and chemicals.

Vulcan-Laval has recently been re-organized and will probably show normal profitability in the 1970´s. SKF and to some extent also the other Swedish companies are over-invested, which makes for a low profit ratio in the beginning. SKF started the production of bearings as late as 1965, but already in 1968 it had become the most profitable bearing company in India, with a steadily rising profit ratio. Atlas Copco, Sandvik and SF have all been very profitable, with profit ratios around 20 per cent. These high ratios are only to a small extent the result of tax concessions, and the Swedish companies may therefore be said to earn profits that are "too high" - the Government´s Tariff Commission usually tries to limit the profits of protected industries to 8-12 per cent.[1] At the same time, high profits, according to my reasoning here, are tantamount to high social benefits.

Profit distribution

Net profits can be either re-invested or distributed as dividends. The re-investment of profits has the positive effect that the possibilities of greater future production and thereby greater economic benefits to the country are increased. Re-investment also reduces the immediate foreign-exchange burden of foreign capital, because less foreign exchange leaves the country as dividends. At the same time, the future foreign-exchange burden is likely to be increased.

Moreover, while the insistence on reinvestment does reduce the immediate demand for foreign exchange to pay dividends abroad, it raises, at the same time, the amount of foreign investment on which further dividends may be earned and transferred in the future. The equity interest of the foreigner is increased, without new funds flowing in from abroad. If the intangible benefits - the managerial and technical assistance - from the original investment are realized within a short period of time, then the continued expansion of the foreign enterprise

---

1) Myrdal, G., op. cit., p. 920.

through retained earnings ceases to make any special contribution to the economy.[1]

Continuous re-investment also increases the value of the foreign-owned share of the economy, with possible negative consequences.[2] The dilemma is drastically put by Baran: " ... it is very hard to say what has been the greater evil as far as the economic development of underdeveloped countries is concerned: the removal of their economic surplus by foreign .capital or its reinvestment by foreign enterprise."[3] The problem is quantitatively important, as re-investments constitute a large part of the foreign-owned capital stock in India.

The solution of the dilemma proposed by Gerald Meier is that the expansion of the productive capacities of foreign companies should as far as possible be financed from local equity sources.[4] The Indian Government has to some extent followed this line of action by insisting that companies with a relatively high proportion of foreign ownership (usually companies more than 60 per cent foreign-owned) should sell part of their share capital to Indian investors as a condition of expansion. More important is probably the initial requirement that only in exceptional cases should foreigners be allowed to own more than 49 per cent of the share capital in new investments. There have been many "exceptional cases", but the restrictive policies of the Indian Government have undoubtedly had some effect in cushioning the potential negative effects of foreign capital.[5]

It has been argued that equity investment is better than loans with fixed interest, because dividends fluctuate with economic cycles, while interest and amortizations do not.[6] But it seems that foreign companies in India, like most big companies in the west, try primarily to keep dividends consta or rising, while re-invested earnings are instead allowed to fluctuate:

" ... distribution abroad is normally the first charge on profits after tax,

---

1) Meier, G. M., The International...,p. 156. Cf. Kindleberger, C. P., American Business Abroad, New Haven 1969, p. 171, where the term "pyramiding technique" is used for continuous re-investment. Such a pyramid must, of course, be imagined as standing on its apex.
2) Cf. p. 183 and Griffin, K., op. cit., p. 131.
3) Baran, P.A., op. cit., p. 184.
4) Meier, G.M., op. cit., p. 156.
5) Cf. pp. 266-267.
6) See, for example, India. Fiscal Commission 1949-50, Report, Vol. I Delhi 1950, p. 216.

and retained earnings are more or less residual, subject to most of the fluctuations in over-all earnings."[1]

Most foreign companies seem to re-invest during the first few years of operation the better part of their earnings, and then settle down to a policy of re-investing,on an average, one-third or one-half of their net profits.[2] Both foreign and domestic companies in India seem to follow the same policy of re-investing in normal years somewhat less than half the net profits (see Table 33). The new Swedish companies do not normally have any fixed distribution policy, but they seem to have retained a larger share of profits than the average. The Swedish parent companies are primarily interested in the long-term stability of their Indian subsidiaries, but they are not adverse to high dividends, as other payments (royalties etc.) are more difficult to effectuate. Local shareholders are said to be more keen on dividends than their European counterparts. For the reasons stated above, the the proportion of undistributed profits will probably decrease in time in the new Swedish companies.

In the late 1960´s WIMCO very generously distributed more than 90 per cent of its net profits in cash to the shareholders. The policy of the company is to pay a steady and rising dividend. One has to go as far back as 1952 to find the retained profits in WIMCO making up more than 40 per cent of the net profit. Before that, however, especially during the Second World War, the re-investment ratio was usually high and only once negative (in 1937). That year the foreign shareholders apparently revalued some assets and sent the proceeds plus the net profit and some reserves home to Sweden, as half the share capital was to be sold the year after to Indian investors.

The Indian Government wants to encourage small-scale investment in equities, and the first Rs. 1,000 of dividend income are therefore exempt from income tax. Dividends from new companies enjoying a tax holiday are also free of tax. The Swedish companies that are quoted on the stock market have many small shareholders, who often go to general meetings and show an active interest in the affairs of the respective companies.

But a large part of the local shares of the Swedish companies is in the hands of prominent Indian capitalists,[3] who usually have a high propen-

---

1) Kidron, M., op. cit., p. 307. Cf. Arndt, H.W., Overseas Borrowing - The New Model, in Economic Record, August 1957, p. 250.
2) Ibid., p. 250; Adler J.H. (ed.), op. cit., p. 184; Reserve Bank of India, Foreign Collaboration..., p. 11.
3) Cf. p. 204.

Table 33. Profits re-invested in Swedish companies

	Re-invested profits as percentage of net profit, average for all years up to 1968		Re-invested profits as percentage of net profit, average 1965-68	
WIMCO	28		8	
Vulcan-Laval	Not available		100	
Atlas Copco	55		48	
Sandvik	71	69	63	72
SKF	100		100	
SF	51		51	
Indian companies, average 1950-66	36			
Foreign manufacturing companies in India 1956-61	40			

Sources. Reserve Bank of India, Financial Statistics of Joint-stock Companies in India 1951-63, Bombay 1966; Reserve Bank of India, Bul-
tin up to 1968; Kidron, M., op. cit., p. 309; company statistics
The figures for Atlas Copco have been arrived at by subtracting
from 100 the percentage of the calculated net profit which the dividend provision represents.

sity to import, which is, however, difficult to realize in India because of
the import restrictions. They consume part of their income, but to some
extent their dividend income from the Swedish companies is probably also
used for investment in equities or productive activities of use for development.[1]   As the consumption of these capitalists is to a large extent concentrated on luxuries, their dividend income from the Swedish firms, if
used for consumption, should perhaps be regarded as a net social cost.[2]
Whatever the use, the dividend income distributed to local capitalists contributes to making the unequal distribution of wealth and income in India
even more unequal.

---

1) There are unfortunately no reliable statistics available to support or
gainsay this assertion.
2) Little, I.M.D. and Mirrlees, J.A., op. cit., p. 130.

Taxes

Given that the gross profits from foreign companies equal the social benefit, the major policy measure for securing a large share of this benefit
for the host country is to tax the profits away from the companies.[1] The
Government then can use the resources gained by the taxation of profits
either for current expenditure or for investment. Current consumption
by the Government may partly be a waste, for example, expenditure on
unnecessary bureaucracy, but a large part of it is as necessary as investment, i.e. money spent on the administration of justice or the police.[2]

Corporate taxes presumably replace re-investments and/or dividends. The
dividend replacement is thereby partly diverted from remittances or private
consumption by Indian capitalists to Government use, which should be
favourable for development. It is probably also better to have taxes at
the free disposal of the Government than re-investments committed in
foreign private companies. The tax issue is complicated by the practice
of many firms of passing the tax burden on to the consumer, and also for
other reasons, but I leave it here with the contention that the conversion
of gross profits into taxes is, on the whole, favourable to development.[3]

In India, only 0.5 per cent of the population pays any personal income tax.[4]
Tax evasion on a large scale is common - a minimum of 600 per cent of
the income stated in tax returns is said to be withheld from taxation.[5]
Taxes on agricultural income and property have, for different reasons,
been kept very low in India and their relative share of the total tax revenues
is decreasing.[6] Customs duties were for a long time a major source of
revenue, but when the import tariffs were replaced by practically absolute
protection through quantitative restrictions, customs duties declined in
importance. Instead, excise duties and other indirect taxes have become
the principal means of financing Government activities.

---

1) Meier, G.M., The International..., p. 153.
2) Little, I.M.D. and Clifford, J.M., International Aid, London 1965,
   p. 140.
3) Cf. Little, I.M.D., and Mirrlees, J.A., op. cit., p.76.
4) Indian Investment Centre, Seminar on International Investment, Speech
   of the Minister of Finance, Mr. Morarji Desai, November 27, Delhi
   1968, p. 13.
5) India. Taxation Enquiry Commission 1953-54, Report, Vol. III, Delhi
   1955, p. 189.
6) "For all practical purposes, Indian agriculture is outside the scope
   of the income tax" (Kust, M.J., op. cit., p. 346).

Corporate taxes have increased in importance since Independence, but in 1967-68 they still constituted only some 10 per cent of the combined tax receipts of the Union and State Governments.[1] The Government is therefore not dependent on such taxes, and the present and future amount of corporate taxes paid by Swedish and other foreign companies are not therefore of crucial importance.

Company taxation is beset with many complicated rules, and constant changes are taking place to the detriment of long-range corporate planning. "These constant changes in corporate taxation are, perhaps, the most persistently disturbing feature in India for foreign enterprise. At times it appears as if the tax on companies depends upon the personal whim of the finance minister."[2] The normal tax rate for Indian and foreign companies alike is 55 per cent of profits, plus surtax on a certain part of the profits. A ceiling of 70 per cent of total income has been set as a maximum total tax liability. But all companies normally enjoy tax holidays and other concessions which bring down the taxes considerably. In later years, however, the effective rates of tax in India seem to have increased, and on an average more than half the corporate income is now appropriated in the form of taxes.[3]

The high tax rates inspire some companies to engage in tax evasion. "It can be taken as axiomatic that the bulk of business in India evades taxation", says Kidron but adds that there is a certain difference between domestic and foreign companies:

> Foreign firms are generally thought to have a cleaner record than indigenous in this respect; and indeed their greater size and the fact that they are exposed to special, politically inspired scrutiny make it unlikely that they would resort to the more blatant methods known. At the same time there is less incentive for them to do so, since many of them are in a uniquely favourable position to modify their accounts to their advantage.[4]

But there is no evidence of any kind that the Swedish companies have modified their accounts to evade taxation, and for the reasons stated in the quotation above, it is also unlikely that they would do so. Instead, they pay taxes which seem to be relatively high, even in the Indian context. As is shown in Table 34, WIMCO, Atlas Copco and SF in 1968 paid taxes at an effective rate of 58-59 per cent, as compared with the Indian average of

---

1) India. Ministry of Finance, Pocket Book of Economic Information 1969, Delhi 1970, p. 153.
2) Kust, M.J., op. cit., Supplement, p. 81.
3) Commerce, Annual Number 1968, Bombay 1968, p. 22.
4) Kidron, M., op. cit., p. 226. Cf. Myrdal, G., op. cit., p. 2102.

Table 34. Income taxes paid by Swedish companies

	(1) Total income taxes paid up to 1968 (Rs. million)	(2) Income tax for 1968 (Rs.million)	(3) Income tax plus net profit for 1968 (Rs. million)	(2) : (3) Effective tax in 1968 (per cent)
WIMCO	177.2	8.1	13.8	59
Vulcan-Laval	3.7	0	0	0
Atlas Copco	10.8	1.9	3.2	58
Sandvik	5.5	1.1	2.9	38
SKF	0.2	0	0	0
SF	3.7	0.7	1.2	58
	23.9	3.7	7.3	
Indian companies, average 1963-66				51

Sources. Reserve Bank of India, Financial Statistics of Joint-stock Companies in India, Bombay 1966; company statistics. All direct taxes,
including taxes on dividends and royalties, are included. For Vulcan-Laval there is no information available before 1953. The figures show the tax provision in the profit and loss account, except
for Atlas Copco, where the tax provision in the balance sheet has
been used.

51 per cent. SKF, Vulcan-Laval and to some extent also Sandvik still enjoyed in 1968 the major tax concession, a tax holiday, and therefore paid
low taxes or no taxes at all.

About half the retail price of matches in India is an excise levy. The levy
was introduced in 1934, as one of the first excise duties of quantitative importance. It would not be correct to regard the match excise as a benefit
from the activities of the match companies.[1] The demand for matches is
anyway quite inelastic,which implies that the match excise is just a transfer of income from the match consumers to the Government.

As is shown in Table 34, up to 1968 WIMCO had contributed a total of Rs.

[1] Prest, A.R., and Turvey, R., op. cit., p. 165. Cf. Little, I.M.D.
and Mirrlees, J.A., op. cit., p. 76.

177 million in income taxes to the exchequer. The corresponding figure
for the new Swedish companies is Rs. 24 million. Together with the total
net profits of Rs. 142 million, WIMCO had thus in 1968 earned a total profit before taxes of Rs. 320 million. The new Swedish companies show a
total pre-tax profit of only Rs. 47 million, but, on the other hand, their
profits are increasing at a much faster rate than WIMCO's. Altogether,
the Swedish companies had thus earned up to 1968 gross profits of about
Rs. 366 million. According to my earlier reasoning, this figure of Rs.
366 million could, properly adjusted, be used as an indicator of the total
economic benefit to India from the activities of the Swedish companies.

Tax concessions and wage benefits

Tax concessions. The Governments in underdeveloped countries sometimes
incur extra fiscal costs to promote foreign investment. To some extent these
costs show up in the accounts, for example, when the Government agrees
to provide infrastructure (roads etc.) for a foreign company. In Chapter 3
I concluded that the new Swedish companies have had a net social cost in
connection with infrastructure. [1] But there are also costs that do not show
up in Government accounts, namely, tax concessions.

Tax concessions usually take the form of tax exemptions on certain parts of
the income and liberal depreciation allowances for tax purposes. They represent "the major legislative effort to promote private investment" in underdeveloped countries, and they have a cost in forgone tax revenue.[2]
From the development point of view, the cost is, of course, not equal to
the total tax forgone. Profits not appropriated as taxes are either re-invested or distributed as dividends, and tax concessions represent a cost
only to the extent that alternative uses are less valuable to the country than
taxes.

Tax concessions also have a cost in the additional administrative burden
which they cause. It has been discussed whether the benefits reaped from
tax concessions are really worth the costs incurred, which is not self-
evident: "So far as we know, no one has ever asked whether enterprise and
investment need encouragement in the form of tax exemptions; it is simply
assumed that this is the case."[3] The available evidence actually indicates

---

1) Cf. p. 80.
2) Meier, G. M., The International..., pp. 143 and 147.
3) Myrdal, G., op. cit., p. 2103.

232

that tax concessions are normally not worth while.[1] The tax system in underdeveloped countries is relatively ineffective as an inducement for investment, temporary tax relief is usually inverse to need and may attract only speculative investment, and the competing concessions of several underdeveloped countries will largely cancel out, to the benefit of no one country.

India has since Independence continuously introduced tax concessions for different purposes.[2] The main concession is a five-year tax holiday, under which an annual income of up to 6 per cent of the capital employed is deducted. Companies investing in "priority industries" are also, on top of normal depreciation, allowed a special deduction of up to 35 per cent of the cost of new plant and machinery. No special concessions are made to foreign enterprise, but some of the tax concessions seem to be of special value to foreign companies.[3]

The Indian Investment Centre has calculated that a normal foreign company with high profitability would have to pay an average tax of 38 per cent of pre-tax profits during its first five years of operation in India.[4] Less profitable companies would pay much less.[5] After the five-year tax holiday, the effective tax goes up and may exceed 50 per cent of the profits. This may seem a high ratio, but one must always take the high price and profit level in India into account when tax levels are compared.[6]

The new Swedish companies have from the start been quite profitable, and they therefore paid as much as 30-40 per cent of their profits in taxes during the first few years. But this is still lower than the present normal rate of 58 per cent, and the difference - the effective tax concession - could be considered in part to be a social cost. This cost has been implicitly included in the previous analysis of the economic benefits of the Swedish companies, in the sense that taxes now are lower and re-investments and dividends higher than they would have been without concessions. Tax concessions are

---

1) See Meier, G.M., The International..., pp. 148 ff; United Nations. ECOSOC, Financing of Economic Development, Promotion of Private Foreign Investment in Developing Countries, Summary and Conclusions, E/4293, March 6, 1967, p. 26.
2) The Indian Investment Centre lists no less than 28 "main tax incentives". Indian Investment Centre, Taxes and Incentives, Delhi 1968, pp. 29-30.
3) Kust, M.J.,op. cit., pp. 363-64.
4) Indian Investment Centre, Taxes and Incentives, Delhi 1968, p. 78.
5) Kust, M.J., op. cit., p. 386.
6) "It, therefore, stands to reason that the burden of Indian taxation, when viewed against the levels of profitability, has not been a negative factor to capital inflow" (Subrahmanian, K.K., op. cit., p. 72).

really not a cost that is specific to foreign investment, as they are general and are given to domestic and foreign companies alike.

Wage benefits. We have seen that much of the increase in productivity broug about by the Swedish investments is either appropriated by the Government as taxes or re-invested or distributed as dividends. But, according to my earlier reasoning, some part of the productivity increase may also accrue to the employees in the form of higher wages. The difference between the wages paid to the employees in the Swedish companies and their wages in former occupations can be regarded as a social gain.[1]

Little is known about the wages of the Swedish employees in former occu-pations, but I have estimated that the difference in average wage levels between the Swedish companies and the firms that supply them with fresh labour is some 25 per cent of the wages in the Swedish firms.[2] Adding 25 per cent of wages to the total economic benefits in the form of the pre-tax profits of the Swedish firms would increase the total benefits considerably. One-quarter of the wages in WIMCO constitutes some 50 per cent of the total pre-tax profits, and the corresponding figure for the new Swedish companies is around 30 per cent. With the inclusion of the wage benefits, the total benefits would increase from Rs.366 million to more than half a billion rupees.

Some difficulties should be pointed out. The figure of 25 per cent is a very rough estimate, based on unreliable statistics, and it is questionable if it is valid over a long period. We also cannot prove that the figure of 25 per cent is equally applicable to the salaries of both workers and staff. We furthermore have to assume that the basic relationship is valid – that the wage differences included here reflect real differences in social opportunit costs.

We must also assume that the transfer costs of labour are negligible,[3] and the secondary events in the companies which supply labour to the Swe-dish firms have not been satisfactorily analyzed. The wage issue may be complicated further, and one may even question the appropriateness of in-cluding wage benefits of this kind in any cost-benefit analysis.[4] The ques tion of wage benefits is thus worth study on its own. I shall here use the

---

1) See pp. 12,126.
2) This is not true of WIMCO in the early years, but I shall for the mo-ment ignore that.
3) Cf. p. 120.
4) Prest, A.R. and Turvey, R., op. cit., pp. 166-67.

figure of 25 per cent to calculate the social wage benefits for the Swedish companies, in spite of the many possible objections to such a procedure.

Outflows and Costs

Dividend outflows

The wage benefits discussed in the previous section arise as a difference between the social and the private costs. Besides wages, the major private costs are expenditure on indigenous and imported raw materials.

There is no reason to assume any difference between social and private cost, as concerns indigenously produced raw materials. But the price of imported materials includes a fair amount in duties paid to the Indian Government, which should perhaps be excluded.[1] But it can be argued that a price that includes the duties is the best measure of the social cost, and the import content of the production of the Swedish companies is anyway so small that it does not make much difference.[2] I shall therefore consider the private costs for all raw materials and components as appropriate indicators of social costs.

There remains one major divergence between the social and private valuations of costs and benefits: to a private concern, remittances of dividends and other foreign payments are only transfer transactions, but to the host country, they represent a real loss.[3] From the foreign investor's point of view, it is natural that the sum of dividends earned on the original capital and on subsequent re-investments should after some time exceed the original investment - the idea of investing is, of course, to get more back

---

1) Chenery, H.B., The application of investment criteria, in Quarterly Journal of Economics, Vol. LXVII, February 1953,. p. 82.
2) Ibid., p. 82; Prest, A.R., and Turvey, R., op. cit., p. 165.
3) There is no reason to regard also profits re-invested in a foreign company as a cost, because for direct investments there is usually no expectation that the principal will be repaid. Re-invested profits are regarded here as a part of the total benefits which may entail indirect costs, in the sense that the basis for earning future dividends is enlarged. Cf. pp. 204,225; Arndt, H.W., op. cit., pp. 253-54.

than you have put in. Spokesmen for the host countries are not always of the same opinion.[1]

Every year about Rs. 200 million leave India in the form of dividends to foreign investors.[2] Dividend remittances are relatively stable, which is probably due to the practice of most companies in India, including the Swedish firms, of keeping dividends steady and instead letting retained earnings fluctuate.[3] Dividends have to be remitted in foreign exchange and may therefore constitute a larger burden to the economy than is shown by their rupee equivalents. Dividend remittances indicate the immediate investment-income liability for the host country, and at the same time measure the "cash profitability" for the foreign investor.

Some countries restrict dividend remittances on foreign capital to, for example, 10 per cent of the original investment.[4] The Indian Government has firmly adhered to the policy of freely allowing both repatriation of capital and dividend remittances. This has been regarded as a prerequisite condition for attracting fresh capital. But re-investment is encouraged in a general way by a dividend tax at source of 25 per cent, a ratio that seems to be relatively high.[5]

The Swedish companies, at least the new ones, have, as we have seen, followed a policy of re-investing a large part of their profits. The figures in Table 35 showing the ratios of dividend remittances to foreign net worth for the Swedish companies therefore do not reflect the real profitability, which is 12 per cent or more (after deduction of all taxes, including the dividend tax).[6] The average remittance percentages for the Swedish companies seem to be normal. The high and early profitability of Atlas Copco and SF shows also in the high percentages of dividend remittance for these companies.

The Swedish investors are interested in getting at least some dividend payments from their Indian ventures. Other payments - for technical services and the like - are severely restricted. Annual dividend remittances are an assurance that the Swedish owners are at least getting some return on their investments.

---

1) "The repatriated profits, in fact, are nothing more than a type of capital flight" (Griffin, K., op. cit., p. 142).
2) Reserve Bank of India, Foreign Collaboration..., pp. 9 and 109.
3) Cf. p. 226.
4) United Nations. ECOSOC, op. cit., p. 20.
5) Cf. Sveriges Allmänna Exportförening op. cit., p. 34.
6) Cf. p. 224.

Table 35. Dividend remittances from Swedish companies

	Dividends remitted to parent company, total up to 1968 (Rs. million)	Dividend remittance to parent company for 1968 (Rs. million)	Average ratio of dividend remittance to foreign net worth, all years up to 1968 (per cent)	Average ratio of dividend remittance to foreign net worth 1965-68 (per cent)
WIMCO	38.2	2.1	5.1	5.6
Vulcan-Laval	0.3	0	0.0 ⎫	0 ⎫
Atlas Copco	2.0	0.2	8.5 ⎪	8.2 ⎪
Sandvik	1.3	0.4	4.9 ⎬ 4.4	4.9 ⎬ 4.4
SKF	0	0	0 ⎪	0 ⎪
SF	1.0	0.2	8.5 ⎭	8.7 ⎭
	4.6	0.8		
Foreign subsidiaries in India 1961-64				6.1
Swedish foreign investments in 1965, world total				4.9
Swedish foreign investment in 1965 in Asia				5.9

Sources. Reserve Bank of India, Foreign Collaboration in Indian Industry, Bombay 1968, p. 18; Lund, H., Svenska företags investeringar i utlandet, Katrineholm 1967, p. 94; company statistics. The remittance for AMCO (WIMCO's Dhubri factory, which is formally a separate company but which here is always included in the statistics for WIMCO) for 1968 is assumed to have been equal to the remittance for 1967. The dividends for Vulcan-Laval (which ceased in 1958) are not available before 1952. Dividend remittances for Atlas Copco have been calculated as dividend provision provision less dividend tax. Remittance percentages for Swedish foreign investments in general are calculated on the Swedish share capital only, which probably yields a bias on the high side.

The benefit accruing to the Swedish investors is enhanced by the structure of the tax regulations. India´s first agreement for the avoidance of double taxation was negotiated with Sweden in 1958. It is based on the method of exclusion, i.e. income in India is taxed in India but not in Sweden and vice versa. The tax treaty was, of course, taken into account when the new Swedish companies made their decision to invest in India. Before 1958, WIMCO had to some extent to pay taxes both in India and in Sweden.

The total dividend remittances for the Swedish companies up to 1968 were Rs. 43 million. If prices, wages and time distribution are not taken into account, the total economic benefit to India of the Swedish companies wou then be Rs. 366 million less dividend remittances, say, Rs. 323 million. The Swedish companies have not taken any substantial loans from their pa rent companies, so there is no possibility of hidden profit transfers throu interest payments that do not show up in the figures for dividend remittan ces.[1]

Royalties and fees

Dividends are the major foreign payments of the Swedish companies, but there are also other remittances in the form of royalties and fees for tech nical and organizational services. To the Swedish concerns,royalties and fees paid by the Swedish companies to their parent firms are only intra-company transactions, but to India these payments represent a real loss. Sometimes the royalties and fees sent out of India may be just transmuted profits - foreign companies may prefer not to show too high nominal profi in the country, and royalties and fees are also less heavily taxed than pro fits.

Over the years, the Indian Government has adopted certain norms for accepting the terms of technical-collaboration agreements between an Indian and a foreign party. Royalties are generally maximized at 5 per ce of net sales, subject to Indian taxes.[2] The payments for technical servi have risen rapidly during the last ten years, and the Indian Government has therefore become stricter about terms and conditions. Collaboration agreements for longer than 10 years are nowadays seldom permitted. The Government prefers lump-sum technical fees to royalty agreements with higher foreign-exchange liabilities in the future. The Government´s pre-

---

1) Cf. p. 199.
2) Additional royalties of 2-3 per cent are permitted for export sales when the foreign collaborator provides special services for export purposes. India. Industrial Licensing Policy Inquiry Committee, Report, Delhi 1969, p. 135.

ference is evident from the fact that technical fees are tax-free, while royalty payments to foreign collaborators are subject to a tax of 50 per cent.

In the case of foreign financial collaborations, royalties over 3 per cent are seldom allowed.[1] Majority-owned foreign companies should in principle not be allowed any royalty or fees at all: "As a rule, where majority or greater equity participation is granted, it is felt that the dividends and capital appreciation to be derived from the sheltered market provided by the Government of India for new industries should include the technology and technical and managerial assistance required by the project".[2] The protected Indian market yields relatively high profits and dividends, and also the nominally low royalty rates normally permitted for foreign collaboration may produce a substantial remuneration when applied to the inflated Indian sales figures.

The tougher conditions for foreign subsidiaries have only been seriously implemented in the last few years. More than 30 per cent of the collaboration agreements of foreign subsidiaries in India have a duration of more than 10 years, as against an average of 13 per cent of all agreements. Most of the subsidiary agreements date from before 1955.[3] Nearly 40 per cent of the subsidiaries have royalty rates over 3 per cent, in spite of the fact that 3 per cent is officially the maximum royalty permissible.[4] The Government's leniency as concerns royalty rates to subsidiaries is well known, and there are very few agreements that have not come about just because the Government has not approved the royalty rate.[5]

Still, the total remittances of royalties and fees from foreign subsidiaries in India in the early sixties were only about 15 per cent of the dividend payments, and as a percentage of the net profit, the remittances were thus well below 15 per cent.[6] Large hidden profit transfers through payments of royalties and fees can therefore be ruled out as a general feature, although there are certainly individual instances of such malpractices. The international experience is that remittances of royalties and fees are, on an average, 10-15 per cent of net profits.

---

1) Reserve Bank of India, Foreign Collaboration in Indian Industry, Bombay 1968, p. 104.
2) Kust, M.J., op. cit., pp. 154-55.
3) Reserve Bank of India, Foreign Collaboration..., pp. 27 and 104.
4) Ibid., p. 105.
5) Cf. Kidron, M., op. cit., p. 269.
6) Reserve Bank of India, Foreign Collaboration..., pp. 17 and 27.

As is shown in Table 36, the Swedish companies generally conform to the normal pattern of taking moderate technical-collaboration payments, remittances being 11.5 per cent of the net profit. But quantitatively the remittances are half the size of the dividend payments, and the average figures conceal wide variations. WIMCO and Sandvik stand out as having made relatively large remittances of royalties and fees.

Table 36. Remittances of royalties and technical fees for Swedish companies

	Remittances of royalties and fees, all years up to 1968 (Rs. million)	Remittance of royalties and fees in 1968 (Rs. million)	Remittances of royalties and fees as percentage of net profit, all years up to 1968	Remittance of royalties and fees as percentage of net profit in 1968
WIMCO	14.2	0.1	24.2	1.3
Vulcan-Laval	0.2	0.0	0.5	4.5
Atlas Copco	0.4	0	7.5	0
Sandvik	5.0	2.1	34.8 } 11.5	120.8 } 33.0
SKF	1.0	0.4	2.3	10.3
SF	0.4	0.2	12.4	29.4
	7.0	2.7		
U.S. and U.K. foreign investments			10-15	

Sources. Gårdlund, T., op. cit., pp. 63-64 (based on data from the "Reddaway Report", the U.S. Dept. of Commerce and Oregon University); company statistics. The remittance for 1968 for WIMCO is taken as being equal to the remittance in 1967. The 1968 payments for SKF and SF are payments for several years lumped together and are therefore abnormally high. Sandvik´s percentage figure for 1968 is also high, because of the very small profits in that year.

WIMCO is a special case. The remittances for WIMCO shown in Table 36 are not strictly royalties or technical fees but the net amount of the "managing agent´s commission". The managing-agency system in India has been treated in Chapter 2. It started as a means of utilizing scarce resources of capital and, above all, management, but it was slowly transformed into a means of controlling big industrial empires.

Since 1929, WIMCO has been "managed" by Swedish Match in Bombay, a branch office of the Swedish Match Company in Sweden (STAB). Swedish Match in Bombay has not had any other function than to "manage" WIMCO. In practice, Swedish Match has only paid the salary of the managing director of WIMCO and a very small part of WIMCO's office expenses, and in return for this it has received a managing agent's commission of considerable size. Like the other Swedish companies, WIMCO also received technical services from its parent company, and some little part of the "managing agent's commission" may be regarded as payment for these services.

WIMCO's managing agency was terminated in 1969, together with many other such agreements in Indian business, on the initiative of the Government. This was actually no great loss to STAB, as the maximum rates of managing agent's commission had been drastically reduced in the 1960's. The commission did not during the last few years cover STAB's actual expenses for technical services. But before that, particularly in the early years, the larger part of the commission was received without any corresponding services being rendered.

In STAB's terminology, the managing agent's commission from India has always been called "the surplus from the Bombay branch", and it has not been related to the costs of technical or other services. The larger part of WIMCO's "managing agent's commission" remitted to Sweden must therefore be considered as part of its profits. Barring one extreme value, the commission remitted has, on an average, been equivalent to 60 per cent of the dividend remittances from WIMCO. It is an internal transfer to the STAB concern, but a net loss to India.

The other Swedish company with large remittances, Sandvik, had up to 1968 remitted royalties and fees of an average amount of 35 per cent of the net profits. At the time of investment, Sandvik had a very strong negotiating position and was therefore able to get Government approval for quite an unusual collaboration agreement. It has a duration of 15 years and stipulates, to start with, that Sandvik shall, net of all Indian taxes, pay to Sweden a 10 per cent royalty on all exports. Furthermore, Sandvik shall every year pay part of the parent company's research expenses, corresponding to an annual fee of 5 per cent of Sandvik's annual turnover. The research payments are classified as technical fees and are therefore free of Indian tax, which makes them very valuable to the parent company. In 1968, the research fee was three times as large as the dividend remitted.

From a business point of view, the research fee is probably adequate. The research costs of the parent company are shared according to a special formula, based on turnover figures, by all companies in the Sandvik concern. But the Indian Government usually takes the view that majority-owned foreign companies should not have any sizeable fees or royalties at all, as their parent companies normally receive quite satisfactory payments in the form of dividends from the profitable Indian market. Sandvik's royalty and research fees are therefore largely an "unnecessary" cost to the Indian economy.

Vulcan-Laval pays only a symbolic annual fee to its parent company. But as Vulcan-Laval is developing into a general engineering company, with several collaborations with different foreign parties, its collaboration payments will probably increase in the future. In contrast, Atlas Copco paid technical fees only during the first five years and will, in all probability, not pay any such fees in the future. SF started out with a 5 per cent royalty, which in 1967 was reduced by the Government to 3 per cent, on the argument that SF was a majority-owned company. SKF pays a royalty of 2.5 per cent, while the Indian ball-bearing companies pay 5-6 per cent.

Generally, the Swedish companies in India pay less for technical services from their parent firms than their sister companies in other countries. The payments are thus from a business point of view inadequate, perhaps grossly inadequate. But from India's point of view all remittances of royalty and fees can be regarded as sheer losses.

WIMCO and Sandvik make, as we have seen, relatively large payments, but these are not of a secret nature. WIMCO's managing agent's commission has, at least in late years, been calculated on a maximum formula laid down by the Indian Government, and the basis for the computation of fees for Sandvik is also known to the Government. The other Swedish companies make relatively modest collaboration payments, and any large-scale transfer of concealed profits through payments of royalties and fees is therefore ruled out for the Swedish companies. On the whole, it can thus be said that the Swedish companies do not make much use of the possibilities of secretly transmuting profits into other payments.

Foreign-exchange costs

The dividend and royalty payments leaving India from the Swedish companies are remitted in foreign currencies and therefore not only lessen the increase of domestic income but also reduce the foreign-exchange reserves of the country. The foreign-exchange drain reduces the immediate import opportunities, but there may also be more long-term and more serious effects.

India has for some time had a very small foreign-exchange reserve, and an increased pressure on the balance of payments may force the Govern-

nent to undertake deflationary measures, which would hamper growth and
:ause unemployment of resources. [1] A not uncommon response to a pressure
on the balance of payments is a tightening of import restrictions, with ineffi-
iency and higher costs as a result. Devaluation is probably not of much
help in the Indian context, but, when undertaken, it may have social costs.
Rerurrent foreign-exchange difficulties may also result in an increased
dependence on foreign lenders.

f an increasing proportion of India's foreign-exchange receipts is
ommitted to the servicing of foreign capital, the country becomes more
ulnerable to economic changes involving foreign-exchange pressure. As
ve have seen, dividend remittances in foreign companies are usually the
irst charge on profits, and remittances do not therefore vary with busi-
ess cycles or export earnings. An indirect cost of foreign investments
n India, including the Swedish companies, is therefore that they may
precipitate and prolong a crisis in the balance of payments.

Many underdeveloped countries with balance-of-payment problems restrict
ransfers of dividends and repatriation of foreign private capital. India's
official policy is to freely allow both dividend remittances and capital repatriation. In practice, dividends (and approved royalties) can be remitted
vithout difficulty, while capital repatriation is sometimes obstructed. [2]

The monetary foreign-exchange outflows from foreign companies in India
seem to outweigh the inflows, in spite of the fact that new investments
are on the increase. [3] A simple foreign-exchange balance for the Swedish
companies is shown in Table 37. WIMCO is an old company and therefore
has a negative balance, while, for example, SKF, which started the production of bearings as late as 1965, has not yet remitted any dividends and
therefore shows a positive balance. One may note that not less than three
of the new Swedish companies had as early as 1968 "turned the corner"
and changed from a positive to a negative foreign-exchange balance.

1) Cf. MacDougall, G.A.D., op. cit., p. 205.
2) Cf. p. 56.
3) Kidron, M., op. cit., p. 310.

Table 37. Foreign-exchange inflows and outflows for Swedish companies

	(1) Foreign-exchange inflows up to 1968 (Rs. million)	(2) Foreign-exchange outflows up to 1968 (Rs. million)	(1) - (2) Foreign-exchange balance in 1968 (Rs. million)
WIMCO	7.4	55.9	-48.5
Vulcan-Laval	7.0	0.5	6.5
Atlas Copco	1.8	2.4	-0.6
Sandvik	6.0	6.3	-0.3
SKF	25.4	1.0	24.4
SF	1.3	1.4	-0.1
	41.5	11.6	29.9

Sources. Company statistics (see Tables 24, 35 and 36). Investment in
kind is included in inflows, but not re-investments. Exports and
imports are not included. Foreign-exchange outflows comprise
remittances of dividends, royalties, fees and Rs. 3.5 million of
repatriated capital for WIMCO.

We found earlier that in India foreign exchange is a very scarce resource
and a "primary bottleneck" to development.[1] The general shortage of
foreign exchange also increases the possibility of indirect costs of the
types enumerated above. A simple foreign-exchange balance, as shown
in Table 37, is not very informative as an indicator of the positive and negative foreign-exchange effects of the Swedish companies. We have to
allow also for price differences and the time distribution of payments,
and the foreign-exchange effects ought to be related to other economic
effects.

The easiest way to do this is to incorporate the foreign-exchange effects
in a more general cost-benefit analysis of the Swedish investments. Share
capital inflows are benefits to India, together with pre-tax profits, and
remittances of dividends and royalties are costs. To allow for the foreign-
exchange effects, the benefits and costs in foreign exchange (share-capital

---

1) Cf. p. 197.

inflows and remittances) may be included in the cost-benefit analysis at a premium that reflects the scarcity of foreign exchange.[1]

The premium should reflect the average over-valuation of the rupee at existing rates of exchange. It is very difficult, not to say impossible, to arrive at a correct figure for such a foreign-exchange premium. But we should perhaps not be too concerned about the detailed accuracy of a factor that is at least measurable in money values. If the cost-benefit outcome is sensitive to changes in the premium rate, alternative calculations may always be made. To start with, I shall allow for a foreign-exchange premium of 100 per cent, which is probably not too high at least.[2] A premium of 100 per cent thus means that the values of benefits and costs of Swedish investments expressed in foreign exchange should be doubled in the cost-benefit analysis.

A foreign-exchange premium of 100 per cent may be realistic now, but we may always ask if this figure is relevant also for earlier periods. The first severe balance-of-payments crisis in independent India occurred in 1956-57, when the sterling balances accumulated during the war were run down, and it may be argued that there should not be any premium on foreign exchange until then. On the other hand, the war period may be considered to have been abnormal, and it may also be maintained that foreign exchange was scarce even when India had its sterling balances, although it was not sufficiently realized at the time.

Before the Second World War there was in India a general shortage of foreign exchange, and one has to go as far back as 1928 to find stable conditions of surplus.[3] Here I shall ignore the war conditions in my calculations (for WIMCO). Foreign-exchange inflows and outflows after 1928 in the cost-benefit analysis will be given double the nominal value, while no premium will be used for earlier payments. These assumptions are, of course, quite arbitrary.

Benefits and costs

The foreign-exchange benefits and costs that will be included in the cost-benefit analysis attempted here are of a direct nature and largely reflect

1) Chenery, H.B., The application of investment criteria, in Quarterly Journal of Economics, Vol. LXVII, February 1953, p. 81. The premium measures the potential usefulness of the foreign exchange, not the actual use.
2) Cf. Myrdal, G., op. cit., pp. 924 and 2084.
3) India. Fiscal Commission 1949-50, Report, Vol. I, Delhi 1950, p. 20.

actual payments. It would be correct to include also the indirect foreign-exchange effects, for example, exports, import substitution, use of foreign-exchange loans from indigenous institutions, etc.

It would theoretically also be possible to include in the cost-benefit analysis the employment effects, the income-distribution effects, the cultural effects, and so on.[1] But it is impossible to assign any sensible money values to these effects, and I therefore prefer to call them "indirect" or "external". This is just to say that we have no common quantitative measure for such effects; it does not mean that these effects are less important than the profit and foreign-exchange effects - perhaps the contrary.[2] A normal cost-benefit analysis of the kind I shall attempt here only lumps together a few disparate effects that happen to be readily expressible in money terms.

My reasoning in this chapter started from the notion that it was possible to use private gross profits - properly adjusted - as an indicator of the economic benefits accruing to the society as a whole from the Swedish investments. It was decided that all private costs for indigenous and imported materials and components should be treated as adequately reflecting social costs. The difference between social-opportunity costs and private outlays for wages may be added as a benefit, and a downward adjustment of private profits must be made on account of dividends and other foreign payments. This downward adjustment should be increased by 100 per cent to allow for a higher social valuation of foreign-exchange resources. The same procedure would be used to increase the nominal benefit from foreign-exchange inflows.

To make the money values of costs and benefits for different years comparable, we must allow for time and price differences. As long as all prices are reckoned on the same basis, it is irrelevant which year´s prices are chosen as a basis. I shall here use an index with the prices for 1963 = 100, which happens to be the latest basis used in the UN statistics. It is an index of wholesale prices, which I consider to be useful for my purposes.[3]

To compare the benefits and costs accruing at different points in time, we have to discount them to a common base year. The actual starting year for

---

1) Cf. Wells, D.A., op. cit., p. 493.
2) See pp. 23 ff.
3) I am aware of the statistical difficulties in using old price indices. Changes in international prices will not be taken into account here, i.e. I shall disregard the Indian devaluations of 1931, 1949 and 1966 and the revaluation of 1925.

the company in question seems a natural choice - it approximates to the point of time when the investor decided to invest and the Indian Government decided to allow the investment. The subsequent choice of a discount rate is, as always, very difficult. [1] I shall here use a 10 per cent discount rate, which I think is not too far out of line. [2]

I shall thus sum up for each company each year its total benefits: gross profits, 25 per cent of wages and the foreign-exchange inflow. The inflow is given double its nominal value (after 1928). From this is subtracted the foreign-exchange outflow for each year, also at double its nominal value. The result is converted to 1963 prices and then discounted back to the respective base year, using a discount rate of 10 per cent.

The outcome is shown in Table 38. The main result is that benefits outweigh costs for all the Swedish companies. This was, of course, to be expected. High tax rates in India secure a substantial part of the profits for the Government, and the wage effect is always positive. Nominally, the foreign-exchange outflows gradually outweigh inflows, but inflows come earlier in time, at lower prices and with practically no discount.

The wage effect is important for WIMCO, because of its relatively labour-intensive production. For the other companies, the profit benefit is much more significant, except for Vulcan-Laval, which shows a nominal net loss over the period. Consequently, the foreign-exchange outflow for Vulcan-Laval is much smaller than the inflow. The other new Swedish firms had, as we have seen, just reached a balance between nominal inflows and outflows in 1968, except for SKF, with its heavy initial investment.

A substantial part of the large foreign-exchange outflow for WIMCO occurred in the early years. The total discounted value of benefits minus costs for WIMCO is therefore relatively low. For several years in the thirties, when large amounts of managing agent´s commission were sent to Sweden, the discounted value for WIMCO is negative, reaching its lowest point in 1939, just after the repatriation of half the share capital.

---

1) Prest, A.R., and Turvey, R., op. cit., pp. 171-72.
2) Wells, D.A., op. cit., p. 495; India. Ministry of Finance, Pocket Book of Economic Information, Delhi 1970, p. 102; Little, I.M.D., and Mirrlees, J.A., op. cit., pp. 96 and 184.

Table 38. Benefits and costs for the Swedish companies (Rs. million)

Company and base year	Gross profit (net profit + + taxes)	25 per cent of total wages	Foreign--exchange inflows (double value after 1928)	Foreign--exchange outflows (double value after 1928)	Benefits minus costs in 1963 prices, discounted back to base year
WIMCO (1923)	319.5	150.1	7.4	-112.1	52.
Vulcan-Laval (1961)	-0.7	6.4	14.0	-0.3	11.6
Atlas Copco (1962)	17.0	3.2	3.6	-4.8	12.3
Sandvik (1962)	16.0	3.6	12.0	-12.6	13.1
SKF (1965)	6.8	2.8	50.8	-2.0	42.3
SF (1961)	7.7	2.1	2.4	-2.6	6.2
	46.8	18.1	82.8	-22.3	

Sources. Company statistics. For WIMCO, detailed profit figures before 1929 are not available, but the recorded decrease in net worth in 1923-28 is assumed here to be on account of losses, and has been spread out evenly over the years 1923-27. It is also assume that WIMCO did not pay any taxes before 1929. The wages paid by WIMCO before 1956 are not known but are assumed to have be 13.6 per cent of turnover, which is the (stable) average for 1956-68. Before 1936 the resulting value for wages is doubled, becaus the match excise was then not included in turnover figures. Turn over figures for 1924-28 are calculated from the production figu res and the prices prevailing at the time. For the new Swedish companies, the base year chosen is usually identical with the year when the main production started. Losses are included in profit figures. Foreign-exchange flows before the base year are included in the figure for the base year. Profits, losses and wage before the base year are not included (if they were, the figures for Vulcan-Laval would be adjusted a little upwards, and the SKF figures a little downwards, but without any significance for the end result). Wages for SF in 1961-63 have been assumed to have represented the same proportion of turnover as the average for 1964-68.

Summary. Private profits - properly adjusted - may serve as an indicator of the economic benefits accruing to the society as a whole from foreign investment. The Swedish companies have had relatively high profits. A large part of the profits in the new Swedish companies has been re-invested, while WIMCO has followed a somewhat more adventurous dividend policy.

Dividends to local Indian shareholders are partly consumed and partly invested. Taxes are an important part of the gross economic benefits from the Swedish investments, and the Swedish firms seem to pay relatively high taxes after their tax holiday has expired. A wage benefit of 25 per cent of total wages is included in the total benefits for the Swedish companies.

The remaining major divergence between social and private costs is that foreign dividends, royalties and fees are a social but not a private cost. The Swedish companies seem to have normal dividend and royalty remittance ratios, but the fees paid by WIMCO and Sandvik are relatively high. The payments from the Swedish companies in foreign exchange may entail costs of a direct and indirect nature, and the foreign-exchange costs (and benefits) may therefore be included at a premium in a cost-benefit analysis. All other benefits and costs may theoretically also be included in such an analysis, but as most effects cannot be quantified, they must be left out. When the remaining measurable effects are discounted in fixed prices to a base year, all the Swedish companies show a surplus of benefits over costs.

Chapter 9.

COMPETITION AND OPPORTUNITY COST

Competition

The result of the quantitative cost-benefit analysis is not conclusive, and in Chapter 10 the totality of advantages and disadvantages of the Swedish investments will be discussed. But first the relations between the Swedish companies and their competitors will be dealt with. In this connection the general market performance of the Swedish firms will be discussed, and I shall start with the possible benefits to the consumers from the Swedish investments.

Benefits to consumers

The increase in productivity resulting from foreign investment may be pas sed on to the employees through higher wages, to the Government by way taxes and to local and foreign shareholders in the form of distributed divi-dends. But the consumers of products from the industry in question may also benefit from lower prices, better quality and a wider range of produc The only reason why the consumers´ benefit was not included in the cost-benefit calculation in the previous chapter was that it is not calculable in practice in the case of the Swedish companies. [1]

Except for the matches from WIMCO, the products of the Swedish compani are not used directly in final consumption but are sold to other industries. But we may still speak of consumers´ benefit being indirectly realized. [2] A consumers´ benefit may perhaps also be spoken of when the Swedish pro ducts are used by priority industries and when the availability of products from the Swedish companies induces fresh investments in new lines. Thes effects have already been discussed in Chapter 3 in connection with indust linkages and priority sectors. [3] A further general benefit, of an indirect nature, may accrue to consumers if the price and product policies of the

---

1) Chenery, H.B., The application of investment criteria, in Quarterly Journal of Economics, Vol. LXVII, 1953, p. 82.
2) Prest, A.R. and Turvey, R., op. cit., p. 163; Little, I.M.D. and Mirrless, J.A., op. cit. p. 26.
3) See pp. 82-87.

Swedish companies force other Indian companies to adopt more progressive policies in these respects.[1]

As for prices, the Indian Tariff Commission has uncovered several cases in which foreign-dominated industries have charged exorbitant prices.[2] The Indian Government has used extensively the device of price control, but in later years the price ceiling has been removed for most industries. It is still in force, however, for such necessities as vanaspati (bread), drugs, and kerosene - products which it is thought to be important to supply to the common man at a fair price.[3] Matches are also considered a necessity, and the Government has controlled the prices of matches in an informal way. WIMCO has always been a price leader with somewhat higher prices than its competitors, and the informal control measures have therefore been addressed directly to WIMCO.

When the match industry started in India in the 1920's, the prices were brought down rapidly by competition. They reached a minimum in 1933-38, when WIMCO showed very low profits and most other match companies had to shut down. With competition eliminated, WIMCO raised its wholesale prices again, but after Independence the increase has been very gradual and in fact has amounted to a voluntary price control. This voluntary control is evidently considered satisfactory by the Government - a proposal by the Tariff Commission of 1963 that price control of matches should be introduced was turned down by the Government:

> ... due to changing costs of raw materials and labour charges, a rigid price control on the ex-factory and wholesale prices of matches cannot be maintained over a reasonably long period. As the evidence brought before the Commission has established that the Central Excise Rules and the voluntary control on prices exercised by the principal producers has been able to ensure the availability of matches to consumers at a reasonable price, Government have decided that it is not necessary to fix any ceiling ex-factory or wholesale price for matches. However, should there be an undue increase in prices, Government will consider suitable steps for keeping the prices under control.[4]

WIMCO:s new products, paper and chemicals, follow the same pricing pattern as the products of the new Swedish companies. As a rule, the new Swedish firms have 10-20 per cent higher prices than their competitors. The Swedish

---

1) McDougall, G.D.A., op. cit., p. 209.
2) Kidron, M., op. cit., p. 250.
3) India. Planning Commission, Fourth Five-year Plan, op. cit., p. 234.
4) India. Tariff Commission, Report on Fair Selling Prices of Safety Matches, Bombay 1963, p.v.

companies state that they could easily lower their prices - which would be of benefit to the consumers - but that the higher prices are more profitable The conclusion is that the general pricing policy of the new Swedish firms, considered in isolation, is not beneficial to the consumers.

Even if the consumers of products from the Swedish companies do not benefit from lower prices, they might do so from better products. A large part of the rise in living standards in the developed countries has taken this form - better quality at constant prices. In India, there is a widespread feeling that foreign goods, imported or produced within the country, are of higher quality than Indian products. To some extent this is true, but it is also a question of a prejudice in favour of everything foreign:

> ... foreign firms enjoy a number of advantages. An important one is the xenophile prejudice which suffuses Indian society. An imported article is ipso facto preferable to one "made in India"; a foreign brand manufactured locally by a foreign firm is better than one made by an Indian firm; and so down the line with decreasing value accompanying receding foreign-ness. [1]

The quality of matches depends to a large extent on the kind of wood that is used. In the beginning, the Indian match industries used imported aspen of high quality. It is possible that WIMCO´s products were then of a higher quality than those of its competitors, because of its good connections with aspen-producing Sweden and on account of its better storage methods. Later when Indian wood was substituted for imported, the general quality of match in India deteriorated, and the cottage industries have since then had a growing quality advantage because of their easier access to suitable indigenous wood. In later years, several cottage factories seem to have produced better quality matches than WIMCO.

The new Swedish companies, except perhaps for Vulcan-Laval, appear to produce goods of better quality than the average on the respective markets. The Swedish products perform according to specifications, are technologically perhaps a little more advanced, and have better finish. But even if the quality of the Swedish products is better than the average, the Swedish companies all have at least one competitor, sometimes a foreign-owned company, that also maintains high quality. Only SKF seems to have no serious competition on the score of quality; this is reflected in the fact that none of SKF´s competitors is allowed to use the brand name of its foreign collaborator. The new Swedish firms also tend to offer better-than-average service facilities to their customers.

---

1) Kidron, M., op. cit., p. 229. Cf. Baranson, J., op. cit., p. 106.

There are many plausible reasons for the higher quality observed in the products of Swedish and other foreign companies in India. The foreign technicians are usually brought up in a tradition of quality, which they stick to also in India. Incidentally, this may explain the fact that several Indian competitors of the Swedish companies now producing low-quality goods produced high-quality goods in the beginning, when the foreign technicians were still there. International companies, like the Swedish firms, also try to keep the quality high because they have to live up to a reputation - there is often an international trade-mark to defend.

A prerequisite for exports from the Swedish companies in India is that the components made shall be interchangeable with those manufactured in other countries. This is usually a major reason why the foreign owners are so anxious to keep works management and quality control in their own hands. Foreign companies generally have the advantage over Indian firms that they can test their products in the factories of the respective parent company, and at least SKF and Atlas Copco have made use of this facility. Furthermore, India has for a long time been a sellers' market, which discourages attempts to keep up quality. The Swedish companies have not adjusted to this type of market - instead they have in most cases deliberately invested heavily to get high quality from the beginning, as this was thought to be the most profitable policy in the long run.

Apart from price and quality, there is a third way for consumers to benefit from new investments, namely, when new products are offered on the market. A wider range of products - what the welfare economists call an "expanded choice" for the individual consumers - can increase standards of living even at constant levels of consumption.[1] The Swedish companies did not, as we have seen, introduce any new products or new technology at the time of the original investment.[2] But, later on, both the Swedish firms and their competitors have offered new varieties of the original products on the market, and in some cases the Swedish firms have been one step ahead of their competitors. Certain bearing sizes, Sandvik's TEMAX tools, couplings from Atlas Copco and WIMCO's luxury matches are examples of such new varieties from the Swedish companies.

As a further positive effect of the price and product policies of the Swedish companies, their Indian competitors may be forced to lower their prices, raise the quality of their products and expand their product range. As concerns price, the effect has probably been in the other direction - the high prices charged by the Swedish companies seem to have served as an

---

1) Mishan, E.J., Welfare Economics: An Assessment, Amsterdam 1969, p. 36.
2) Cf. p. 163.

"umbrella" for the Indian competitors. But the relatively high quality and the widening range of products from the Swedish firms have probably forced their competitors to be more alert than they would otherwise be. Atlas Copco, for example, maintains that its export performance makes it possible for the Government to put pressure on its competitors to start exporting too.

Competition and monopoly

By their competitive strength, foreign companies may end up in monopoli positions. The general effect of monopolies is usually that products are more expensive than is necessary, and that development in a monopoly industry is slower than under competitive conditions.[1] A foreign monopoly is regarded in India as more detrimental than a domestic monopoly. Monopolies in general are so abhorred that a kind of anti-trust clause was even included in the Constitution: "The State shall, in particular, direct its policy towards securing... that the operation of the economic system does not result in the concentration of wealth and means of production to the common detriment."[2]

At an early stage, the Indian Government tried to avoid monopolies by licensing as many new units as possible in every industry. But the result of this was only that economies of scale could not be realised, and prices in the prevailing sellers' market were generally high instead of competitively low. In addition, economic power was not diluted, because the big business houses were allowed to diversify freely into all industries, and they therefore grew rapidly. In later years, measures were introduced to restrict the activities of big business.[3] Apart from the concentration in certain business houses, the Government is still against concentration in separate industries, but already at the beginning of the Third Five-yea Plan, the policy of freely issuing industrial licences was discontinued. Th means that economies of scale and thereby also a certain degree of conce tration have been accepted.

In 1964, the Government appointed a Monopolies Inquiry Commission, wh reported in 1965. The Commission took a not very fruitful line in conside ing the growth of the big business houses as a necessary evil and directed

---

1) Cf. Johnson, H.G., The efficiency and welfare implications of the international corporation, in Kindleberger, C.P. (ed.), The International Corporation, Cambridge 1970. It is, of course, possible that monopolies may be advantageous from a theoretical world economic point of view, because of economies of scale in research etc.
2) The Constitution of India, Allahabad 1968, p. 12.
3) Cf. p. 43.

its main attention to concentration in specific industries. It defined a "mono-polistic undertaking" as a company that either produced or distributed more than one-third of the goods of a certain kind, or a company which, together with not more than two other companies, was responsible for more than half the production or distribution of a product.

India is a relatively small market, and under the above definition nearly all big companies in India are monopolistic. In an illustrative list drawn up by the Commission of companies producing goods of special importance for or-dinary consumers, not less than 83 per cent were monopolists according to the above definition. Besides concentration in production, the Commission also enumerated other monopolistic practices, like exclusive dealing and price leadership. The Commission's definitions and recommendations have, with some additions, been formally adopted by the Government. In cases of monopolistic practices, the Government can now either stop a company from producing or divide it up into smaller units. But the Government could legally do this before and, with the all-inclusive definition of monopoly, no new policies not practised before came into being as a result of the report of the Monopolies' Commission.

WIMCO was at a very early stage accused of monopolistic practices, and the Tariff Board of 1928 examined the question in detail.[1] The Swedish Match concern was at the time undoubtedly trying to build up a world mono-poly in matches, but for several reasons the urge to monopoly seemed less strong in the Indian operations than elsewhere. In the opinion of the Tariff Board, WIMCO had not tried to establish a monopoly in India.

In 1928 the Tariff Board forecast that WIMCO's market share would be gra-dually reduced. The forecast did not come true. After a period of cut-throat competition in the 1930's, when about 20 large firms were forced to leave the market, WIMCO emerged as the dominant producer. At the time of Independence, WIMCO controlled some 80 per cent of the market, and it could at that time certainly be called monopolist. The remaining few per cent of the market were then served by the cottage industry ope-rating in South India, where conditions for match production on a cottage scale were particularly favourable.

The national Government decided after some time to check the monopolistic expansion of WIMCO. During the First Five-year Plan the future expansion of match production was reserved for the cottage industries, and further expansion of WIMCO's factories was banned. But, in spite of the ban, WIMCO kept its share of the growing market until the 1960's, when the increasing competitive strength of the cottage industry forced WIMCO to relinquish

---

1) See p. 64.

part of its market share. The Monopolies Inquiry Commission of 1965 took note of the growing strength of the cottage industries and mentioned the match trade as an example of the de-monopolizing effects of small-scale industries:

> The production of small-scale industries has been of some importance in combating the effect of concentration in certain industries. In match for example, though Western India Match Co. is by far the largest producer, and has immense resources, a restraining influence on its pow and its conduct is undoubtedly exercised by the numerous small producers of matches, operating mostly in cottages without even the assista of any mechanised factory. [1]

The market share of WIMCO in 1969 was down to 42 per cent, which does not seem to be enough to justify further use of the term "monopolist" with reference to WIMCO. Also, the voluntary price control exercised by WIMC during the last few decades has not permitted any undue exploitation of the monopoly position, as concerns prices. The only monopolistic practice still attributable to WIMCO seems to be exclusive dealing - some match dealers do not dare to take other brands than WIMCO's for fear of losing their WIMCO quotas. [2]

The new Swedish companies

The new Swedish companies have never had such a predominant position in their respective fields as WIMCO has had. In 1968 their average market share was 25 per cent (see Table 39). Vulcan-Laval has the largest share with 40 per cent of the market for its main product line, dairy machinery. For certain individual products outside the main lines, the market share of the new Swedish firms is sometimes very large. Vulcan-Laval had in 1968-69 65 per cent of the market for plate heat exchangers, Atlas Copco 63 per cent for 160-cm compressors, Sandvik 80 per cent for drill steels, SKF 100 per cent for certain bearings and SF 100 per cent for special marine air-conditioning equipments. The existence of such large market shares is not uncommon in the small and well-protected Indian market.

---

1) India. Monopolies Inquiry Commission, Report, Delhi 1965, p. 144.
2) Cf. ibid., p. 130.

Table 39. Swedish companies' market shares for main products in 1968

	Market share for main products in 1968 (per cent)
WIMCO	46
Vulcan-Laval	40 ⎫
Atlas Copco	17 ⎪
Sandvik	30 ⎬ 25
SKF	19 ⎪
SF	20 ⎭

Sources. Company statistics. The figures are not exact.

According to the definition of the Monopolies Inquiry Commission, all the new Swedish companies are monopolists in one or more of their production lines. But with the very wide definition used by the Commission, the statement that a company is monopolistic is not very informative, and to get a more refined picture we have to look at individual companies and their specific competitive situation.

Vulcan-Laval has in the dairy field two strong competitors, Larsen & Toubro and APV. They started production before Vulcan-Laval, and they both have foreign collaboration. Larsen & Toubro is a big Indian-controlled company with a very diversified production, while APV is a relatively small subsidiary of a British company concentrating on dairy equipment. Also in Vulcan-Laval's other production fields there are strong competitors, and the general picture is that Vulcan-Laval faces competition regarding both quality and prices.

Atlas Copco started production in 1962, when its main competitors had been in the market for almost five years. The compressor industry in India is crammed with producers, and Atlas Copco, with less than 20 per cent of the market, therefore has the largest share. Next in the market comes CPT, a British-controlled company with a sizeable minority of Indian shareholders. CPT has not - in contrast with Atlas Copco, which has insisted on full ownership - had any difficulties in expanding its range. CPT makes good-quality goods at competitive prices and may get ahead of Atlas Copco on the Indian market in the 1970's.

The main Indian competitor of Atlas Copco is Kirloskar Pneumatic, which belongs to the well-known business house of Kirloskar. It started up in 1958 in Poona and has at present a very wide range. In spite of its having technical collaboration with a reputable foreign company, it seems that the quality of its products is not always very high, and the company has had difficulties in withstanding the competition from Atlas Copco and CPT. There are on the market also other Indian companies, another two foreign firms and a new public-sector project. Atlas Copco has a very large share of the market within its relatively narrow range, but this market share has been acquired in competition with several other companies, and Atlas Copco could not therefore be called monopolist.

Sandvik and its main competitors were licensed at the same time. Most of the tungsten-carbide metal manufactured in India is produced by India Hard Metal, which, together with Sandvik, supplies the other manufacturers of tungsten-carbide tips and tools with raw material. India Hard Metal belongs to the powerful Shri Ram business group. The quality of its products is allegedly not as good as Sandvik´s, and it has had problems with its foreign collaborators. But India Hard Metal is a viable company and a member of a strong group, and it will therefore in all probability stay in the market. But two other fairly important competitors of Sandvik have during the last few years sustained heavy losses and seem to be on their way out of the market as independent companies. Sandvik´s share of the market will therefore probably grow to more than 40 and perhaps more than 50 per cent.

When SKF started the production of bearings in India, there were already three companies in the market and more in the offing. The oldest company, National Engineering Industries, belongs to the Birla group, till now the most powerful business house in India. It has manufactured bearings since 1952 and had in 1969 more than 50 per cent of the market. There are, besides SKF, four other sizeable competitors and some smaller factories on the market. SKF is the only foreign-owned firm, but all the other companies have foreign technical collaboration. The bearing industry is rather capital-intensive, and the Indian market is really too small for all the existing factories. SKF makes good-quality goods at reasonable prices and its market share has risen rapidly. Several and perhaps all the bearing companies other than SKF and the Birla company will in due course have great difficulties in meeting competition from SKF and Birla, and many liquidation or take-overs are to be expected.

All the products made by SF are based on a specialized technology of air treatment. No other company in India specializes in air treatment, but there are a number of firms that make one or two of SF´s type of products. The competition for SF is therefore product-based and not technology-based. All but one of the competitors started production before SF, and the main competitors of SF are established Indian firms with different foreign collaborators for different products.

The general competitive position of the new Swedish companies is favourable, because, like other foreign firms, they have several advantages over Indian companies.[1] Foreign companies are favoured in the Indian market by a xenophile prejudice, and they have much easier access to cheap finance in the form of loans from Indian financial institutions and from the parent companies or home governments.[2] They are also favoured in attracting local equity.[3]

The most important competitive advantage of the Swedish companies is probably that they can freely use the name and know-how of their respective concerns. The use of international trade-marks gives the Swedish firms an edge over their competitors in the market. The Swedish companies normally also have a technological advantage – there is usually a time lag before the competitors get fresh know-how from their foreign collaborators.

The existence of foreign subsidiaries like the Swedish firms in an industry may force the competitors to seek foreign collaboration just to be able to compete with the favoured foreign companies.[4] This may result in technological duplication and a waste of foreign exchange. Every single one of the competitors of the Swedish companies has foreign collaborators, which would perhaps not have been the case if the Swedish firms had not invested in India. According to Kidron, the argument is valid at least for one of the competitors of SKF:

> ... a well-known Indian firm which favours a more "nationalist" line than most had very nearly completed arrangements to manufacture ball- and roller-bearings independently of outside help. Machinery had been copied and trials completed. A decision had been taken to start produc-

---

1) "... relative to domestic enterprise in the underdeveloped countries, it enjoys certain superior advantages. They are the experience developed in the mature industrial tradition of the advanced countries, the access to and command over better technique, technical and managerial personnel and greater financial resources. It has all the research facilities of its parent organisation at its disposal with little or no extra fees or cost. It has access to the money market of the advanced economies and can draw upon it at a cheaper rate" (Islam, N., Foreign Capital and Development: Japan, India and Canada, Tokyo 1960, p. 150).
2) Cf. Kidron, M., op. cit., p. 231.
3) Cf. p. 203.
4) More than half the industrial licences approved in 1964-66 included foreign collaboration (India. Planning Commission, Industrial Planning and Licensing Policy, Final Report, Bombay 1967, p. 42). Cf. Subrahmanian, K.K., op. cit., p. 20; Behrman, J.N., Economic effects of private direct investment, in Mikesell, R.F., op. cit., p. 149.

tion (but to wait until the product was fully proved before marketing)
when the news of the Tata-SKF project - Associated Bearings Co. Lt
broke. Knowing how difficult it would be to compete against an inter-
nationally-known brand, it felt compelled to enter into an agreement
for technical collaboration with another foreign firm - solely to acqui
the use of its trade mark.[1]

Because of their advantages, the new Swedish companies have increased
their sales relatively faster than the average in respective industries. In
the absence of new entrants this means that their market share is on the
increase. But it seems unlikely that firms like Atlas Copco and SF, havin
to compete with several big companies, will in the near future become
very dominant in their respective fields. Vulcan-Laval has, it is true,
about 40 per cent of the dairy-machinery market, but the company tries t
diversify into other product lines to avoid the growing Government contro
in the dairy field, and it is therefore also unlikely that Vulcan-Laval will
end up in a monopolistic position.

In 1968, SKF had 20 and Sandvik about 30 per cent of the respective mark
Their market shares are rapidly growing and they will probably soon reac
the sensitive point at which the Government begins to take an interest. Ba
bearings and tungsten carbide are important industrial products of nationa
significance, and the Indian Government would probably not like their pro
duction to be wholly dominated by foreigners. The policy of SKF and Sand
vik is therefore to advance slowly, with frequent checks with Government
circles. If the companies became too dominant, they might be required to
export more or to take up new, not very profitable products. Rather than
end up in this sort of situation, SKF and Sandvik would prefer to abstain
from further increases of their market share of the main product and instead diversify into profitable new products of their own choice. A paralle
can be drawn here with WIMCO, which refrains from trying to keep up its
share of the market in ordinary matches and instead concentrates on luxu
matches, paper and chemicals.

Opportunity Costs

Foreign and domestic companies

The competitive behaviour of the Swedish firms described in the last sect

---

1) Kidron, M., op. cit., p. 303.

may restrict the amount of business done by Indian companies. I shall treat here the possible negative effects of foreign investments on local industry. These negative effects were not included in the limited cost-benefit analysis in Chapter 8. They can conveniently be called opportunity costs, in the sense that it is usually a question of forgone opportunities of domestic production.

When a foreign company invests in an industry in an underdeveloped country, its technical and economical superiority is likely to carry it to a prominent position on the market. With a limited market, the prominence of the foreign company may be gained at the expense of existing domestic firms, and this may then be regarded as a cost caused by the foreign company. When domestic firms are pushed back by a foreign intruder, their reduced sales usually result in lower domestic profits.[1]

If the foreign company is very aggressive and the competitors weak, one or more of the domestic firms may have to shut down. This may imply not only loss of income and savings, but also a capital loss and increased foreign control over industry. A domestic initiative may be lost. "In bidding for domestic resources and cutting costs (and prices), foreign enterprise may edge the domestic producer out of business and stifle that very (domestic) initiative which foreign private enterprise is supposed to foster."[2]

There is also a possibility that foreign investment, by its mere presence in an industry, may deter indigenous entrepreneurs from entering it. The prospect of having to compete with a strong foreign company cannot be alluring for domestic capitalists, who have safer alternatives in hoarding, residential investment and trading activities. Without spectacular liquidations of local competitors, foreign investments may thus inhibit domestic industrial growth.

> Indigenous entrepreneurs may be discouraged. Foreign investors
> may leave domestic entrepreneurs on the margin of economic activity;
> they may preempt the most profitable opportunities and retard the de-
> velopment of an investing class. Should the presence of investors from
> economically advanced societies frustrate the growth of an indigenous

---

1) The presence of a foreign company in an industry may, of course, be qualitatively beneficial, because local competitors may be forced to pay more attention to questions of efficiency, quality and product development. See p. 253.
2) Behrman, J.N., op. cit., p. 145.

entrepreneurial group, the chances for long-run development will be
seriously prejudiced.[1]

To assess the extent of the opportunity costs of the type described above,
we have to know the alternatives, the opportunities forgone. This, of course
poses serious problems. The situation with foreign investment should be
compared with an imaginary situation without it. The relevant comparison
is then not with an ideal situation of resource utilization, but with a realistic
estimate of what would have happened in the absence of foreign investement.
Such estimates are very difficult to make, especially for larger areas and
longer time periods.

It is not enough to estimate the direct opportunity costs in terms of reduced
income and capital loss. If the resources brought in by foreign investment
substitute for investment and the use of domestic resources, these domestic resources may be used for other purposes - domestic resources may
be "released" by foreign investment. It would be ideal if one could follow
the use of such released resources throughout the economy, preferably in
a general equilibrium approach. The better the use of the resources released, the lower the opportunity cost of foreign investment.

The extent to which foreign investment in general substitutes for domestic
investment is disputed.[2] In the case of India, the alternative events in
colonial times to the actual investment-cum-trade system run by the British are very difficult to assess. At the very beginning, the opportunity
costs of British industrial investments were probably very low, but later

---

1) Griffin, K., op. cit., p. 125. Marxist writers have taken a special
   interest in this type of opportunity costs: "What is more, once an undertaking of that scope had taken place in an industry, both the limitations
   of demand and the magnitude of the required investment reduced greatly
   or eliminated entirely the chances of another enterprise being launched
   in the same field. The amount of capital required to break into the
   monopoly's privileged sanctuary, the risks attendant upon the inevitable
   struggle, the leverages that the established concern could use to harass
   and to exclude an intruder - all tended to decimate the inducement for
   merchant capital to shift to industrial pursuits. The narrow market
   became monopolistically controlled, and the monopolistic control became an additional factor preventing the widening of the market"
   (Baran, P.A., op. cit., p. 175). Cf. Frank, A.G., Capitalism and
   Underdevelopment in Latin America, New York 1967, passim.
2) Meier, G.M., The International..., p. 232. Lewis, A.W., op. cit.,
   p. 258; Humphrey, D., op. cit., p. 928; Wells, D.A., op. cit., p.
   496; Singer, H.W., op. cit., p. 476; Adler, J.H.(ed.), op. cit., p.
   234; Griffin, K., op. cit., p. 122; Baran, P.A., op. cit., p. 188.

one can find examples of all the types of negative effects described above.[1]

There have been quite a few examples of such negative effects since Independence, mainly due to administrative mistakes.[2] Non-essential and repetitive foreign collaborations that have endangered the position of already existing domestic producers have been allowed into the country, and "genuine Indian parties" have sometimes been prevented from entering an industry by the appearance of a foreign company or an Indian company with foreign collaboration.[3] Generally speaking, India is one of the more industrialized underdeveloped countries, and the possibility of foreign investment replacing existing or forthcoming domestic investment there is proportionately greater than in other such countries. At the same time it is relatively more likely in India than in other underdeveloped countries that the resources released by foreign investment will be put to productive use.

The negative substitution effects of foreign collaborations since Independence have been contrary to official policy. The idea was from the beginning that foreign investment should supplement and not supplant domestic investment, and that it should not be permitted to enter if it would jeopardize existing of forthcoming local industries.[4]

When foreign investments grow older, their contribution of technology and know-how may be relatively less significant than in the beginning.[5] It has been proposed that in such cases the foreign investor should be compulsorily bought out by domestic interests.[6] In India, nationalization has never been used for this purpose, but other policies may be said to work in this

---

1) "The price that the Indian economy had to pay consisted not only of the destruction of the indigenous industries by the competitive power of British investments, but also in the ' opportunity cost' incurred in forgoing the natural process of domestic industrial development which would have taken place if the foreign investments were not there" (Kurian, K.M., Impact of Foreign Capital on Indian Economy, Delhi 1966, p. 60). Cf. pp. 33 ff.; Islam, N., op. cit., p. 185.
2) Cf. pp. 60-61.
3) India. Industrial Licensing Policy Inquiry Committee, op. cit., pp. 131 and 138.
4) India. Planning Commission, Fourth Five-year Plan, op. cit., p. 241.
5) Cf. Meier, G.M., The International..., pp. 156 ff.
6) "It can be argued that the host country is making available foreign exchange to pay the foreign firms without economic justification, if the activities of foreign firms can well be replaced by local firms without loss of efficiency" (Subrahmanian, K.K., op. cit., p. 431). Cf. Tarapore, S.S., Some aspects of foreign investment policy, in Reserve Bank of India Bulletin, May 1966, p. 510.

direction. When majority-owned foreign companies want to expand, they are
sometimes forced to sell part of their share capital to Indian investors. [1]
The Government sometimes puts pressure on foreign firms to make
them take up new and complicated products, thereby increasing the technological benefit to the society from the presence of the foreign company.

Opportunity costs of Swedish companies

In a discussion of the total benefits and costs to India of the presence of the
Swedish companies, the opportunity costs are very important. We have to
find out the probable alternatives, to ascertain what would have happened
if the Swedish firms had not invested in India. Such constructs are necessarily uncertain, especially as regards WIMCO, where alternative events
for almost half a century have to be imagined.

When tariff protection for matches was introduced in the early twenties,
several full-size Indian companies started production, and a large number
of cottage industries also entered the market. According to the Tariff Board
Report of 1928, during its first few years of production WIMCO did not
force any other producers to shut down, but there appears to have been,
even at that early stage, a "pre-empting effect", in the sense that some
domestic companies refrained from setting up new factories for fear of
the competitive and monopolistic strength of WIMCO. [2] During the 1930's
all the major Indian match producers were forced out of the market by
WIMCO, and the only remaining competition came from a few cottage industries in the south. Since Independence, the cottage industries have been
favoured by the Government, but not until in the 1960's did they actually
manage to encroach upon WIMCO's share of the market.

If WIMCO had not invested and started production in India, Indian producers would probably have continued to produce and sell matches in competition with each other. A few of the early Indian companies had technical
collaboration with Japanese firms, and there is a possibility that the Japanese or other foreigners would have invested instead of WIMCO. But the
Japanese firms actually refrained from investing in the 1920's although
they had ample opportunities to do so, and after that the indigenous companies would probably have been strong enough to keep out any possible
foreign investors.

---

1) Cf. p. 201.
2) India. Tariff Board, Match Industry, Vol. II, op. cit., p. 195.

Hence, the most likely alternative development without WIMCO would have been a continued expansion of the domestic match industry.[1] In the opinion of WIMCO, the mechanization of the industry would in that case not have been carried as far as it has now. Besides the full-sized companies, the cottage industry would probably have had better prospects than under the aegis of WIMCO, and it might have stayed on in more places than in the south only. The policy of the national Government of favouring cottage match factories at the expense of large-scale producers would in all probability have been the same, even without the presence of WIMCO.[2]

If the investment and production of WIMCO in the 1920´s had a "pre-empting effect", this means that resources about to be invested in the match industry were released for other purposes. The buoyant condition of the match industry at the time and the tough conditions in other industrial fields make it very likely that some part of these released resources were "wasted", i.e. consumed or invested non-productively. The resources sunk in the match factories of WIMCO´s competitors, practically all of whom were forced out of the market in the 1930´s, were probably lost almost entirely. In later years, WIMCO has substituted for potential investment in the cottage industry, and the resources thus not used for investment in cottage factories in the south have probably not been used for industrial purposes. From the point of view of economic development, WIMCO thus seems to have had relatively high opportunity costs.

If the new Swedish companies had not invested in India, there would probably have been just more domestic production. The competitors of the new Swedish firms were in the market first - none of the new Swedish companies. was a pioneer in its field.[3] The primary effect of the investment of the new Swedish firms was impaired business prospects for already existing local enterprises. In the opinion of the new Swedish companies, other foreign investments would not have replaced the Swedish investments if these had not been made, but the number of Indian firms with foreign technical collaboration might have been greater.

In the case of SKF, an offer was made at the time by the Soviet Union to put up a ball-bearing factory, which allegedly did not fructify because of the investment of SKF. If it had, it would have been a purely technical colla-

---

1) India. Tariff Board, Match Industry, Vol. IV, op. cit., pp. 340 and 500.
2) The duty of the Government to encourage and promote cottage industries is inscribed in the Constitution (The Constitution of India, Allahabad 1968, p. 13).
3) See pp. 256-58.

boration with a company in the public sector, with much higher priority than a private foreign-majority investment like SKF.[1] The investment of SF would probably not have been replaced by a single domestic company because of the special character of SF´s production. Instead, several Indian firms, among them the present competitors of SF, would have secured separate collaborations for different types of SF products.

The resources bound up in the form of fixed capital in the factories of tho competitors of the new Swedish firms which are gradually edged out of the market will probably largely be lost. But most of the resources released for the viable competitors of the new Swedish companies are likely to be used for industrial production of some type, a priori as valuable as the production forgone in favour of the production of the Swedish firms. The resources at the disposal of the Indian capitalists who would have invested had not the new Swedish companies pre-empted the market would probably have to some extent been used for other productive investment, but also for luxury consumption, residential investment, hoarding, etc. Part of th resources released by the investment of the new Swedish firms thus seem to be used productively, and the opportunity costs for the new Swedish com panies are probably lower than for WIMCO.

By its general policies the Government has secured or tried to secure som what greater benefits from the Swedish companies than were originally en visaged. WIMCO in 1938 had to sell half its shares to Indian investors, an in 1969 Vulcan-Laval sold 25 per cent. Atlas Copco has for a long time re tained full ownership but only at the price of compulsory exports as a con dition of expansion. SKF is being pressed to start the manufacture of mor complicated and unprofitable bearings, and the Government also seems to regard it as natural that SKF should export more than the other bearing manufacturers. SF´s royalty rate has been reduced from 5 to 3 per cent, and the other Swedish companies have also met difficulties when applying for the renewal of their royalty agreements.

It is - in retrospect - possible that the Indian Government could have secured even greater benefits from the Swedish companies from the beginnin by tougher negotiations and by the more forceful implementation of its own policies. We have seen that the Swedish majority and its size, the rates of royalties and fees and other conditions were negotiable at the time of the investment, and a tougher attitude on the part of the Indian Government would probably have resulted in greater benefits to the country.[2]

In the 1920´s the Swedish Match concern was not very particular about the

---

1) Cf. also p. 259.
2) Cf. pp. 201–203.

conditions of entry, as long as it was allowed into a country, and it is there-fore quite probable that WIMCO could have been replaced by a technical-collaboration agreement. It is also likely that Sandvik and SKF would have entered even if they had only been able to secure a collaboration agreement. But it appears that the parent firms of Vulcan-Laval and Atlas Copco would, as a matter of policy, rather have abstained than started production in India with only technical collaboration. The parent company of SF is in principle willing to consider all solutions, but a purely technical collaboration would probably not have been possible, because SF thinks it necessary to have quite a large number of foreigners to run the sales, the design work and the organizational activities, and under a technical-collaboration agree-ment enough foreigners would probably not have been allowed by the Govern-ment.

During the present swing left in Indian politics, it seems that the Govern-ment's policies in relation to foreign investments have become a little tougher, which shows, for example, in the increased pressure on foreign companies to further Indianize their capital. Hypothetically, the pressures could continue to the point of total relinquishment of foreign ownership. What would be the reaction of the Swedish companies to such pressures?

As regards WIMCO, the result is not known, because the parent company has no stated policies on this matter. But it seems probable that further Indianization would to some extent be tolerated. Most of the new Swedish companies seem to draw the line at 50 per cent foreign ownership - below that they would either ask for large royalties and fees or simply pull out, in which case their factories in India would soon have to close down be-cause of the lack of fresh know-how (as the Swedish companies in India do not develop and store any know-how of their own). One company sets no lower limit, however, and another claims that it will stay on, as long as it can control the quality of the products. The actual share-holding seems to be less important to the Swedish investors than the possibilities of control.[1]

Transformed benefits and costs

I shall try to illustrate the opportunity costs in the context of the quantita-tive cost-benefit analysis. If the production of the Swedish companies sub-stitutes for domestic production that would otherwise have taken place, the main economic benefit from the Swedish firms, the gross profit, then also substitutes for benefits in the form of profits from the alternative do-

---

1) Cf. pp. 8-9.

mestic production. The sum of the gross profits could therefore be deducted from the total benefits for the Swedish companies as a measure of the maximum opportunity costs.

The profit ratio for the Swedish companies is somewhat higher than the average for Indian industry, and it may therefore be argued that only profits corresponding to the average should be deducted. But we do not know enough about the profit ratios which would prevail in the respective industries in the absence of the Swedish companies, and therefore I shall deduct the actual profits made by the Swedish firms. Gross profits include taxes.

The wage benefit included in the total benefits of the Swedish companies is in itself an "opportunity benefit", where the opportunity costs have already been taken into account. The Swedish companies pay more than the going wage, which, I have assumed, is not the case with the average Indian companies. Without the Swedish companies, the wage benefit would therefore not materialize. It is a benefit uniquely associated with the Swedish firms and should therefore not be deducted from the total benefits of the Swedish companies.

The foreign-exchange inflow is also uniquely associated with the Swedish companies. The imports of machinery to the Swedish subsidiaries in India have largely been financed by the foreign investors. Indian firms have to import machinery and equipment from abroad too, but they cannot supply the foreign exchange themselves. The foreign exchange brought in by the Swedish companies in cash in excess of their import needs goes directly into India's foreign-exchange reserve. The foreign-exchange inflow caused by the Swedish companies is therefore a net benefit, which would not materialize in their absence.

By the same type of reasoning, the foreign-exchange outflows in the form of dividends are a net cost that would not have materialized if there was only domestic production, and the cost of dividend outflows should therefore still be included in the total costs of the Swedish companies. As regards royalties, the Indian companies that would have replaced the Swedish firms would in all probability have had technical-collaboration agreements with foreign concerns. For this they would have incurred costs in foreign exchange for royalties and fees. The royalties and fees paid by the Swedish companies should therefore not be included in the total costs, except for the managing agent's commission for WIMCO and the research fee paid by Sandvik, which are abnormally high and in reality are to a large extent part of the profits.[1] It may be argued that the alternative Indian compa-

---

1) Cf. p. 240 ff.

nies might have secured somewhat higher royalty rates than are permitted for the foreign-controlled Swedish firms, but the resulting adjustment upwards of the net benefits of the Swedish companies would be very marginal.

The inclusion of maximum opportunity costs thus results in a transformation of the quantitative cost-benefit analysis summarized in Table 38 (p. 248). Gross profits are deducted from total benefits, but the wage benefits and the benefits of foreign-exchange inflows are retained, as they would, according to my earlier reasoning, not have materialized without the Swedish companies. The dividend costs is retained and a few exorbitant fees but not normal royalty payments. The result of the transformation is shown in Table 40.

Table 40. Benefits and costs for the Swedish companies, exclusive of gross profits and royalties (Rs. million)

Company and base year	25 per cent of total wages	Foreign-exchange inflows (double value after 1928)	Foreign-exchange outflows, exclusive of royalties (double value after 1928)	Benefits minus costs in 1963 prices, discounted back to base year at 10 % interest rate
WIMCO (1923)	150.1	7.4	-112.1	9.4
Vulcan-Laval (1961)	6.4	14.0	-	11.4
Atlas Copco (1962)	3.2	3.6	-4.1	2.7
Sundvik (1962)	3.6	12.0	-11.0	6.0
SKF (1965)	2.8	50.8	-	40.3
SF (1961)	2.1	2.4	-1.7	2.6
	18.1	82.8	-16.8	

Sources. See Table 38, p. 248. The remittances of the managing agent´s commission for WIMCO and the research fee for Sandvik are included in the outflow figures.

The most striking feature of Table 40 is that the discounted benefits still outweigh the costs, in spite of the exclusion of gross profits. The main benefit from the new Swedish companies, according to the table, is the foreign-exchange inflow, and not the wage benefit. To WIMCO, however, wages are more important. Together with the initial foreign-exchange inflow, they outweigh by a narrow margin the high costs of WIMCO´s foreign-change remittances in the 1930ś.

Vulcan-Laval has made little profit, and the exclusion of profits does not therefore result in any significant change in the discounted value of bene-fits minus costs for this company. The same is true of SKF, where the initial foreign-exchange inflow is very dominant. For the other new Swe-dish companies, the exclusion of gross profits means that the discounted net benefit is heavily reduced but is still positive.

It is possible that for some of the new Swedish companies the negative eff of foreign-exchange remittances will in the future predominate over the w benefits and in due course make the discounted value negative, but that is not a likely outcome. For WIMCO, it might be argued that the relevant ba year should be 1947, when the national Government obtained decision-mal power. At that time the sum of wages in WIMCO had already become so high as to totally predominate over remittances, and the discounted value for WIMCO in 1947 would therefore also be positive.

The result is not, as regards any of the companies, sensitive to changes in the discount rate from 10 to, say, 5 or 15 per cent or even larger va-riations. Altering the assumptions about the premium on foreign exchang will have no effects on the new Swedish companies. As regards WIMCO, a smaller premium yields the same result but with a premium of about 200 per cent, instead of 100 per cent, the discounted value in 1923 would be negative.

Summary. Consumers may benefit from foreign investment through lowei prices and through better and new products. WIMCO has exercised a volu tary price control on matches but not on other products, which, like the products of the new Swedish companies, are sold at a relatively high price. The Swedish products, matches excluded, are of a relatively high quality and the Swedish firms widen the range of choice for the customers by off ing new kinds of product.

There is a danger that through their competitive strength foreign compan may develop into monopolies. Before the cottage industry grew strong enough to offer serious competition, WIMCO had a monopolistic position. The new Swedish companies had in 1968 an average market share of 25 p cent. They all have at least one serious competitor, but, because of thei market advantages, they tend to increase their market shares continuously. Sandvik and SKF may soon reach a point at which the Government will begin to fear monopolistic tendencies.

Foreign investment may have negative effects on local industry by reducing profits, by precipitating close-downs and by deterring prospective local investors from investing. To ascertain these opportunity costs for the Swedish companies, one should find out what would have happened if the Swedish firms had not invested in India. With reasonable assumptions, it seems likely that the opportunity costs are rather high for WIMCO but, relatively speaking, lower for the new Swedish companies. If maximum opportunity costs are included in the quantitative cost-benefit analysis, the benefits still outweigh the costs for all the companies.

Chapter 10.

CONCLUSION

The result of the transformed cost-benefit analysis is not conclusive -
there are certainly many other factors that are of importance in a discussion
of the development effects of the Swedish companies in India. I shall here
recapitulate briefly the non-quantitative effects of the Swedish companies,
but first the effects included in the quantitative analysis will be discussed
somewhat further, in order to diversify the picture a little.

Benefits and costs again

The total gross profits of the Swedish companies were excluded from the
benefits as a measure of the opportunity cost. This is an over-statement of
the negative effects, especially as regards the new Swedish companies.
Also, the possible differences in distribution and use of profits by the Swedish companies and the local producers who would be their likely alternatives were not taken into account in the quantitative analysis. The Swedish
firms, with the exception of WIMCO, have re-invested a larger part of the
profits than the average, and it is therefore probable that the alternative
producers would have distributed more of their profits as dividends. The
larger re-investments of the Swedish companies are a positive effect, but
at the same time they create a long-term foreign-exchange liability. As
for dividends, the share-holders of the alternative companies and the owner
of the resources released by the Swedish investments would probably be the
same type of capitalists who now own a large part of the Indian shares in
the Swedish firms. Without the Swedish firms, these capitalists might get
somewhat larger dividends from the alternative Indian companies than they
get now, with ensuing social costs in the form of increased inequality of
incomes. Taxes and tax concessions are the same for foreign and Indian
companies.

The Swedish companies are mainly run on Indian capital in the form of
equity, long-term loans and short-term bank borrowings.[1] In comparison
with the Indian capital employed, the addition of savings by the Swedish
firms is therefore not very important, but as an addition of foreign exchange
the capital inflows are of more consequence, and this has been taken into

---

1) Cf. p. 200.

consideration in the quantitative analysis. Most of the inflow is in kind, which is sometimes less valuable than cash, but the Swedish companies have generally not imported more than was necessary, and the alternative companies - including those that would have been set up with the resources released - would probably have run a relatively greater risk of importing excessively from unscrupulous foreign collaborators.

The indirect foreign-exchange effects through exports and imports were not included in the quantitative analysis. The Swedish companies export more than their competitors - spurred on to do this by pressures from the Indian Government and encouragement from their parent firms - but the quantity of exports is generally small. Indian companies of the type that would have been set up with the resources released by the Swedish investments have in general somewhat better export performances than foreign companies. The exports of the Swedish firms cannot therefore be added as a net benefit, in spite of the fact that they are relatively larger than the exports of their present competitors. Whether positive or negative, the net foreign-exchange effects of exports from the Swedish companies are probably quantitatively insignificant.

The Swedish firms are found in import-substituting industries, but this is the case also with their Indian competitors, who started production before the Swedish companies. The direct import-substitution effects of the Swedish firms are therefore cancelled out. The resources released by the Swedish companies may be invested in import-substituting industries, but to what extent is not known.

The import content of production for most industries in India is determined by objective technical requirements, because the Government maintains a constant pressure on producers to substitute local manufactures for imports. There is, therfore, little scope for differences between Swedish and Indian companies with respect to import content. Hence, the net foreign-exchange effects for the Swedish companies in connection with imports are probably positive and dependent on the extent to which the resources released are invested in import-competing industries.

The wage benefits pose special problems. The fact that a company pays higher wages than others has effects both on growth and the distribution of income. The inclusion of wage benefits in a cost-benefit analysis is perhaps not always warranted.[1] Also, the actual wage benefits included in the quantitative anlysis should be corrected on at least one point. For all the Swedish companies I have assumed a constant wage benefit of 25 per cent as a mea-

---

1) Cf. p. 234.

sure of the higher wages in the Swedish firms. But it is more realistic to assume that WIMCO paid only average wages up to 1947.[1] If the wage benefits before 1947 are excluded from the transformed cost-benefit analysis for WIMCO presented in the previous section, only capital inflows and outflows remain for the early years, and the discounted net value of benefits minus costs for WIMCO then turns negative.

Non-monetary benefits enjoyed by the employees in industrial firms seem to be marginally preferable to wages, because of their more direct effects on the workers' productivity and well-being. WIMCO has followed and still follows the local practices in the respective factory areas, while the new Swedish companies provide uniforms, transport subsidies and free tea, over and above normal practice. Indian firms replacing the new Swedish companies would probably have followed the prevailing practices, and the extra welfare provided by the new Swedish firms should therefore be considered as a net gain. It is only a question of a net value of a few per cent of the total wages, but as a measure of the qualitative advantage of welfare as compared with wages, the value of the extra welfare measures could perhaps be set at, say, 5 per cent of the total wages. The wage benefits for the new Swedish companies would thereby increase from 25 to 30 per cent of the total wages, a change that would, of course, not alter in any way the result of the quantitative analysis.

Location and employment

Of the many effects not included in the quantitative analysis, some are connected with the location of the Swedish companies in the country and within industry. The WIMCO factories were from the beginning located in non-industrial areas, but at present most of them, in company with the new Swedish firms, tend to aggravate the industrial congestion in already developed areas. This is contrary to the present industrial-dispersal policy of the Government.

Indian companies are not as prone as foreign firms to establish themselves in the old industrial centres and, compared with the probable alternatives, at least the new Swedish companies seem therefore to some extent to have had negative locational effects.

The distribution of the Swedish companies between industries and within the industrial structure is, on the whole, favourable to development. This would, of course, also have been the case with the Indian companies replac by the Swedish firms, but it would not be applicable to the investment and

---

1) See p. 121.

se of the resources released in non-industrial pursuits. The linkage effects are a consequence of a company's position within the industrial system. WIMCO is largely an "industrial enclave", while the new Swedish companies stimulate in varying degrees production in other industries through backward and forward linkages. The linkage concept is dubious, and the net effects of the Swedish companies in this context are uncertain.

WIMCO for a long time had a monopolistic position on the match market, and a few of the new Swedish firms may eventually get into a similar position. The Swedish companies are so strong and have so many advantages over their competitors that the latter have difficulties in holding their own, in spite of their having in some cases acquired costly foreign collaborations and trade-marks just to fight the Swedish companies. The Indian companies replaced by the Swedish firms would probably not have had as much marketing strength as the Swedish companies and the risk of a production monopoly arising would have been proportionately smaller. At the same time the Indian capitalists owning the replaced industries and in command of the resources released by the Swedish investments would to a considerable extent have been members of the large industrial houses, which have had a special type of monopoly effects.

The monopolistic position of WIMCO had, at least in the later stage, no drastic effects on the prices of ordinary matches, because of the voluntary price control exercised by the company. As regards other products, WIMCO's prices are higher than the prices of its competitors. Also the new Swedish companies have higher prices than the average, but, on the other hand, the quality of their products is probably higher than that of Indian companies. The introduction of new kinds of product may proceed somewhat faster with the Swedish companies than without them, and, on the whole, the consumers of the Swedish types of products would probably be somewhat worse off in the absence of the Swedish firms.

Employment. The Indian Government has accepted industrialization and modern industries, even though they do not in the short run create very much in the way of employment opportunities. But in the modern sector itself, other factors being disregarded, companies employing more people are preferred to those that employ fewer people. More employment is still one of the basic independent goals of the Indian Government. An increased number of wage-earners is sometimes also regarded as a means of accomplishing a desirable redistribution of income.

At the same time, the Government wants increased productivity, and it therefore follows a cautious policy of promoting rationalization. Capital-intensive techniques are accepted in the long-range view, while at the same time a strong preference for labour-intensive techniques is shown in fields where the use of such techniques does not lead to smaller aggregate production.

The new Swedish companies are very capital-intensive in the Indian conte and they do not actively try to exploit the few possibilities available of usi more labour-intensive techniques. They also have high productivity, the consequences of which have already been treated. The ultimate employme effects of the new Swedish companies are likely to be small but positive. WIMCO, on the other hand, competes with the very labour-intensive cotta industry and has therefore probably strong negative employment effects.

External economies

A large part of this book has been taken up by an analysis of what I have called "external economies". The linkage effects mentioned in the last section are of a type that I have called "external economies in a narrow sense". Besides the linkage effects, I have included in this category the external economies of a physical nature.

It is likely that the costs incurred by the Swedish companies for investme in roads, electricity, etc. to some extent exceed the social costs. But the resources disemployed by the new Swedish investments are probably partl used for industrial investment, and this implies further use of underprice public utilities. The ultimate effects of the Swedish companies in connecti with the infrastructure are therefore difficult to determine. The Swedish firms have caused little in the way of pollution, and their well-kept factor buildings and gardens offer a pleasant sight. In comparison with the avera Indian companies, the Swedish firms seem to give more attention to envir mental effects.

The more important external economies are those that I have called "external economies in a wider sense". This category is a somewhat obscure concept, comprising almost everything that is usually omitted or only me tioned in the analysis of foreign investment: labour policies, educational effects, and cultural impacts. I have tried to penetrate a bit deeper into these areas but have certainly not gone deep enough. The lack of data sho perhaps have kept me from trying at all.

Labour policies. The Swedish companies do not at present recruit any far mers. They pay high wages and can therefore recruit already trained labo from other big companies, who in their turn recruit from smaller establis

276

ments. The burden of initial "industrial socialization" is therefore not borne by the Swedish companies. The Indian companies that would replace the Swedish firms would probably also recruit already trained labour, although not to the same extent.

Several WIMCO factories give preference in recruitment to the sons of workers, and some of the new Swedish companies have set an upper age limit for new workers. But, on the whole, at least the new Swedish companies appear to have more progressive recruitment policies than the average Indian company. New applicants are not discriminated against on account of their religion, race or caste. The male hegemony in typewriting jobs has to some small extent been broken by the new Swedish firms, and they also seem to keep relatively few workers in non-permanent positions.

The new Swedish companies appear to use formalized channels of recruitment relatively more than other firms, which will give skill and experience fuller play - recruitment becomes less personal and arbitrary. Also after recruitment, within the factory, skill and experience seem to be more appreciated in the new Swedish companies than in the average Indian firm. Horizontal mobility is encouraged, and also to some extent promotion within the company.

Skill and experience are also relatively well reflected in the wage-fixing of the Swedish companies, as most of them have introduced or are introducing piece-rate systems of payment. But even though most of the employees would earn more with piece-rates, they are usually not in favour of such systems. The general wage policy of the Swedish companies is relatively progressive - the clerk category, for example, seems to be less pampered in the Swedish companies than in other firms.

The workers in the Swedish companies are usually organized in trade unions. The majority of the trade unions are affiliated to Left-wing political parties, and half of the unions in the Swedish firms have outside leaders. The managements of the Swedish companies seem to have a much more positive attitude to trade unions and serious negotiations than that of the average Indian company. They know from Swedish experience that strong unions and open-minded negotiations are as profitable or even more profitable for the company than for the workers themselves. WIMCO still has many strikes, but the new Swedish companies have a good record of industrial peace. They also appear to have in general better and more democratic management-labour relations than most Indian firms.

The Swedish companies, at least the new ones, thus seem to have generally more progressive labour policies than the Indian firms that would have existed in their absence. They are also likely to be more progressive than the companies started with the resources released by the Swedish investments. This is favourable for the Swedish companies and also for their employees. But to be an external economy in the usual sense of the word the effect must be external, i.e. the progressive policies in the Swedish companies should be spread to other companies and bodies and there produce growth and development.

The satisfactory labour-management relations in the Swedish companies seem to spread relatively easily. The personnel officers and trade-union leaders in an area are usually in constant touch with their counterparts in other companies, and in this way a continuous harmonization of labour-management relations in different companies is accomplished. But the progressive recruitment policies in the new Swedish companies are apparently not spread in this way. There must, of course, be some "rub-off" effects from the contented employees in the Swedish firms.[1] But the most efficient medium of communication of new recruitment ideas still seems to be the employees leaving to take up posts in other companies. As these employees are leaving, they are not always enthusiastic about the Swedish firms. Besides, the turnover in the Swedish companies is relatively low. The progressive recruitment policies in the Swedish companies do not therefore appear to be of much benefit to other companies.

This seems to be true also of most other labour policies. The trade unions may be interested in the promotional policies of the Swedish companies, but the encouragement of horizontal mobility and increased flexibility meets with little appreciation from the workers. In the Indian context this is understandable - jobs are so scarce that, once acquired, they are looked upon as pieces of property that should not be unnecessarily tampered with. The wage policies and piece-rate systems of payment introduced by the managements in the Swedish companies are also regarded with suspicion by the workers, and they do not therefore have much reason to spread the message. With the exception of the labour-management relations, the good habits and progressive policies of the Swedish companies therefore tend to some extent to stay within the walls of the respective firms, and the "external economies" remain largely internal.

Training, culture and politics

An obvious example of what I have called the "external economies in a wider sense" of foreign investment is the training of the workers. But, in India, the Government is responsible for practically all organized training of workers. Private companies have generally not shown any interest in

---

1) Cf. p. 168.

the training of workers, and their main contribution - the training of apprentices - was forced upon them by the Government. The Swedish companies have in the main followed the general passive trend. In the early years
WIMCO provided - as would any replacing industry - its workers with basic on-the-job industrial training, but later, when other companies became
the main source of recruitment, the task of initial socialization was passed
on to others. Some of the Swedish firms have a very specialized production,
turnover of labour is generally low, and the possible spread effects of
workers' training are therefore apparently not greater than in the case of
most of the labour policies.

Also as regard staff-training, the Swedish companies have taken very few
initiatives. A few employees have been sent to Sweden, but in India little
is done. In WIMCO, many of the higher posts were for a long time reserved
for foreigners, which restricted the opportunities of advancement for
Indian nationals. At present both WIMCO and the new Swedish companies
seem to be moving effective company control from India to Sweden, and
this is one reason why the number of foreign personnel in India can be reduced. The Indian companies that are replaced by the Swedish firms would
probably have followed the same passive policy, as regards staff-training,
but there would not have been any restrictions on staff promotion, and the
net effect of the Swedish companies in respect of training is therefore likely to be marginally negative.

The external economy most frequently mentioned in connection with foreign
investment is that foreign companies can bring in new technology and know-
how. The Swedish companies did not bring in any new technology at the
time of investment (this follows from the fact that the Swedish firms replaced local production), but later, new kinds of product have been introduced, perhaps more rapidly by the Swedish companies than by their competitors. The latter effect has already been taken into account as a
consumers' benefit.

The existing technology is probably spread somewhat more actively through
sales and service activities by the Swedish companies than would be the
case with alternative Indian companies. On the purchase side, there is
also a benefit derived from the foreign contact - perhaps more of a cultural than a technological nature - suppliers are taught to be time and quality conscious. But a major cost is also associated with the foreign companies only: all research necessary for the production of the Swedish companies is done outside India. Alternative Indian companies would not be in
a position to rely so completely on their foreign collaborators as the
Swedish subsidiaries do on their parent firms. In the long run, the external economies in connection with technology will, on the whole, therefore
probably be more of a diseconomy than an economy.

Except for WIMCO, the Swedish companies have probably used more modern and efficient management tools and methods than the companies that they have replaced. It is also likely that business standards and personnel policies in the Swedish firms are relatively more conducive to growth than in Indian firms. But the problem is, again, that these effects are more internal than external. The diffusion of business standards and management know-how is largely dependent on a small trickle of Indian staff leaving their employment in the Swedish companies.

Culture. In India, religion, as such, is apparently not as important an obstacle to growth as the caste system. Although at least the extremes of the caste system show up also in the Swedish factories, their activities and policies seem to work in the direction of a weakening of the system. Caste, for example, is not taken into account in the Swedish firms in recruitment and promotion matters. In contrast, many small-scale Indian companies are run on a caste or family basis. The likely alternatives to the Swedish firms, except in the case of WIMCO, would be large-scale Indian companies which would probably pay almost as little attention to caste as the Swedish companies.

The characteristics of the early industrialization process in India, such as extremely high turnover figures and generally unstable conditions, are gradually disappearing. The industrial labour force is settled in the factory areas and is gradually becoming committed to industrial work. But commitment to factory jobs is not necessarily the same as commitment to industrial values and incentives. Low figures of absenteeism and turnover may indicate that the work force, at least in the new Swedish companies, is more stable than the average, but from this fact no firm conclusions can be drawn about cultural changes.

But the workers in the Swedish companies have to some extent to conform to the "logic of industrialization". The industrial order forces them to accept changes in dress, discipline, attitudes to business careers etc. But more fundamental values do not seem to change much as a consequence of employment in the Swedish firms. The changes resulting from the industrial order are largely part of the all-pervasive western influence in India, where the role played by industry is probably less significant than other westernizing influences. But it is still likely that industrial culturization and general westernizing proceeds a little faster in the Swedish firm than in Indian companies.

Political effects. The political effects treated in Chapter 6 were mainly of a negative nature. The Swedish investments in India add to an already relatively large foreign sector and as a marginal addition they have a proportionately high political "cost". New foreign investments represent increased foreign control over industry. Also, the higher the percentage of foreign-owned equity in a firm, the larger the present and future share of industry that will be controlled by foreigners. All the Swedish companies were at the time of investment allowed majority ownership, which was perhaps not necessary.[1]

The initial 99-100 per cent foreign ownership of Vulcan-Laval and Atlas Copco certainly seems unjustified. The policy of the new Swedish companies of re-investing a larger part of the profits than the average also has a political cost; although less income is siphoned away to Swedish or Indian capitalists, their wealth is increased, a future foreign-exchange liability is created, and foreign control over Indian industry is enlarged. Control of the Swedish companies is also qualitatively becoming increasingly foreign - refined budgeting and reporting systems are leading to the locus of decision and control being moved outside India.

The foreign sector in India - sometimes backed up by the respective foreign governments and aid agencies - has some influence on the policies of the Indian Government in a direction favourable to foreign capital, which is a restriction on the freedom of the Indian Government to formulate its own policies. The Swedish companies seem to have more influence as members of the total foreign sector than individually or as a group of Swedish firms. The foreign sector also gives support to the Indian big-business sector. In the absence of the Swedish firms, the political effects in connection with the "foreignness" would not have materialized. The alternative Indian companies and the resources released would probably also have been to a large extent used to further the cause of big business, and the negative political effects of the Swedish companies appear therefore to be a net addition.

Final considerations

The political effects of the Swedish companies are not quantifiable, nor are most of the external effects treated earlier. In a few cases a quantitative indication can be given, for example, the extent to which formal channels of recruitment have been used. But this is not enough for what would have been appropriate at this stage, namely, a precise comparison of all the different positive and negative effects of the Swedish firms.

---

1) Cf. pp. 266-67.

Ideally, such a comparison should take the form of a summation of quanti
tative indicators, which should be given due weightings.[1] But not even th
quantitative cost-benefit analysis in Chapters 8 and 9 can be considered to
include satisfactory weightings (actually, no weightings at all were used
for widely different uses of the social income). It is practically impossibl
to give satisfactory quantitative weightings to most of the other effects of
the Swedish companies. Many effects cannot, in the first place, be given
any quantitative indication, much less any weightings.

A precise comparison of effects is therefore impossible. But instead of
leaving matters at that, I would like to proceed a little further. The decisions of the Indian Government on foreign investments involve all the type
of effects described here, and it may be of interest to discuss somewhat
further in what direction an assessment of the total effects of the Swedish
investments might go.

The case of WIMCO is fairly straightforward. With realistic assumptions,
the quantitative analysis for WIMCO yields a negative result in the form
of a negative value of the sum of discounted benefits and costs.[2] In addition to this, there is a very strong negative employment effect. It is really
not necessary to add that the net positive external economies for WIMCO
in the form of technology, labour effects and cultural impact have not been
very significant, and that the long-term political effects also seem to be
negative. One does not need any refined analysis to conclude that the
net effect of WIMCO's presence in India has been negative.

In the case of the new Swedish companies, no such clear-cut conclusions
emerge. The quantitative analysis yields a net economic benefit for all
of them, which has then to be set in relation to other effects.

The positive net effects of the new Swedish companies on their physical
environment appear in comparison to be quite insignificant. As regards
the location of the Swedish firms in the country, an also not very significant negative effect of increasing industrial congestion and inequality between states may be assigned to the new Swedish companies. More import
are perhaps the employment effects. The ultimate employment effects of
the new Swedish companies are likely to be small but positive.

The high quality of the Swedish products is matched by high prices, but
it is possible that the consumers may benefit from a somewhat faster introduction of new kinds of product by the Swedish companies than would
otherwise be the case.

---

1) Cf. p. 22.
2) See p. 274.

The labour policies of the new Swedish companies are, on the whole, more progressive than the average. Relatively speaking, very little discrimination is shown in recruitment, promotion and wage-fixing. Labour-management relations are generally good. But with the possible exception of labour-management relations, the good practices in the Swedish companies do not seem to have spread extensively to other companies - they remain largely internal to the Swedish firms.

The spread effects from the scanty training given in the new Swedish companies are apparently also of little significance. When compared with alternative Indian companies, the Swedish firms are even likely to have a marginally negative educational effect, on account of their having reserved certain higher posts for foreign nationals.

The new Swedish companies utilize more modern management know-how than Indian firms, but this know-how is, on the whole, not spread to other companies. Also, the Swedish firms have not introduced any new technology, but existing technology and quality consciousness are probably spread to customers and suppliers more actively than would be the case with purely Indian companies. But the latter positive effect may be more than cancelled out be the negative effect on indigenous research produced by the presence of the new Swedish firms.

The net cultural effect of the new Swedish companies includes a weakening of the caste system. Superficial but not fundamental cultural habits and values are affected in a direction positive to economic growth, and the net cultural effect is probably positive. But the political effects are all negative. The Swedish companies come on top of an already "too large" foreign sector and strengthen the bargaining position of the total foreign sector vis-à-vis the Indian Government. They also strengthen the position of Indian large-scale business interests. Foreign control through the Swedish companies is increasing both quantitatively and qualitatively. The monopoly tendencies of a few Swedish companies and the unnecessary acquisitions of foreign collaboration by their competitors may also be included among the negative political effects.

To summarize the non-quantified effects, the new Swedish companies have small but positive employment effects, and they to some extent offer qualitative benefits to the consumers. The cultural effects are, on the whole, likely to be positive, and the progressive labour policies may to some small extent be beneficial to other companies. Against this should be set the somewhat negative locational effects, the possible indirect costs pertaining to training and know-how, and the negative political effects.

The adding up of incommensurables in the preceding paragraph yields no obvious results. I invite the reader to go back to the main body of the text to make his own judgments and draw his own conclusions. As the quantitative analysis shows a positive result for the new Swedish companies, the more interesting case would be when the sum of the non-quantified effects is negative, because this would necessitate a comparison between the quantified and the non-quantified effects.

The quantitative result, as shown in Table 40 (p. 270), should be slightly modified in the light of the subsequent discussion of the various benefits and costs.[1] The opportunity costs for the new Swedish companies are lower than those included in Table 40, and secondary benefits may occur in connection with the profit distribution, the import-substitution effects and the non-monetary wage benefits of the new Swedish firms. The total quantitative benefits are therefore probably larger than is shown in Table 40.

The final result of weighing up the totality of the quantified and non-quantified effects depends very much on the weight given to the political effects. In calculating the quantitative benefits, I have made use of a discount rate, which makes effects in the distant future appear very unimportant. But it does not seem that the long-term effects of foreign control can be discounted in this way.[2] The Swedish companies, however small in the aggregate, are part of the total foreign sector, they grow faster than Indian companies, and they therefore represent a threat of growing foreign control over industry and increased foreign influence on national policies. We have seen earlier that the effects of foreign investment should be seen in a long-term perspective,[3] and the short-term economic benefits then may become relatively less important than the long-term negative effects of a political nature.

The political effects seem particularly important in the Indian case, because there is in India an alternative to foreign control through the Swedish companies. The Swedish companies started production in fields where Indian companies were already well established, and the main effect of the Swedish investments was therefore that they replaced the already existing production of local companies. It therefore seems probable that the Indian Government, faced with a clear-cut choice, would not have preferred the Swedish foreign-majority-owned companies to domestic production and

---

1) See pp. 272 ff.

2) Nor, really, can the long-term pressure on the balance of payments caused by foreign investment, and the discussion of the long-term political effects is also applicable to the long-term balance-of-payments effects.

3) See pp. 24-25.

increased possibilities of long-term self-sustaining growth, even though
the foreign companies might offer larger short-term economic benefits.
If the Indian Government had at the time of decision had access to the type
of material on a number of actual and future events presented in this study,
it seems likely that it would not have allowed the new Swedish companies
to invest in India.

Foreign investment in general. The total result of the past activities of
the Swedish companies in India may be of interest with regard to future
policies. In the current situation, with the Swedish companies in production in India, a new examination ought to be made in the light of past experience of the future effects of these and other foreign investments in
India. It may be appropriate to give as much attention to the effects of
foreign investments as to the activities of the large-scale Indian business
houses, which were scrutinized in detail by the Dutt Committee. [1]

The actual results of the presence of the Swedish companies and the consequent policy conclusions are not the major possible outcome of this study.
The total development impact of the Swedish firms is anyway so difficult
to determine that really no firm conclusions can be drawn. The present
study should rather be regarded mainly as a case study of the possible
development effects of foreign private investment - an example of which
types of effects could be taken into account in an analysis of foreign investment and perhaps also which effects one may expect to be relatively
more important than others. If one is to judge from the example of the
Swedish companies, it seems, for example, that the "external economies
in a wider sense" - the indirect spread effects in connection with technology, training and know-how - are generally given undue importance in
the theoretical literature on private foreign investment.

It is not possible to generalize about the impact of private foreign investment in underdeveloped countries. It all depends on the country and the
industry concerned. But one may always speculate, even in connection
with the slender evidence from the Swedish companies. It seems that in
the case of the Swedish firms in India, we have come across a rather
favourable example, at the upper end of the scale, as it were. In comparison with firms from other countries, the Swedish companies in India

---

1) India. Industrial Licensing Policy Inquiry Committee, op. cit. Foreign
   companies were also to some extent discussed by the Dutt Committee,
   and the policies towards foreign investments have subsequently become
   a little more restrictive. The Swedish firms were exposed in 1970-71
   to more pressures than before to further Indianize their share-holdings,
   to export more, etc.

appear to be fairly "well behaved". This seems also to be the case with some Swedish companies in Latin America.[1]

Also, India seems to have extracted almost the maximum practicable contribution from the Swedish firms: investment in priority sectors, relatively low foreign-majority ownership, import substitution, high taxes, etc. If the Swedish companies are in comparison keenly alive to the development needs of the respective host countries, if India is an underdeveloped country that secures a relatively high contribution from its foreign investments, and if one may still question the value to India of the presen of the Swedish companies, one may ask what contribution other foreign companies in other underdeveloped countries are expected to make.

---

1) Sveriges Allmänna Exportförening, op. cit.

BIBLIOGRAPHY

ADLER, J.H. (ed.), Capital Movements and Economic Development, New York 1967.

ALEJANDRO, C.F.D., Direct Foreign Investment in Latin America, in Kindleberger, C.P. (ed.), The International Corporation, Cambridge 1970.

The American Economic Review, May 1950, Papers and Proceedings.

The American Economic Review, 1965:1.

ANSTEY, V., The Economic Development of India, London 1957.

ARNDT, H.W., Overseas Borrowing - The New Model, in The Economic Record, Vol. 23, August 1957.

ARROW, K.J. and Scitovsky, T. (eds.), Readings in Welfare Economics, London 1969.

BARAN, P.A., The Political Economy of Growth, New York 1967.

BARANSON, J., Manufacturing Problems in India. The Cummins Diesel Experience, New York 1967.

BEHRMAN, J.N., Economic effects of private direct investment, in Mikesell, R.F. (ed.), U.S. Private and Government Investment Abroad, Eugene 1962.

BERNSTEIN, M.D., Foreign Investment in Latin America, New York 1968.

BOPEGAMAGE, A. and VEERARAGHAVAN, P.V., Status Images in Changing India, Delhi 1967.

BUCHANAN, D.H., The Development of Capitalist Enterprise in India, New York 1934.

CAIRNCROSS, A.K., Factors in Economic Development, London 1962.

CHENERY, H.B., Foreign assistance and economic development, in ADLER, J.H. (ed.).

CHENERY, H.B., The application of investment criteria, in Quarterly Journal of Economics, Vol. LXVII, 1953.

CHOPRA, P., Uncertain India, Cambridge 1968.

CHOUDHARI, A., Oligopoly and industrial research in India, in Monopolies and Their Regulations in India, Bombay 1966.

CLAIRMONTE, F., Economic Liberalism and Underdevelopment. Studies in the disintegration of an idea, Bombay 1960.

Commerce, Annual Number 1968, Bombay 1968.

The Constitution of India, Allahabad 1968.

COOPER, R.N., The Economics of Interdependence, New York 1968.

DAS GUPTA, S.C., The story of matches and the match industry of India, All India Khadi and Village Industries Research Institute, Bombay, no date.

DESAI, A.V., Potentialities of collaboration and their utilisation, in Hazari, R.K. (ed.), Foreign Collaboration.

DHAR, P.N. and LYDALL, H.F., The Role of Small Enterprises in Indian Economic Development, Bombay 1961.

DIWAN, G.R., Working Paper on the Poona Metropolitan Region, Poona 1968, p. 5 (mimeographed).

DIWEDY, S., and BHARGAVA, G.S., Political Corruption in India, New Delhi 1967.

DORFMAN, R., (ed.), Measuring the Benefits of Government Investments, Washington 1967.

DUTT, R., The Economic Development of India, London 1957.

Economic Journal, June 1956.

Economic Record, Vol. 23, August 1957.

Economic Times, March 28, Bombay 1969.

Economic Times, March 31, Bombay 1969.

EDWARDES, M., British India, London 1967.

EISLER, H., En saklig betraktelse, Uddevalla 1969.

Employers Federation of India, Handbook of Labour Statistics 1968, Bombay 1968.

EPSTEIN, T.S., Economic Development and Social Change in South India, Manchester 1962.

Foreign Affairs, July 1967.

FORSTENIUS, E., Swedish Collaborations in India, Swedish Embassy, New Delhi 1970 (mimeographed).

FRANK, A.G., Capitalism and Underdevelopment in Latin America, New York 1967.

GABRIEL, P.P., The International Transfer of Corporate Skills. Management Contracts in Less Developed Countries, Boston 1967.

GAGDIL, D.R., The Industrial Evolution of India in Recent Times, London 1933.

GEIGER, T., The General Electric Company in Brazil, New York 1961.

GIESECKE, H., Betrachtungen zum Entwicklungsbeitrag überseeischer Privatinvestitionen, in Wirtschaftsdienst, 43, 1963:1.

GRIFFIN, K., Underdevelopment in Spanish America. An Interpretation, London 1969.

GÅRDLUND, T., Främmande investeringar i u-land, Stockholm 1968.

HARBISON, F. and MYERS, C.A., Management in the industrial world. An International Analysis, New York 1959.

HAZARI, R.K. (ed.), Foreign Collaboration, University of Bombay, Bombay 1967.

HIRSCHMANN, A.O., The Strategy of Development, Yale 1958.

HUMPHREY, D., Direct foreign investment and economic growth, in Economic Weekly, Special Number, June 1960.

HYMER, S.H., International Operations of National Firms. A Study of Direct Foreign Investment, Diss., Massachusetts Institute of Technology 1960.

India, Central Statistical Organisation, Annual Survey of Industries 1965, Volume 1, Delhi 1969.

India, Estimates Committee, Report 1967-68, Delhi 1967.

India. External Capital Committee, Report, Calcutta 1925.

India. Fiscal Commission 1949-50, Report, Delhi 1950.

India. Industrial Licensing Policy Inquiry Committee, Main Report, Delhi 1969.

India Labour Bureau. Indian Labour Statistics 1969, Simla 1969.

India. Ministry of Finance, Pocket Book of Economic Information, Delhi 1970.

India. Ministry of Labour, Report of the Committee on Fair Wages, Delhi 1963 (1949).

India, Monopolies Inquiry Commission, Report, Delhi 1965.

India. National Commission on Labour, Report, Delhi 1969.

India. Planning Commission, The First Five-year Plan. A Summary, Delhi 1952.

India. Planning Commission, Fourth Five-year Plan 1969-74, Draft, Delhi 1969.

India. Planning Commission, Second Five-Year Plan, Summary, Delhi 1956.

India. Planning Commission, Third Five-year Plan. A Draft Outline, Delhi 1960.

India. Planning Commission, Industrial Planning and Licensing Policy, Final Report, Delhi 1967.

India. Tariff Board, Report of the Indian Tariff Board regarding the grant of protection to the match industry, Calcutta 1928.

India. Tariff Board, Match Industry, Vol. I-IV, Calcutta 1928.

India. Tariff Commission, Report on Fair Selling Prices of Safety Matches, Bombay 1963.

India. Taxation Enquiry Commission 1953-54, Report, Vol. III, Delhi 1955.

Indian Investment Centre, Seminar on International Investment, Speech of the Minister of Finance, Mr. Morarji Desai, November 27, Delhi 1968.

Indian Investment Centre, Taxes and Incentives, Delhi 1968.

ISLAM, N., Foreign Capital and Development: Japan, India and Canada, Tokyo 1960.

JATHAR, G.B., and BERI, S.G., Indian Economics, Bombay 1959.

JOHANSSON, H., Utländsk företagsetablering i Sverige, Uddevalla 1968.

JOHNSON, H.G., The efficiency and welfare implications of the international corporation in Kindleberger, C.P. (ed.), The International Corporation, Cambridge 1970.

KERR, C., et al., Industrialism and Industrial Man, London 1962.

KIDRON, M., Foreign Investments in India, London 1965.

KINDLEBERGER, C.P., American Business Abroad, New Haven 1969.

KINDLEBERGER, C.P. (ed.), The International Corporation, Cambridge 1970.

KOTHARI, M.L., Industrial Combinations, Allahabad 1967.

KRISHNAMACHARI, T.T., Inaugural speech at the All-India Economic Conference, December 1963 (mimeographed).

KUMARASUNDARAM, S., Foreign collaborations and Indian balance of payments, in Hazari, R.K. (ed.), Foreign Collaboration, Bombay 1967.

KURIAN, K.M., The Impact of Foreign Capital on the Indian Economy, New Delhi 1966.

KUST, M.J., Foreign Enterprise in India, Bombay 1966.

KUST, M.J., Foreign Enterprise in India, Supplement, Bombay 1967.

LAMBERT, R.D., Workers, Factories and Social Change in India, Princeton 1963.

LEWIS, A.W., The Theory of Economic Growth, London 1965 (1955).

LITTLE, I.M.D., and CLIFFORD, M.J., International Aid, London 1965.

LITTLE, I.M.D. and MIRRLEES, J.A., Manual of Industrial Projects Analysis in Developing Countries, Vol. II, Social Cost-Benefit Analysis, OECD, Paris 1968.

LUND, H., Svenska företags investeringar i utlandet, Stockholm 1967.

LUNDBERG, E. & BACKELIN, T. (eds.), Ekonomisk politik i förvand-ling, Stockholm 1970.

MacDOUGALL, G.D.A., The benefits and costs of private investment from abroad: A theoretical approach, in Oxford University Institute of Statistics Bulletin, 22:1960.

MASON, R.H., An Analysis of Benfits from U.S. Direct Foreign Investments in Less developed Areas. Diss., Stanford Univ., no date.

McKEAN, R.K., Efficiency in Government through Systems Analysis, New York 1958.

McLAUGHLIN, R.U., Foreign Investment and Development in Liberia, New York 1966.

MAY, S. and PLAZA, G., The United Fruit Company in Latin America, New York 1958.

MEADE, J.E., Efficiency, Equality and the Ownership of Property, Cambridge 1964.

MEHTA, B., Oil and Self-reliance, Delhi 1965.

MEHTA, G.L., Development and Foreign Collaboration, Indian Investment Centre Publication, Delhi 1968.

MEIER, G.M., The International Economics of Development, Tokyo 1968

MEIER, G.M., International Trade and Development, Tokyo 1964.

MEIER, G.M., Leading Issues in Economic Development, Stanford 1970.

MIKESELL, R.F. (ed.), U.S. Private and Government Investment Abroad Eugene 1962.

MISHAN, E.J., Welfare Economics: An Assessment, Amsterdam 1969.

MODEL, L., The politics of private foreign investment, in Foreign Affair July 1967.

Monopolies and Their Regulations in India. Bombay 1966.

MYERS, C. A., Labor Problems in the Industrialization of India, Cambridge 1958.

MYRDAL, G., Asian Drama, New York 1968.

NAMJOSHI, M.V., Monopolies in India, Bombay 1966.

NIEHOFF, A., Factory Workers in India, Milwaukee 1959.

OHLIN, G., Den ekonomiska teorin inför u-ländernas problem, in LUNDBERG, E. & BACKELIN, T. (eds.), Ekonomisk politk i förvand-ling, Stockholm 1970.

The Oxford History of India, Oxford 1958.

Oxford University Institute of Statistics Bulletin, 1960:22.

PANT, S.C., Indian Labour Problems, Allahabad 1965.

PAZOS, F., The role of international movements of private capital in promoting development, in ADLER, J.H.

PENROSE, E., Foreign investment and the growth of the firm, in Economic Journal, June 1956.

Poona Metropolitan Regional Planning Board, Industries in the Poona Region 1964-65, unpublished.

PREST, A.R. and TURVEY, R., Cost-Benefit Analysis: A Survey, in Surveys of Economic Theory III, New York 1967.

Quarterly Journal of Economics, Vol. LXVII, February 1953.

Bank of India, Bulletin, May 1966.

Reserve Bank of India, Bulletin, June 1968.

Reserve Bank of India, Foreign Collaboration in Indian Industry, Bombay 1968.

Reserve Bank of India, India´s Foreign Liabilities and Assets 1961 –
Survey Report, Bombay 1964.

REYNOLDS, L.C., Wages and Employment in a Labour–Surplus Economy,
in The American Economic Review, 1965:1.

ROSEN, G., Industrial Change in India, Bombay 1966.

SABADE, B.R. Poona, the New Industrial City, no date, p. 3 (mimeographed).

SCITOVSKY, T., Two concepts of external economies, in ARROW, K.J.
and SCITOVSKY, T. (eds.), Readings in Welfare Economics, London
1969.

SEGAL, R. The Crisis of India, London 1965.

SEN, A.K., Choice of Techniques in a Labour Surplus Economy, in
MEIER, G.M., Leading Issues...

SEN, S.K., Studies in Industrial Policy and Development of India (1858–
1914), Calcutta 1964.

SHAH, N., Industrial development in India since 1947 survey, in Commerce, Annual Number 1968, Bombay 1968.

SHETH, N.R., The Social Framework of an Indian Factory, Bombay
1968.

SHILS, E., The Intellectual between Tradition and Modernity: The
Indian Situation, The Hague 1961.

SINGER, H.W., The distribution of gains between investing and borrowing countries, in The American Economic Review, May 1950, Papers and
Proceedings.

SPENCER, D.L., India: Mixed Enterprise and Western Business. The
Hague 1959.

STRACHEY, J., The End of Empire, London 1959.

STREETEN, P.P., Economic Integration, Leyden 1961.

STREETEN, P.P. and LIPTON, M. (eds.), The Crisis of Indian Planning,
London 1968.

SUBRAHMANIAN, K.K., A Study of Foreign Private Investment in India
since 1950. Diss., University of Bombay 1967 (unpublished).

Surveys of Economic Theory III, New York 1967.

Sveriges Allmänna Exportförening, Svenska produktionsinvesteringar i
Latinamerika, Stockholm 1970.

SÖDERSTEN, B., International Economics, Stockholm 1969.

THORBURN, T., Nyttokostnadskalkyler, in LUNDBERG, E. & BACKELIN T. (eds.), Ekonomisk politik i förvandling, Stockholm 1970.

United Nations, ECOSOC, Financing of Economic Development. Promotion of Private Foreign Investment in Developing Countries, Summary and Conclusions, E/4293, March 6, 1967.

VAID, K.N., The New Worker, New Delhi 1968.

WELLS, D.A., Economic Analysis of attitudes of host countries towards direct private investment, in MIKESELL, R.F. (ed.), U.S. Private and Government Investment Abroad, Eugene 1962.

WIGGINS, G.A., Private Foreign Investment in the Development of India since 1900, M.Sc. (Econ.) thesis, unpublished, London 1956.

Wirtschaftsdienst, 43, 1963:1.

THE SCANDINAVIAN INSTITUTE OF ASIAN STUDIES

Founded 1967

2, Kejsergade   1155 Copenhagen K   Denmark

Board

Professor Pentti Aalto, Finland (Vice-Chairman)
Professor Jussi Aro, Finland
Dr. Philos. Otto Chr. Dahl, Norway
Professor Kristof Glamann, Denmark
Professor Henry Henne, Norway
Professor K. G. Izikowitz, Sweden
Professor Göran Malmqvist, Sweden (Chairman)
Professor Anders Ølgaard, Denmark

Director

Professor Søren Egerod, Denmark

Fellows

Karl Reinhold Haellquist, Fil. lic.
Benedicte Hjejle, M. A., D, Phil. (Oxon)
Trygve Lötveit, M. A., Ph. D.
Poul Mohr, M. A.
Asko Parpola, M. A., Ph. D.
Per Sørensen, M. A.

Librarian

Eric Douglas Grinstead, B. A.

Assistant Librarians

Hanne Balslev
Ib Norel

Secretaries

Setsuko Bergholdt-Hansen
Susanna Harald Hansen
Ulla Kasten